BJÖRK

Icons of Pop Music

Series Editors: Jill Halstead, The Grieg Academy, University of Bergen, and Dave Laing, independent writer, editor and broadcaster. Books in this series, designed for undergraduates and the general reader, offer a critical profile of a key figure or group in twentieth-century pop music. These short paperback volumes focus on the work rather than on biography, and emphasize critical interpretation.

Published

Brian Wilson
Kirk Curnutt

James Brown
John Scannell

Buddy Holly
Dave Laing

Bob Dylan
Keith Negus

Forthcoming

The Beatles
Ian Inglis

Elvis Presley
Mark Duffett

Nina Simone
Richard Elliott

Elton John
Dave Laing

Joni Mitchell
Jill Halstead

BJÖRK

NICOLA DIBBEN

SHEFFIELD UK   BRISTOL CT

Published by
UK: Unit S3, Kelham House, 3 Lancaster Street, Sheffield, S3 8AF
USA: ISD, 70 Enterprise Drive, Bristol, CT 06010

www.equinoxpub.com

This revised edition published 2013.

© Nicola Dibben 2009

All rights reserved. No part of this publication may be reproduced or transmitted in any form or by any means, electronic or mechanical, including photocopying, recording or any information storage or retrieval system, without prior permission in writing from the publishers.

British Library Cataloguing-in-Publication Data
A catalogue record for this book is available from the British Library.

ISBN-13 978 1 84553 184 3 (paperback)

Typeset by S.J.I. Services, New Delhi
Printed and bound in Great Britain by Lightning Source UK Ltd, Milton Keynes

Contents

Acknowledgements	vii
Copyright acknowledgements	viii
Introduction	1
1 Biographical overview	5
2 Nationalism	24
3 Nature	53
4 Technology	72
5 Sound	100
6 Emotion	131
7 Contribution	155
Notes	173
References	199
Discography and Filmography	213
Index	217

Acknowledgements

The majority of this book was written during a period of research leave, funded by the Arts and Humanities Research Council, and the University of Sheffield, UK, to both of whom I am extremely grateful. Thanks are due to my colleagues at the music department of the University of Sheffield, in particular Eric Clarke, Karen Burland and Stephanie Pitts, for their part in making this possible, and for their friendship and support throughout the process. I would also like to thank the people who gave up their time to talk to me about their work with Björk, and shared valuable broader insights, namely Dawn Shadforth, Derek Birkett, Guy Sigsworth, Spike Stent, and Valgeir Sigurðsson. Thanks also to Dick Langham Smith, Julian Johnson, and Daniel Grimley who commented on early drafts of chapters and to Dave Laing and Jill Halstead for their positive and supportive presence throughout the editorial process.

Although the research and writing of this project took place during a limited period of time, it is the product of the influence and support of many people. The ideas in this book were explored in many invited lectures over the past six years, and I am grateful to the staff and students whose questions and comments provoked me to further thinking, particularly Allan Moore, James Brown, Jan Fairley, Mike Jones, and Richard Middleton. I am indebted to my colleagues on the editorial board of *Popular Music* (Cambridge University Press), with whom it has been an absolute privilege to work; and to Philip Thomas whose musical enthusiasms have proved infectious. Lastly, I thank my partner James for his unfailing support and patience, my siblings Susan, Steven, Julia, Rachel and Claire for putting up with years of piano practice in a crowded house, and my parents and grandfather: to Jo and Albert Humphrey, for supporting my musical interests, and to Jim, for the Shirley Bassey enthusiasms.

Copyright acknowledgements

Used by permission of One Little Indian:

Figure 1: Front cover of *Björk* (1977) 12 inch vinyl recording.

Figure 4: Still image from the music video 'Who Is It (Carry my joy on the left, carry my pain on the right)' (dir. Dawn Shadforth 2004). Dress by Alexander McQueen.

Figure 5: Still image from the music video 'Jóga' (dir. Michel Gondry 1997).

Figure 7: Parallel movement in fifths in the string arrangement of the first verse of 'Jóga' (*Homogenic* 1997).

Figure 8: Vocal and violin parts from the chorus of 'Jóga' (*Homogenic* 1997).

Figure 11: Bass and vocal of verse from 'Big Time Sensuality' (*Debut* 1993).

Figure 12: Music box and vinyl scratch in the introduction to 'Scatterheart' (*Dancer in the Dark*, and *Selmasongs*, 2000).

Figure 13: Still image from the music video 'All is Full of Love' (dir. Chris Cunningham 1999).

Figure 14: Vocals from 'All is Full of Love' first chorus (video mix by Spike Stent).

Figure 15: Vocals from 'All is Full of Love' second chorus (video mix by Spike Stent).

Figure 16: Vocal melody of the chorus from 'Ammæli' (*Life's Too Good*, The Sugarcubes 1988).

Figure 18: Vocal melody from 'Mama' (*Life's Too Good*, The Sugarcubes 1988).

Figure 19: First vocal phrase of 'Possibly Maybe' (*Post* 1995).

Figure 20: Vocal melody of '5 Years' (*Homogenic* 1997).

Figure 21: First vocal entry in 'Miðvikudags' (*Medúlla* 2004).

Figure 22: Instrumental loops in 'Human Behaviour' (*Debut* 1993).

Figure 23: Chord sequence in 'Triumph of a Heart' (*Medúlla* 2004).

Figure 24: Front cover of *Homogenic* (1997) CD.

Figure 25: Front cover of *Vespertine* (2001) CD.

Figure 27: Sketch of 'Cocoon' (*Vespertine* 2001).

Other permissions:

Figure 3: Commemorative postcard sold by Bad Taste © Friðrik Erlings, 1986.

Figure 6: 'Skjaldbreiður' 1957–62 Jóhannes Kjarval ©Heirs/Myndstef, 2001.

Figure 10: Performance of 'Oceania', opening ceremony of the Athens Olympic Games. © Mick Hutson / Redferns, 2004. Dress by Sophia Kokosalaki.

Introduction

Perhaps you have encountered Björk in her role as pop star – known for her unique music, bizarre fashion sense and quirky behaviour. Or possibly you know her as an award-winning actress and film music composer. Or maybe you think of her as a singer, either of her own compositions, of jazz standards, or of modern art music. In addition to six solo studio albums, her work includes *Björk* (1977), released when she was eleven years of age, and five other albums: one of jazz standards, two film soundtracks, and two remix albums. Collections of her music videos and performances have been released, and she has toured extensively. Moreover, she contributed to numerous other recordings, including those by the punk influenced bands Tappi Tíkarass, Kukl and the Sugarcubes, an album of works by the classical composer John Tavener, and a performance of *Pierrot Lunaire* by Arnold Schoenberg.[1] She also worked as an actress, most famously in the film *Dancer in the Dark*, directed by Lars von Trier (2000). There have been two "retrospectives": a *Greatest Hits* album (2002) (of tracks selected by fans via an online poll), and the *Family Tree* box-set (2002) comprising hits chosen by Björk, alongside other recordings spanning her career from 1984 to 2001. In sum, she is a vocalist and recording artist who programmed, arranged and produced much of her music; she is a composer of film music, and an actress.

At the time of writing, Björk is forty-two years of age; arguably rather young to be the subject of a critical review. Yet there are many reasons why a book-length study of her artistic output is appropriate. She is a platinum-selling artist cited as an influence by numerous musicians, and is widely respected for the innovative character of her artistic output; she has won international awards for her music, videos and acting. Her music underwent seemingly radical changes in style, from punk, jazz covers, and the prankster-ish pop of the Sugarcubes, to an innovative blend of electronic dance and indie in her early solo career, and subsequent combinations of electronic and acoustic sound sources and styles. Björk's collaboration with other musicians, including those from non-Western and folk idioms, raises questions about the attribution of artistic control and its role in perceptions of emotional authenticity. And in a record industry environment which thrives on classifiable genre distinctions, her artistic output is particularly interesting because it is sometimes uncompromisingly experimental in style yet is not part of an artworld-centred musical avant-garde. Furthermore, two retrospective projects in 2002 marked a significant point in Björk's career when she felt she had "mapped out all the sides of me" that she perceived were in opposition: her classical music education and her identity as a pop musician; her role as a vocalist and as a songwriter; an artist who works alone, and a collaborator (*Miniscule*, dir. Gestsdóttir 2001). Björk described the *Family Tree* compilation as a project in which she took stock of her career, documented it, and moved on with "a clean slate". Writing an account of Björk's artistic output after this time therefore allows us to engage with Björk's own perspective on her output, as well as assess its development since then.

My aim in this book is to examine the cultural significance of Björk's artistic output, its creation, and mediation. This is partly a response to her exoticization by the print and broadcast media, which arguably underplays her achievements. Björk was a child star at the age of eleven, a single mother at the age of twenty, and lead singer for the Sugarcubes before she embarked on her solo career. Much of her reception in the press, and the official information released by her record company, interprets her music in terms of her biography, as illustrated in the headlines and visual images of magazine articles and other publicity material. These representations focus on her motherhood, her sexual relationships, her artistic heritage as a musician, and her Icelandic nationality, which is used both as an explanation of what are seen as her eccentricities, and as a metaphor for the extremes of her music (the "fire and ice" of her home country). Scant attention is generally paid to musical material and processes in the critical reception of popular music, so this book attempts to rectify that situation by attending to Björk's sound. My intention is that greater understanding of how Björk's artistic output has been made, and its significance within a broader cultural context, should increase knowledge and awareness of the cultural significance of popular music more generally, as well as potentially enriching the experience of her music.

My approach is based on music analysis informed by discourse surrounding the music, and information about compositional processes and motivations. The research draws on primary material, such as Björk's recorded music and videos, live performances, and her film roles; secondary sources produced during the process of selling these core products, such as documentaries, interviews, and features, and the official websites (such as the English language site *bjork.com*); and a third type of material which includes her reception in the press, web-based fanzines and forums. The latter includes a huge number of fan-created websites which provide access to information on Björk and her artistic output, original artistic material by Björk, interpretation of lyrics, an outlet for creativity such as art, music, film, and remixes inspired by Björk, and a forum in which to share opinion, including regular polls regarding preferences for her music and visual material. These sources provide an insight into audience reception of her material. I also interviewed a number of musicians and record company personnel in an attempt to better understand the processes and social networks behind Björk's artistic output. The discourse surrounding Björk, her words and those of her collaborators, are treated here as part of the phenomena being studied rather than solely as "fact" to be relayed. Recordings are my object of study more frequently than live performances because they are more readily accessible by readers of this book. Moreover, I treat performances and recordings as separate entities: one song can be the basis for two different tracks (recorded realizations of a song), therefore I focus on each recording as a unique artefact, and I emphasize the sound of the recording not just the form, syntax, words, or performances that make it up.

Rather than present a strictly chronological account of Björk's artistic output, I have chosen to refer to examples from across her career to illustrate different themes in her work. One reason for this is that a number of chronological biographical accounts already exist (Aston 1996a; McDonnell 2001; Gittins 2002; Pytlik 2003), and the official website, *bjork.com*, provides copious documentation regarding the chronology of her career. More significantly, Björk's style seems to have changed radically with each new recording project, but as I will show, her work articulates a number of recurrent themes, which together communicate a vision of unity with and in the world. As a consequence, the chapter themes draw on both her solo career and the years prior to it, rather than treating them as separate periods.

4 Björk

Therefore, Chapter 1 contextualizes subsequent chapters by presenting a biographical overview. In Chapter 2 I show how Björk's Icelandic nationality is fuel for her exoticization by the international press, but also provides a way of understanding the origin and significance of two other themes in her artistic output: namely, the relationship between nature (Chapter 3) and technology (Chapter 4). I argue that Björk's artistic output unifies oppositions between ideas of the natural and the technological. The impetus for this reconciliation arises from widespread cultural anxieties about technology and from Björk's enculturation in Icelandic nationalism, whose ruralist ideology is potentially threatened by technological modernization. In Chapter 5 I examine the sound of Björk's music in more detail, showing the way that many of her songs set up tensions between separate musical elements, which are unified during the course of individual tracks. In discussing the sound of Björk's music, Chapter 5 identifies changes in her compositional style, and the way these have been shaped by technological and biographical factors. The apparent contradiction between Björk's collaborative approach to music-making and the projection of her authorial control is explored in Chapter 6, where I show how her author image is central to perceptions of her music's emotional authenticity, and part of a utopian vision of unity. Furthermore, the emotional character of her music is manifested through particular kinds of virtual soundscapes created in her recordings. The final chapter examines the contribution and significance of her artistic output in relation to the social and political context of her music, and in relation to her vision of unity.

1 Biographical overview

Björk Guðmundsdóttir[1] was born in Reykjavík, Iceland, on 21 November 1965. Her father, Guðmundur Gunnarsson, electrical engineer and, at the time of writing, head of the Union of Icelandic Electrical Workers (Rafiðnaðarsamband Íslands), and her mother Hildur Rúna Hauksdóttir, were in their teens when they married, and divorced within three years of Björk's birth. Björk grew up alternating between her father's and mother's households. During Björk's pre-school years she lived with her father and his parents, and in an interview with Björk's biographer Mark Pytlik, Guðmundur Gunnarsson recalled signs of Björk's early interest in musical performance: singing tunes heard on the radio, picking out melodies on her grandmother's piano and giving impromptu "performances" to gatherings of family and friends, or even passengers on a local bus (Pytlik 2003: 3–4). When Björk was four her mother remarried blues musician Sævar Árnason, with whom she had a son Arna, and Björk joined them living in a shared household. Björk's living situation was unusual in the extent to which she was surrounded by other adults, many of whom were musicians, who played records and held jamming sessions in the house (Connolly 2001).

Björk's own, often hyperbolic, accounts of her early life contrasted her mother's hippie lifestyle with the conservatism of her father and his new family, and emphasized her difference of identity within each household; she recalled "Going to my conservative family and being the really freaky hippie, with the long hair and barefoot, and I go back to my hippie people and … being really down-to-earth practical, conservative" (Broughton 1994: 30). Other anecdotes highlight Björk's self-perceived difference from other children: she described wanting to help the carers at pre-school rather than play with the other children, and being called "China girl" by her peers due to what were perceived as her unusual features and colouring.

Björk attended a part-time music school in Reykjavík (Barnamúsikskóli Reykjavíkur) from the age of five until fifteen, which was additional to the normal school system, and where she studied Western art music history and theory, encountered music by twentieth-century avant-garde composers, sang in school choirs, and learnt the recorder, flute and piano. Björk's experience at music school was an important aspect of her musical identity, as indicated by inclusion of the self-composed flute piece 'Glóra' from 1980 on the *Family Tree* box-set, and numerous references to the influence of her academic training on her musical style in interviews between 1997 and 2003. In addition, she encountered a wide variety of music through her home environments: she heard recordings by Jimi Hendrix, Eric Clapton and other rock musicians in the household that she, her mother and stepfather shared with others until the family moved to an apartment when she was aged six; she heard jazz with her grandfather; and she described being exposed to Icelandic traditional music through both her grandmothers. Björk's musical abilities received public recognition when, in 1976, an Icelandic radio station broadcast a recording of her singing the disco tune 'I Love To Love', which had been a number one chart hit in the UK earlier that year for Tina Charles, and which Björk had performed at a school event. The recording was popular enough that Björk's mother and her musician stepfather, Sævar Árnason, secured a small record deal for Björk for an album with local record label Fálkinn.

Figure 1: Front cover of *Björk* (1977) 12 inch vinyl recording.

Biographical overview

The album *Björk*[2] (1977) was recorded in two weeks at Hljóðriti Studios in Hafnarfjörður with Sævar Árnason and other experienced local musicians. The songs chosen for Björk to record were a mixture of pop covers (typical of the chart covers and bubblegum pop that dominated the Icelandic pop music scene in the 1970s), settings of children's tales,[3] original pop songs, including 'Arabadrengurinn' ('Arab Boy') written by her stepfather, and which the record sleeve, designed by Björk's mother, references (see Figure 1), and an original flute and piano composition written by Björk and titled after Icelandic nationalist painter Jóhannes Kjarval. The resultant album fits the conventions of neither children's nor adult markets; nonetheless, the vinyl-only album sold out its pressing, achieving enormous success in Iceland's tiny music market, and bringing Björk to national attention (see Figure 2). The success of the album *Björk* enabled her to buy a piano, and encouraged Fálkinn to offer her a contract for a second recording, but she refused because she was uncomfortable with the attention it had brought her.[4]

Figure 2: Newspaper report on the recording of *Björk*, 1977. *Tíminn*, September 25 1977: 30.

Björk's classical music training at school sat uncomfortably with her musical tastes. She associated the Germanic canon of composers studied in school, and the rock she encountered at home, with worn-out forms of musicmaking, leading her to describe herself as "the fighter in the school, the odd kid out, with a real passion for music, but against all this retro, constant Beethoven and Bach bollocks" (Bjork 1996). Anecdotes about Björk's early music-making emphasize her experimental approach, which included a drum and popcorn machine duo, a recorded loop of Björk's grandfather snoring used as the rhythmic basis of a track, and "automatic" creative methods (Aston 1996: 47–48). The place where her music schooling and extracurricula interests coincided was in contemporary experimental and electronic music, in the form of avant-garde classical composer Karlheinz Stockhausen (whom she later interviewed for the magazine *Dazed & Confused* in 1996) and electronic bands Kraftwerk and DAF. She recalled that on being introduced to the music of Stockhausen by a school teacher (when she was aged twelve or thirteen), she immediately identified with his pronouncement that people should listen to contemporary music, rather than music of the past (Bjork 1996). In her final years at school she was attracted by the punk scene then emerging in Reykjavík and in 1979 formed an allfemale band with three school friends called Spit and Snot.

For many of Björk's generation in Iceland, punk represented a rebellion against conservatism and apathy and what they saw as its musical incarnation in Anglo-American rock. The years between 1977 to 1979 have been described as a low point in Icelandic popular music: there were fewer opportunities for original live pop music due to the popularity of disco, and, influenced by this, local musicians often recorded covers of Anglophone chart hits rather than wrote original music (Guðmundsson 1990). In the 1970s the State radio station was dominated by bubblegum pop.[5] Only one radio show, directed by Ásmundur Jónsson (later instrumental in the formation of the Sugarcubes), played jazz and rock (from the US), and eventually punk, when it reached Iceland in 1977–8. Punk initially had little success in Iceland: the Sex Pistols-style punk band Fræbbiarnir played in Reykjavík in 1978–9 to small audiences, but interest grew among younger audiences in 1980 with the raw rock sound and political lyrics of Utangarðsmenn (Outsiders).

Björk's diverse musical activities after leaving music school in 1980 included a jazz-fusion band Exodus, formed with music-school friends Ásgeir Sæmundsson and Thorvaldur Thorvaldsson (and who released a home-made recording on cassette and appeared on Icelandic television), and the punk-influenced band Tappi Tíkarrass (which translates as 'Cork the Bitch's Arse'), which emerged from Jam-80, a duo she had formed with bassist Jakob Magnússon, initially to play disco covers. The punk scene of which Tappi Tíkarrass formed a part was supported by the launch of the independent record label Gramm in 1981 by Einar Örn Benediktsson (singer with Purrkur Pillnikk), and radio DJ Ásmundur Jónsson (the first to play punk on Icelandic radio). Gramm provided new opportunities for less commercial music: prior to and after Gramm's demise due to bankruptcy in 1987, the majority of Iceland's music was released by just two record labels. Iceland's tiny population (fewer than 300,000 people) and the costs of recording led Gramm to market its bands through tours to Scandinavia and the UK. As a consequence, Purrkur Pillnikk supported The Fall on tour in England in 1982, during which singer Einar Örn became friends with Derek Birkett. Birkett, who was at this time a member of the English anarcho-punk band Flux of Pink Indians, subsequently became Björk's long-time friend and record company head. Gramm released Tappi Tíkarrass' extended single *Bitið Fast Í Vitið* (Bite Hard in Your Mind) in 1982, and an album *Miranda* a year later. Tappi Tíkarrass also featured in the seminal documentary *Rokk Í Reykjavík* (dir. Friðriksson 1982), dispelling Björk's pre-teen image as a cover artist, and making her the iconic visual image of Reykjavík's music scene in poster advertising.

Icelandic punk was influenced by its English counterpart, but it encompassed a more diverse range of influences than the 1970s English punk epitomized by the Sex Pistols, partly due to different social circumstances. Whereas English punk had emerged from high unemployment, and a repressive social sphere, there was steady economic growth in Iceland throughout the 1970s and unemployment was rare. Whereas English punk criticized society, sometimes suggesting solutions to ills, the lyrics of Icelandic punk complained about mundane aspects of everyday life. Other differences between the English and Icelandic punk scene were illustrated by Derek Birkett's account of his first meeting with Björk when they were both in their respective punk bands:

> It was the first time we'd ever met and we played records: they played Abba, The Sex Pistols, Shostakovich, Messiaen, and then they were reading excerpts from NME and laughing about it, and then somebody would read a bit of Baudelaire or Rimbaud, and then someone would play the piano. I was like …. I'm in a punk band in England and we drink cider and we sniff glue when we're together. (Birkett 2006)

Derek Birkett attributed the eclecticism of the Icelandic punk scene at that time to the limited amount of television ("three hours a day, and not on Thursdays 'so the Symphony Orchestra played on Thursdays'"), the lack of foreign influence ("ninety percent of the television had to be in Icelandic and Icelandic generated"), heightened by a determination to preserve the Icelandic language ("foreign words were illegal, so everything had a translation: computers were called 'Numberprophetress'"), a lack of bars and clubs resulting from a prohibition on beer, and extreme seasonal variation in the amount of daylight, which encouraged indoor pursuits in the dark winter months. The artistic liberalism and eclecticism, which might have been perceived elsewhere as the pretentious preoccupation of a small elite was (for some in Iceland, at least) part of an emerging punk scene. The main similarity between Icelandic and Anglophone punk lay in its reaction to musical inertia, and its do-it-yourself aesthetic, where effort was more important than technical competence.

The Icelandic punk scene lasted three years, perhaps due to the small market, the cancellation of the only show on Iceland State radio to play alternative music, and the launch of a second State radio station, which played easy listening pop. After Tappi Tíkarrass split up in 1983 Björk continued to play piano and sing in cover bands, which she had been doing for the past summer, and played with a variety of other local bands. The most famous of these was Kukl ("Sorcery"), formed when two DJs (one of whom was Ásmundur Jónsson) brought together who they perceived to be Iceland's most cutting-edge musicians to play live on the final programme of their radio show. The collection of musicians comprised Björk, vocalist and trumpeter Einar Örn Benediktsson from Purrkur Pillnikk, keyboardist Einar Melax from Van Houtens Kókó, guitarist Guðlaugar Kristinn Óttarson and drummer Sigtryggur Baldursson from Þeyr, and bassist Birgir Mogensen. The musicians enjoyed playing together and a few weeks after the radio show performed in

Iceland with the English anarchist punk rock band Crass whom Einar Örn met during his time at a British polytechnic studying Media. Kukl's aim was to avoid "mediocrity, materialism and a narrow-minded small town mentality", as Björk later reflected (Gittins 2002: 19), which manifested itself in obscurely metaphysical liner notes, avoidance of strophic (verse-chorus) song structures, a collage of samples of everyday sounds and music, and emphasis on the individuality of instrumental lines and the textures they created, resulting in a dissonant harmonic style: Guitarist Óttarson recalled that "we wanted to demonstrate for people that you don't always have to play two chords with always [sic] the same melody" (Pytlik 2003: 22). During their time in Kukl, Einar Örn and Björk also developed the complementary vocal roles which later characterized the Sugarcubes: a combination of melodic and half-sung, half-spoken and shouted vocal styles.

Kukl's two albums were recorded in London: *The Eye* (1984), whose title referenced George Bataille's surrealist erotic novel *Story of the Eye* (cited by Björk as an important influence), and *Holidays in Europe (The Naughty Naught)* (1986), the tracks of which are named after different countries.[6] Kukl also toured Western Europe, playing with other bands such as the English anarcho-punk activists Flux of Pink Indians (which included Derek Birkett), and renowned Icelandic oppositional rock and roll singer-songwriter Megas (Magnús Þór Jónsson), to whose tracks she and other members of Kukl contributed in 1990. Björk's DIY ethic is evidenced by her selling of 100 hand-written and coloured copies of a fairytale, *Um Úrnat frá Björk* ('About Úrnat by Björk'[7]) to supplement income from casual manual and factory work between Kukl's tours.

Björk continued to perform while pregnant in 1985, including an infamous televised performance with Kukl while seven months pregnant, which caused outrage and shock among more conservative members of the audience (Pytlik 2003: 32). Between 1984 and 1986 Björk also recorded eleven songs with Guðlaugar Kristinn Óttarson under the name The Elgar Sisters, a reference to the English composer Edward Elgar suggested to them by recording engineer Mel Jefferson who thought their music sounded classical (Óttarsson 2005). The songs with The Elgar Sisters were more melodic and lyrical in style than those of Björk's previous collaborations and expressed greater emotional gravity. Their significance is indicated by the appearance of some of these tracks as B-sides to singles released during Björk's later solo career (but credited to The Elgar Sisters), and inclusion of the hauntingly dissonant, 'Siðasta Ég', performed by guitar, voice and harpsichord on the *Family Tree* retrospective.

In the summer of 1986, with Einar Örn back in Iceland, members of Kukl and their friends from surrealist poetry group Medúsa, formed the organization Smekkleysa SM SF (Bad Taste Ltd), who organized theatrical performances and exhibitions and whose ambitions included a restaurant, radio station and series of awards for bad taste. Inspired by an aphorism attributed to Picasso that "The worst enemy of creativity is good taste", Bad Taste's aim was to redefine what was then accepted as good taste, as declared in their manifesto:

1. As "good taste" and "frugality" are the main enemies of creativity and well-being, Bad Taste aims to fight everything that can be branded "good taste" and "frugality".
2. In the fight against the above ("good taste" etc.), Bad Taste will use every imaginable and unimaginable method, e.g. inculation [sic], extermination, tasteless advertisements and announcements, distribution and sale of common junk and excrement. ("The somewhat complete Bad Taste saga" n.d.)

In the context of 1980s Reykjavík, "good taste" was exemplified by fashions and styles associated with a culture of corporate profit-making and individual gain. The fashion for shoulder-padded suits and geometric hairstyles sanctioned the values of consumer culture, and the dominance of bubblegum pop in Icelandic music suggested a pursuit of profit: both implied a compliance with authority by endorsing commercialism (Jenkins 2004). Bad Taste reacted against the values of corporatism with a combination of pranksterism and surrealism (embodying their concern for absolute freedom), a do-it-yourself approach to all their projects, and a disregard for financial gain. The eclecticism of media encompassed by Bad Taste, and its reaction to consumerism was akin to that of the English anarcho-punk collective, Crass, who combined graphics, music and film to promote an anarchist political ideology.

The musical branch of Bad Taste was launched on 8 June 1986, the day Björk gave birth to her son Sindri whose father was fellow musician Þór Eldon Jónsson. Sykurmolarnir, anglicized to the Sugarcubes, comprised Björk and Einar Örn on vocals (with Einar playing trumpet as well), Þór Eldon on guitar, Purkurr Pillnikk's guitarist Friðrik Erlings, Bragi Ólafsson on bass and former Kukl member Sigtryggur 'Siggi' Baldursson on drums. The poet Sjón (Sigurjón

Birgir Sigtryggur, who co-wrote some of Björk's lyrics during her subsequent solo career) also occasionally performed with the Sugarcubes as Johnny Triumph. The Sugarcubes aimed to play less serious music than Kukl and create a pop band to make money to fund Bad Taste's other projects. Björk also made her acting debut during this period: a few weeks after giving birth she played the role of a thirteen-year-old child in the Icelandic film *The Juniper Tree*, directed by Nietzchka Keene (1987), and a year later she appeared in an Icelandic television drama by Matthias Johannesen called *Glerbrot* (*Broken Glass*).

The Sugarcubes' first single was funded by a hugely successful Bad Taste project: on hearing that Ronald Reagan and Mikhail Gorbachev were meeting in Reykjavík for a summit in October 1986 Bad Taste commissioned and sold 5,000 copies of a commemorative postcard, shown in Figure 3. The kitsch postcard, reminiscent in style of Stalin-era graphics, and designed by Friðrik Erlings (a founder member of Bad Taste and graphic designer as well as band member of the Sugarcubes), earned Bad Taste enough money to record two songs in Icelandic: 'Köttur' and 'Ammæli'. Members of Bad Taste also coloured and assembled the record sleeves and sold copies from the back of a car and in bars and cafes.

Figure 3: Commemorative postcard sold by Bad Taste © Friðrik Erlings, 1986.

Like other punk cover art, such as that of the Sex Pistols' record sleeves, the Sugarcubes' early graphics used the device of detournément, in which elements of a well-known media are used to convey a message opposite that of its original meaning (Jenkins 2004). The single 'Einn Mol' á Mann' has on its reverse the logo for Dansukker, a well-known Danish Sugar company, which, in conjunction with the band's name, suggested they were a "product" defined by their corporate sponsorship, ironically playing with the idea of commercialism. For example, Bad Taste's logo of a pig and trumpet, and still used twenty years later, parodies the dog and gramophone logo of music industry giant His Masters Voice.

The single had little success in Iceland, but it attracted the attention of their friend Derek Birkett, who released an English-language version on his recently founded label, One Little Indian. The track 'Birthday' (Ammæli) was declared Single of the Week in the British magazine *Melody Maker* a week after its release in August 1987 and received huge interest from press and record companies. The Sugarcubes' guitar-based pop followed conventions of song structure and an indie sound, but had a playful, subversive character due to its surreal lyrical and visual imagery, pastiche references to other musical styles and the contrast between Einar Örn's vocal style (a cross between speaking and singing in which the vocal line followed approximate melodic contours) and Björk's imploring angular vocal lines. Björk's critical reception as a child-woman can be attributed partly to her occasionally childlike vocal timbre, her lyrics sung in the first person often from the perspective of a child and about seemingly distasteful subject matter (the erotic attraction felt by a five-year-old child towards a fifty-year-old man, on 'Birthday'; the story of a young girl who takes home a victim from a road accident on 'Motorcrash'): the first English-language reviews of the Sugarcubes describe her as a "disarmingly youthful singer and lyricist" who has a "childlike frankness" (Gibson 1987: 41), and "a dangerously cross-eyed chanteuse who resembles both Denis Lavant and the little girl who *cuts your lips off*" (Roberts 1987).

Although they were offered lucrative recording contracts with major record labels, the Sugarcubes retained their anarchist roots and recorded instead with independent record label One Little Indian (the company to which Björk is still signed) and money earned was put back into Bad Taste projects. British success was followed by success in the United States, where the

Sugarcubes' recordings were licensed to the record label Elektra: in 1988 they toured the United States and appeared on the comedy-variety show *Saturday Night Live* (NBC). The Sugarcubes released three albums: *Life's Too Good* (1988), *Here Today, Tomorrow, Next Week!* (1989) and *Stick Around for Joy* (1992). A second American tour (*Monsters of Alternative Rock*) with New Order and Public Image Ltd in 1989 was followed by a world tour in 1990.

However, their quick success coincided with the development of complicated personal relationships within the band: Björk and Þór divorced, and Þór married and had a child with Margaret ('Magga') Örnolfsdóttir, who joined the band in 1988 as keyboardist after Erlings left. Media attention focused on Björk, treating her as the main creative force in the band, even though the band was fronted by both Björk and Einar Örn and worked collectively (Björk wrote her vocal melodies and lyrics).

During the six years the Sugarcubes performed and recorded together, Björk's musical tastes increasingly diverged from those of the other band members as she became interested in the electronic dance music scene then happening in England. The collective working process meant that no one person had creative precedence, and left no room for individual members to develop their musical ideas within the band. Despite Björk's attempts to interest band members in her musical ideas by playing them the new music she was listening to, or bringing ideas for the band to develop, the Sugarcubes never diverged from their indie-pop style. Björk's interests led her to approach Manchester-based producer Graham Massey of 808 State to add beats to songs she had written over a ten-year period, including 'Anchor Song' which later appeared on *Debut*, and which she had written in summer 1990 when she cycled between farmers' churches in Iceland, writing songs on the harmoniums and recording them on her Walkman (Bailie 1993). Massey provided Björk with a supportive friendship and their later collaborations included two tracks released on the 808 State album *Ex:El* (1991), a track for the Sugarcubes' remix album *It's It* (1992), and co-written tracks which appeared on Björk's solo albums.

Returning to Reykjavík in 1990, after a world tour promoting the second album, *Here Today, Tomorrow, Next Week!*, Björk recorded an album of jazz standards with the Trió Guðmundur Ingólfssonar, with whom she had previously sung after the demise of Kukl: *Gling-Gló* (1990) made the number one place in the Icelandic chart. By the time of the Sugarcubes' final album, and a tour with U2, the band members' musical ambitions had totally diverged and they effectively disbanded, although they remained friends and continued to manage Bad Taste. Björk humorously recalled that having started as something of a joke between friends "five years later it was taking up all our time; all we were doing was, like we had an empty office and piles of unsold books. And what was supposed to be the most promising poet of his generation hadn't written a book for four or five years because he was doing sound checks in Texas" ("About & About: The Sugarcubes" 1995–2007).[8] The Sugarcubes failed to provide a forum within which Björk could pursue her changing musical ideas.

In 1993 Björk moved to London with her son Sindri to work on her solo album, with the support of Derek Birkett from One Little Indian. Her musical ideas were developed in sessions with Graham Massey and US jazz harpist Corky Hale, with arrangements by the US jazz composer and saxophonist Oliver Lake. Her original intention had been to work with different producers on separate tracks for an album provisionally titled *Björk's Affairs*. In the end the majority of the album was produced by British dance music producer Nellee Hooper,[9] and the title *Debut* was chosen to mark the idea that, despite the existence of the 1977 album, this was her first genuinely "solo" recording project. *Debut*, released in 1993, was an innovative mix of dance, jazz, and indie influences, which combined acoustic and electronic sounds. The music videos and cover art for *Debut* were to define her image for years to come: the cover art by photographer Jean-Baptiste Mondino presents Björk in vulnerable, retiring pose; and the animation-like style of the video for 'Human Behaviour', the first single from the album, projects a child-like Björk in surreal surroundings – a realization she reached with the then little known director Michel Gondry.[10]

Whereas One Little Indian had budgeted for sales of 40,000 records based on the popularity of the Sugarcubes, *Debut* sold many times more than that within a few months of its release (Birkett 2006). A tour was quickly put together with what Björk described, from her perspective as an Icelander living in England, as a collection of "immigrant musicians": tabla player and DJ Talvin Singh who had contributed to 'Venus as a Boy' (the second single from the album), keyboardist Leila Arab, bassist Ike Leo, drummer Tansay Omar, Guy Sigsworth on keyboards and Dan Lipman on flute, tambourine and saxophone. Offers of work at this time included a request for Björk and Nellee Hooper to write for Madonna, which resulted in 'Bedtime Story' released on *Bedtime Stories* (1994) and a show for *MTV Unplugged*, which comprised live performances of tracks from *Debut*, involving glass harmonica, Corky Hale on harp, Talvin Singh on percussion, classical percussionist Evelyn Glennie, and the South Bank Gamelan Orchestra. The re-versioning apparent in the live performances of these tracks is a practice which Björk continued throughout her career. Other activities during this time included a performance at the Brit Awards with PJ Harvey, and modelling for Jean-Paul Gaultier in Paris.

Whereas *Debut* had featured songs written over a ten-year period in Iceland, Björk's second studio album, *Post* (1995), consisted of songs created within a shorter time period: some were tracks she had previously co-written with Graham Massey but which hadn't fitted within the *Debut* concept, namely 'Army of Me' and 'The Modern Things'; others were new compositions, such as 'Possibly Maybe'. A further difference from *Debut* was that Björk wanted to co-produce this album rather than rely so heavily on Nellee Hooper. Other collaborators included Bristol triphop artist Tricky (Adrian Thaws), with whom she co-wrote 'Enjoy' and 'Headphones', and to whose album *Nearly God* (1996) she contributed, and British musician and producer Howie B (Howard Bernstein). Although the album was recorded in the Bahamas, it underwent further changes on Björk and Nellee Hooper's return with the addition of live instrumental performances to some tracks. Björk also called upon the skills of Brazilian musician Eumir Deodato (renowned for his fusion of jazz and big band with popular and classical genres), having heard his string arrangements for 'Travessia' by Brazilian singer-songwriter Milton Nascimento. Despite the commercial success of *Post*, it was 'It's Oh So Quiet', a song originally recorded by Hollywood actress and singer Betty Hutton in 1948 under the title 'Blow a Fuse', which was Björk's biggest hit, aided by Spike Jonze's exuberant Hollywood musical-style video treatment.

Björk's success was marked by a number of awards: in 1994 she won Best Breakthrough Act and Best International Female at the Brit Awards. She won the latter award again in 1995 and 1998, and was nominated for it in 2001, 2004, 2006 and 2008. However, other events were less positive: a sample from the album *Mass Observation* (1994) by British experimental musician Scanner (Robin Rimbaud) used at the beginning of 'Possibly Maybe' had not been copyright cleared and led to a lawsuit, later dropped, and during the tour of *Post* Björk lost her voice, necessitating her to seek vocal training. The pressure which Björk was under at this time is indicated by an incident at Bangkok airport in February 1996 when, coming off a flight, and surrounded by camera crews clamouring for interviews, Björk lunged out at a reporter, allegedly because the journalist had been trying to interview her then ten-year-old son (a second similar assault on a newspaper photographer was reported in January 2008 on her arrival at Auckland International airport in New Zealand after he persisted in taking photographs when he had been asked not to).

In the intervals of a busy touring schedule during 1996 Björk interviewed Stockhausen for a feature in *Dazed & Confused* magazine, and performed part of Schoenberg's *Pierrot Lunaire* at the Verbier Festival in Switzerland with conductor Kent Nagano and the Opera Orchestra of Lyon. Although Björk rehearsed for three months in preparation (she was coached for this project and John Tavener's *Prayer of the Heart* by musical director Murray Hipkin) and gave a reportedly successful performance, Björk refused to release a recording on the grounds that this was other singers' territory.

Telegram, an album of remixes of tracks from *Post*, released the same year, was not received well by the press, perhaps due to prejudice against the idea of the remix, and the album's less commercial appeal. However, the release of this album illustrates the significance of remixes within Björk's compositional aesthetic, and the way that she perceived her songs to be realizable in different versions rather than as fixed entities.

The media pressure on Björk reached a climax in September 1996 when a fan, enraged by her mixed-race relationship with Jungle DJ Goldie (who unbeknownst to the fan, she had already split up with), sent Björk a letter-bomb and filmed himself committing suicide. The bomb was intercepted and destroyed, but this event, plus the increased media attention it entailed, had a huge impact on Björk's well-being.

Soon after this event Björk moved to Spain to escape the publicity that surrounded her in London and Reykjavík, and began work on material for *Homogenic* (1997). Björk's explicit concept for this album was the creation of an "Icelandic" sound characterized by strings, beats and her vocals, to be produced by Björk with a small number of collaborators, one of the most important of whom was Mark Bell of electronica duo LFO, whose minimal

Biographical overview 19

beats Björk admired. *Homogenic* was much more aggressively extrovert than the previous albums and its tracks are much more consistent in sonic and thematic content: gone are the jazz covers, and instead the songs are much darker in mood. The album cover art depicted Björk as cyber-Geisha, rather than the innocent youth of previous representations, locked into a constricting costume, yet directly meeting the viewer's gaze. A tour followed, along with the release of a number of recordings of live performances, and a volume of music videos.

In 1999 she recorded *Prayer of the Heart*, written for her and the Brodsky Quartet by John Tavener (released on *A Portrait: John Tavener* in 2004), and gave acoustic performances in the Union Chapel in Islington, London, in an attempt to achieve a more intimate performance context, and anticipating the use of venues associated with art music on the *Vespertine* tour in 2001.

Her next project was to act in and compose the film music for *Dancer in the Dark*, filmed in Sweden and Denmark in 1999. Danish director Lars von Trier, the founder of the Dogme cinema movement, had reportedly approached Björk after seeing her performance in the music video 'It's Oh So Quiet' (dir. Jonze 1995). However, work on the music and lyrics (with the poet Sjón, producer Mark Bell, musician Guy Sigsworth, and studio engineer Valgeir Sigurðsson) proved difficult as Björk and Lars von Trier reportedly battled for artistic control. Furthermore, Björk's method of acting meant that her performance was "felt" rather than constructed, with the consequence that Björk experienced the same emotionally harrowing psychological disturbances undergone by the character Selma that she played in the film. Björk also had different plans for the soundtrack album to those of the production company, Zentropa: whereas Zentropa had been planning a straightforward reproduction of the songs, Björk envisaged *Selmasongs* as the realization of Selma's musical fantasies, and so re-recorded some of the music for the album's release. The film received the Palme D'Or and her performance was awarded Best Leading Actress at the 2000 Cannes Film Festival, a nomination for Best Original Song for 'I've Seen It All' from the 2001 Academy Awards, and nominations for Best Actress in a Drama Motion Picture and Best Original Song in the Golden Globe Awards. Yet, at the Academy Awards it was her attire which attracted most press attention – most of it disparaging: the white tulle and feather dress designed by Marjan

Pejowski was constructed to look like a swan draped around her body, and she dropped eggs under her skirt as she walked up the red carpet in a theatrical statement reminiscent of Bad Taste's earlier pranksterism.

Björk's next solo studio album, *Vespertine*, was written at the same time as filming *Dancer in the Dark*. Its introverted, intimate sound and thematic content was influenced by three things: Selma's interior musical world; Björk's acquisition of a laptop computer (which fired an interest in miniaturization of sounds); and the intimacy of her relationship with her partner, US artist Matthew Barney. Björk had already composed the tracks on *Vespertine*, and created its innovative combination of glitch beats, miniaturisation and spatial diffusion, by the time she started working with relatively unknown electronica artists: Thomas Knack (Opiate) from Denmark created the beats for two songs ('Cocoon' and 'Undo'), US duo Matmos were brought in at the mix stage, and British-based Bogdan Racynski provided a remix. The album's introverted sound, lyrics and visual imagery were in stark contrast to the extrovert character of *Homogenic*.

The tour for *Vespertine* took place in classical music venues, and involved string orchestra and choir as well as Matmos' live electronics. The venues, the style of music, and finally the videos for singles from the album were more art-oriented than her previous solo work. The other project released in 2001 was *Björk*, a collection of prose and photographs edited by M/M (Paris) (artists Mathias Augustyniak and Michael Amzalag), and whose multimedia character (in the context of her music) was consistent with Björk's continued involvement with the Bad Taste collective.

In 2002 Björk became pregnant with her second child, and released the *Greatest Hits* album and *Family Tree* retrospective, the latter of which includes Björk's own choice of 'Greatest Hits', previously unreleased material, such as recordings with the Brodsky Quartet, and material from the period before her solo career. After the birth of Ísadóra, in October 2002, Björk continued work on her fifth solo studio album, *Medúlla* (2004), made entirely from vocal materials and involving collaborations with a wide variety of musicians, including Canadian Inuk throat singer Tanya "Tagaq" Gillis, Mike Patton (US musician and lead singer with Faith No More), Robert Wyatt (English musician formerly with the band Soft Machine), and human beat-boxers Schlomo (from England), Dokaka (from Japan), and US hiphop MC and human beatboxer Rahzel (Rahzel M. Brown). The innovative character of the album led to Björk's nomination in 2005 for the BBC Radio 3 World Music award for Boundary Crossing, and for the Inspiration award at the annual *Q Magazine* awards. Björk's largest ever audience was for her performance of the song 'Oceania' commissioned for the opening ceremony of the 2004 Olympic Games in Athens.

After the release of *Medúlla*, Björk became increasingly politicized by her experience of living in the US during the occupation of Iraq after the terrorist attack on the World Trade Towers in New York. The charity album *Army of Me-Xes* was released to raise money for the United Nations International Children's Emergency Fund subsequent to the tsunami which hit parts of Southeast Asia on 26 December 2004. Björk also headlined in Tokyo in July 2005 as part of the series of Live 8 concerts organized by musician Bob Geldof to pressure the world's richest nations to help the poorest.

Contrary to her earlier declarations that she would not act in a film again, Björk appeared in and wrote the soundtrack for *Drawing Restraint 9* (2005). Filmed and set on a Japanese whaling ship in Nagasaki Bay, the central idea of the film is the relationship between creativity and self-imposed restraint. This theme is symbolized by the transformation of a huge Vaseline sculpture during the course of the film, and through the characters of two occidental guests on the ship played by Björk, and director Matthew Barney.

During 2005 and 2006 Björk's artistic profile was further consolidated though the release of three substantial projects. Two of these were archive collections, *Björk: The Television Archive* (2005) and *Björk: The Live Archive* (2005), consisting of live performances, interviews and documentaries. The archive project was followed a year later by the box-set *Surrounded* comprising her first three solo studio albums and two soundtrack albums remastered in 5.1 surround sound, plus *Vespertine* and *Medúlla* which were already available in 5.1 surround sound, repackaged with music videos of associated tracks.

Björk's sixth solo album *Volta* was different again: the combination of primary colours in the artwork is the opposite of *Vespertine*'s monochrome and *Medúlla*'s black cover art; it combines acoustic and electronic sources in contrast to *Medúlla*'s foray into vocal materials; and it employs live percussion and 1990s-style electronic dance beats which are a radical departure from the sophisticated micro-beats of *Vespertine*. Björk's collaborations included US hiphop and r&b producer Timbaland (Tim Mosley), Antony

Hegarty, singer with American band Antony and the Johnsons, Malian kora player, bandleader and composer Toumani Diabaté and the band Konono No.1 from the Democratic Republic of Congo, whose sound uses the likembe (thumb piano), and experimental percussionists Brian Chippendale and Chris Corsano. Performances included live electronics from Mark Bell, and Damian Taylor, classical keyboard player Jónas Sen, and an all-female Icelandic brass ensemble. Other collaborations included work on a piece with performance artist Meredith Monk, whose 'Gotham Lullaby' Björk had performed live on a number of occasions (including the Making Music concert at Carnegie Hall, New York, in November 2005, held in honour of the 40th anniversary of Meredith Monk's career), and continuing her practice of working with other musicians, not all of which resulted in record releases.

Conclusion

This brief overview of Björk's life and career serves to provide a chronological, biographical context for the ideas that the rest of this book explores.

Björk's artistic career can be divided into four main phases: her experience as a child star, as a teenage punk musician, as a member of a successful pop group, and as an international solo artist. Her openness to diverse influences is reflected in the stylistic shifts from one phase of her career to another: the most obvious change was from the punk-influenced styles of Kukl and the Sugarcubes to the influence of electronic dance music during her solo career, but there have also been other changes, such as the extreme contrasts in thematic, sonic and visual identity between successive solo albums, which are conceived of as distinct "projects".

This diversity is aided by her collaborations with a wide variety of musicians, video directors, photographers and designers. These collaborations reveal a tendency to ignore genre boundaries, both within pop, and between low and high art styles, and to ignore divisions between the various artistic media. This reveals a disregard for disciplinary boundaries and a willingness to take what could be perceived as artistic risks. For example, many of the people employed to create the videos for her singles were artists rather than video or film directors: fashion designer Alexander McQueen directed the video for 'Alarm Call' (1998), photographers Inez Van Lamsweerde and Vinoodh Matadin (of M/M (Paris)) directed 'Hidden Place' (2001), and costume designer Eiko Ishioka directed 'Cocoon' (2002). Often her collaborators were relatively unknown artists working with the musical or visual art "underground" at the time. One example is Michel Gondry who was better known as the drummer with the French band Oui, Oui when he directed her first video, yet went on to win an Academy Award with his film *Eternal Sunshine of the Spotless Mind* (2004). Björk's artistic output during her solo career embodies her identity as a "whole artist"; that is, an artist who communicates her ideas through the integrated use of all media at her disposal. Her work also shows enormous creative freedom in which the imagination is given free rein.

Much of the manner in which Björk's artistic output is presented and managed bears the influence of punk's anti-commercialism. Bad Taste subsequently became an independent record company which continues to work on a not-for-profit basis to promote Icelandic music. The artistic control that epitomized Bad Taste is also evident in Björk's loyalty to independent record label One Little Indian, her high degree of artistic control over her music, and the extent of self-documentation (documentaries, the book *Björk*, and the retrospective *Family Tree* box-set) which shapes the perceived history of her artistic development.

Critical reception of Björk's work uses her perceived otherness to "explain" the sounds and style of her artistic output: her appearance and behaviour are often characterized as bizarre and eccentric, and her music as individual and eclectic, and both are most often interpreted in terms of a globally imagined Icelandic identity. Subsequent chapters explore the extent to which it is possible to go beyond such explanations, by investigating the shaping and wider cultural significance of her music.

2 Nationalism

> My theory is that when Iceland got independent in 1944, it still took two generations to develop a real confidence. My parents were born in the late 1940s. But when my generation came along we finally started to ask ourselves what it meant to be Icelandic and how to feel proud of it instead of feeling guilty all the time, like animal creatures colonised by Denmark for 600 years. (Björk interviewed in *Screaming Masterpiece*, dir. Magnússon 2005)

Iceland, an island lying just below the Arctic Circle in the North Atlantic ocean, was settled by Vikings in the late ninth century, who brought with them their religions, customs and poetry, including pre-Christian mythology. Iceland's harsh climate, extreme seasonal variations in daylight, and geological activity due to its location on the Mid-Atlantic Ridge, presented difficulties for settlers and kept the population low. The isolated farming communities governed themselves through annual assemblies held in Þingvellir, south-west Iceland, and the population developed a strong literary tradition which communicated genealogies and pagan mythologies (Christianity was present, but not adhered to). By the late thirteenth century Iceland was under Norwegian, and subsequently Danish, rule. An independence movement emerged in the mid-nineteenth century, influenced by European philosophy, and in 1918 Iceland gained home rule from Denmark after 500 years, declaring itself a Republic in 1944. During the twentieth century there was a rapid shift from rural to urban life, from agriculture to mechanized fishing, the emergence of a class system, and closer economic and political ties to the United States (Karlsson 2000). From being a colony that survived by subsistence farming and fishing, Iceland is today an independent state and, until the economic crisis of 2008, was the fifth richest nation in the world (measured by Gross Domestic Product per capita), despite its tiny population of 300,000 people.

Contemporary Icelandic consciousness is steeped in nationalism, as a consequence of its recent past as a colony of Denmark, and subsequent perceived danger to the Independence it so recently gained. In addition to the risk to Icelandic culture brought by global media, a more immediate cultural threat was that represented by the British military occupation of Iceland in 1940 (in order to protect North Atlantic supply lines during World War II), and subsequent establishment of a United States military base at Keflavík from 1941 to 2006. As Björk indicates in the quotation which starts this chapter, Iceland's past as a colony has significance for contemporary Icelanders' view of themselves. This chapter examines the way Björk's artistic output has been shaped by Iceland's post-colonial situation, by imaginations of Iceland by outsiders, and by Björk's position as a global pop icon.

An Invented Iceland

Contemporary understandings of Icelandic history, circulating in Iceland and communicated abroad, are themselves based on nationalist constructions of Icelandic identity (Hálfdanarson 2000: 15). The period from settlement by Vikings in the late ninth century until the union with Norway in the late thirteenth century is viewed as a Golden Age by contemporary Icelandic cultural institutions and popular culture, and is reaffirmed through an emphasis on Iceland's literary heritage of the sagas, its Viking ancestry, its language, and (in some instances) its non-adherence to Christianity.

From the fourteenth century until the beginnings of the national revival in the nineteenth century, Iceland is commonly perceived to have undergone economic and cultural decline; the eighteenth and first half of the nineteenth century brought disasters, epidemics and famine, such as the Lakagigar eruption of 1783–4 which poisoned grass, caused the death of livestock, and was followed by a twenty percent decrease in the population (Árnason 2005).[1] Danish rule during this period was seen by Nationalists as a wholly negative one which intervened between the imagined Golden medieval saga period, and an imagined better future as an independent nation.

Like other nations, Iceland is an "imagined community" (Anderson 1983); a group of people with a desire to be self-governing, with a shared historic territory, common myths and historical memories, communicated through cultural artefacts and processes. In the case of Iceland, this identity draws on its land, language and literature (Sigurðsson 1996), to create the idea of a "natural" relationship between the land of the nation-state and the people that inhabit it.

An important means by which Icelandic identity has been conceptualized historically is through its landscape. Early Icelanders' ideas about nature were influenced by animist pagan religion and became increasingly negative and fearful post-settlement, perhaps in response to real hardships, such as those engendered by the Lakagigar eruption of 1783–4. Against this background, a number of reformists sought to educate the nation towards a better life, and part of this appears to have been an attempt to change Icelanders' views of nature. Hence, a more benign view is reflected in the poetry of naturalist Eggert Olafsson (1726–68), and that of early romantic poets such as Jónas Hallgrímsson (1807–45), both of whom place greater emphasis on the beauty of Icelandic nature rather than on its utilitarian function. Its landscape of volcanoes, lava fields and glaciers subsequently came to be understood in terms consistent with a nationalist agenda. For example, the Lakagigar eruption in the eighteenth century and the famine that followed were linked by the idea that the management of these disasters would have been better had Iceland not been under Danish rule, and as a consequence, the lava fields left after the eruption represented for nationalists economic and social atrophy under Danish rule. Only later were perceptions of the "barren" and "static" landscape reimagined by nationalists within themes of renewal and restoration of Iceland's social and cultural history (Oslund 2002: 324).

This rural landscape ideology was circulated in the nineteenth and early twentieth centuries through Icelandic poetry and art; in particular landscape painting was seen by politicians as a primary means to communicate nationalist ideals at home and abroad (Sigurðsson 1997).[2] This view of Icelandic nature was tied to the nationalist movement, and a spiritual vision, sometimes called the "Nordic sublime" (Swain 2001), was articulated in painting at the turn of the nineteenth to twentieth century through the work of Þórarinn B. Þorláksson (1867–1924), Ásgrímur Jónsson (1876–1958) and Jóhannes Kjarval (1885–1972). Icelandic nature was idealized in these paintings as serene and peaceful, despite the threat the natural landscape had posed to Icelanders' survival at various times: the paintings depict wide open spaces and mountains, often without human presence or intervention into the landscape, as appropriate to nationalist imaginings of the nation as a timeless entity identical with the land. Notably, the colours of the Icelandic national flag are officially described as "sky blue", "fire red" and "snow white" (Article 1 of the Flag Act No.34/1944 cited in "Icelandic National Flag"). A nationalist movement in music embodied a similar preoccupation with the Icelandic landscape: the majority of music by composer Jón Leifs (1899–1968) is programmatic and draws on the Icelandic landscape and the sagas, and incorporates traditional Icelandic musics believed to have originated prior to Danish influence.

The role of Iceland's landscape as a symbol of historical continuity is epitomized by Þingvellir in the south-west of Iceland, where dramatic ravines mark the zone of geological displacement along the Mid-Atlantic Ridge. It is now a National park, but was originally the location of the Alþingi, Iceland's national assembly and high court from 930 AD to the eighteenth century. Volcanoes and glaciers signified independence and stoicism for nineteenth-century nationalists (the forging of the nation out of adversity) and preserved a continuity with the past throughout the years of Danish rule (Oslund 2002: 323). Even today, Iceland's volcanoes and ice are synecdoches through which it is recognized internationally. However, this version of the Icelandic landscape is difficult to sustain in the face of regions of Iceland which are more pastoral in character, and problematically (for tourism promoters) "un-Icelandic" in their failure to conform to the image of Iceland as the Arctic North (Helgadóttir n.d.).

Iceland's ideological rural national landscape (Edensor 2002) reflects a distinction between urban and rural landscapes: the idea that the rural, peasant class was the heart of national culture prevailed because it preserved the language and mores of the culture more than the city dwellers supposedly corrupted by foreign influence (Hálfdanarson 1995). However, this notion is at odds with Iceland's modernization over the last sixty years: it is now a technologically advanced society with a thriving urban centre in Reykjavík.

There are specific historical reasons why technological advancement is an important aspect of contemporary Icelandic identity. During Danish rule a trading monopoly prevented Iceland from developing its own fishing economy, and a farming elite developed on Iceland which served Denmark's economic purposes. When this system outlived its usefulness, farming became reconstructed by Icelanders as "backward" and fishing became Iceland's primary economic focus, even though this backwardness was a product of Iceland's previous position as a tributary to Denmark rather than an objective truth (Durrenberger 1996). Thus, although the image of the nation as land remains an important facet of Icelandic nationalism, it carries with it retrograde connotations at odds with the modernizing agenda of the industrialized nation Iceland has become. There is therefore a tension within contemporary Icelandic identity between technology, modernity and the urban on the one hand, and nature, tradition and the rural on the other.

A second important aspect of Icelandic national identity was the circulation of the idea of a "natural" relationship between the land, the language and the people – an idea which was central to European nationalist movements in the nineteenth century (Hedetoft and Hjort 2002: xii–xiii). Iceland's literary heritage was central to the Nationalist cause because its language had remained unchanged since settlement, was preserved in literature from the Middle Ages, and was Iceland's main form of cultural expression until the twentieth century. Nationalists played down the links with other cultures, and emphasized its cultural uniqueness. Familial and friendship lineages illustrated in the Family Sagas, which functioned as claims to land, were reinterpreted as evidence of ethnic roots; individual autonomy was linked to national Independence (as ironized in the novel *Independent People* (*Sjálfstaett Fólk*), 1934–5) by Halldór Laxness, in which the main character, Bjartur, puts his existence as an independent farmer – a symbol of frontier mentality, the taming of nature and rural traditions – above health and family); and popular and institutional reception of the sagas highlighted the classless, democratic society seemingly depicted within them, as a means of constructing the Icelandic population as a homogenous one, suited to the nation's claims for Independence. Ideas of equality, independence and purity were imported to serve the interests of the political elite who were working to gain independence from Denmark, but, according to Durrenberger (1996: 185), they later took on an authenticity of their own.[3] Racially essentialist criteria for Icelandic identity in the twenty-first century are facilitated by the establishment in 1996 of an Icelandic medical database by the deCode genomics company, the discourse surrounding which encourages Icelanders to think of themselves as a unique genetic community (Simpson 2000).

The connection between inhabitants of Iceland and the land was further emphasized by Icelandic religiosity. Prior to and even after the adoption of Christianity in Iceland circa 1000 AD, the inhabitants of Iceland practised

Norse paganism, a polytheistic animist tradition, which held that supernatural beings inhabited every natural object. Contemporary Icelanders are exposed to these ideas through the sagas and Eddas (Old Norse poems and tales), as indicated by the emergence of Ásatrú, a form of Germanic neo-paganism, which accounts for less than one per cent of the population, but which was officially recognized by the government in 1973. Thus, although the National Church of Iceland is Lutheran, pagan beliefs form an important part of the Icelandic national identity because they represent a connection to the imagined Golden Age of Icelandic history.

In summary, Icelanders' views of themselves are shaped by a colonial past, such that its language, literature and land are the basis of its historical continuity as a nation: the sites most frequently shown to visitors, and promoted in tourist brochures by the Icelandic Tourist Board, are the Árni Magnússon Institute (which holds the medieval manuscripts of sagas repatriated from Denmark in the 1970s and 1980s), and Þingvellir (the birthplace of the parliament and a symbol of nature) (Sigurðsson 1996). As a nation who only recently became independent, yet who even then remained occupied by a foreign army, Icelanders' ability to feel pride in their nationality, and to make a contribution perceived as at least equal with other nations in a European and global context is a salient issue in contemporary Icelandic consciousness.

Imaginings of Iceland by outsiders have historically viewed Iceland as a place lying culturally, politically, and geographically, on the periphery of Europe, and stuck in the Middle Ages. While it is true that Iceland remained rural much later than other European nations, Iceland had always had contact with the rest of the world and been influenced by European ideas through its connection to Denmark: Copenhagen was the main cultural centre for Icelanders. Iceland's peripheral position in European consciousness is partly due to its geographical location on the North-Western edge of Europe, where it has a historic role as a staging post between Europe and the United States, which dates back to an abortive Viking settlement of Greenland, and subsequently of Vinland (Newfoundland), the first recorded European presence on the North American continent. Iceland continued in this role during the twentieth century by virtue of the re-fuelling of trans-Atlantic flights at Keflavík, the US air force base, and the symbolic status of Iceland as the "mid-way" location for the Reagan-Gorbachev summit in 1986. Its peripheral status is also partly a consequence of its small population, and its previous colonial status.

Icelanders' articulation of pride in their national identity, and perception of Iceland by foreign media and audiences as an exotic periphery to Europe and North America, are shaped by one another. Looked at in these terms, Björk's sometimes whimsical and hyperbolic self-presentation in interviews can be understood as an articulation of nationalist sentiment to an audience largely ignorant of Iceland. So, for example, accounts of her grandmother painting out on the lava fields, and of her own compositional practices outdoors, can be understood as articulating the link to nature central to Icelandic national identity, as well as affirming romantic ideologies of creativity and authenticity (Ahonen 2006). Björk's accounts of her family as, variously, owing their livelihood to fishing or hunting ("my family still hunts for half our food, but using a mobile phone and a laptop to coordinate with other hunters" (Berry 1998)) articulates a link to the rural peasant life, which lies at the heart of Icelandic national identity, simultaneous with a display of Iceland as a developed nation. Her self-avowed stubbornness references long-established notions of Icelanders as a people who have overcome adversity. Her reported habit of collecting model boats, living on boats, and her self-presentation as musical "pioneer" draw upon a perceived continuity between the modern nation and Iceland's Viking past and frontier mentality. Her claim to Icelandic identity is also made on an ethnically essentialist basis of genealogy ("my family tree of the past 1000 years only contains Icelanders" (Rüth 1997)), and genetics: "I am from Iceland. I was born with two legs, two arms, and genes that go 1,200 years back being what I am, with my nose, my eyes, whatever... That is Icelandic" (McDonnell 1997).[4]

This analysis of contemporary Icelandic consciousness would suggest that Björk's work was shaped by a newly emerging patriotism in relation to a colonial past, founded upon a unity of land, language and literature, and its communication of ancient mythology. However, this consciousness is itself part of the global imagination of Iceland, shaped in relation to outsiders' views. The next section considers how ideas of Iceland among outsiders shaped interpretations of Björk's work in the foreign press.

Nationalism   31

Ideas of the North in the Reception of Björk's Artistic Output

Critical reception of Björk's work reflects many of these ideas of Icelandic identity, where they take the form of a generalized northern-ness through mention of Icelandic topography and nature, fairytales and myth, her perceived Viking ancestry, and characterizations of her as "other-worldly." One of the earliest available English-language reviews of Björk, a review of *The Eye* in 1984, refers to Kukl's "glacial world of confused emotions", and subsequent reviews of the Sugarcubes refer to Björk as an "elf" (Dessau 1992). By the time of *Debut* in 1993 English language discourse on Björk was marked by a now-familiar repertoire of references: Björk is variously depicted as an "ice princess", "-queen", or "-fairy" with "elfin looks", and descriptions of her music and voice use metaphors of ice, geysers and volcanoes. Systematic analysis of the critical reception of her music reveals two main themes, landscape and folklore, which I deal with in turn.[5] The prevalence of certain themes differs across the press coverage in different languages[6] (which shows how interpretations are shaped by specific cultural circumstances of reception), and across the chronology of her career[7] (reflecting changes in her output). However, there are many similarities in her work's reception, which reflect shared ideas of the North circulating across cultures, and the influence of promotional material released by One Little Indian (the production of which was subject to, as well as helping to shape, ideas of the North).

Icelandic topography appears as metaphor for her music, voice, and artistic experimentation. A review of *Vespertine* describes her as making "music for laptop and broken ice"[8] (Prevignano 2001); and in *Medúlla* "Her most hushed tracks rouse the laziest ears with the force of icebergs jutting from still water" (Lee 2004). She is described as "geyser-voiced" (Aston 1993: 40), with "a voice at once as steamy and as volatile as her country's famous volcanic hot springs" (Helligar and Griffiths 1995), while her "sources of inspiration gush like the geysers of her homeland"[9] (Rüth 1997), and her "emotional world . . . explodes anew . . . almost like one of the innumerable volcanoes of her homeland"[10] (Frost 2001). The metaphors juxtapose opposites, highlighting the perceived dynamism of the landscape: "*Homogenic* seems on the one hand chilly and restrained, yet at the same time simmering, ready to explode" (Berry 1998); "It's the defect and the excellence of Björk:

not to set limits, to cross the borders of rationality, to convene fire and water in the same swirl of instinctive impudence"[11] (Sabatier 1997). Thus, Björk's critical reception draws upon ideas of the Icelandic landscape as a geologically active land of fire and ice – an image which is central to nationalist constructions of Icelandic identity.

The second recurrent theme is Björk's depiction as a character from (a stereotyped version of) Icelandic folklore and mythology. Hence, Björk is an "elfin-eskimo" (Deevoy 1994: 92), an "Icelandic imp" (Fay 1994), and an "indie-pixie" (Thompson 1997: 66); who "was helped by several elves and goblins devoted to her cause"[12] (Dessange 2004) and "is blessed with a gamine face which should belong to a character from Tolkien" (Harding 1995). These references to the supernatural reflect the importance of myth and magic within perceptions of Iceland. The other aspect of Icelandic folklore which appears in Björk's reception is the characterization of her as a musical "explorer" ("Electronica is the musical territory this thirty-two-year-old pioneer has been exploring since the late 80s" (Herman 1997)) which is reinforced by European imaginations of the heroic north,[13] and authenticated in interviews by her essentialized Viking ethnicity: "Björk loves the radical, and the lack of compromise considered characteristic of her native people"[14] (Rüth 1997). Statements such as this are redolent of an essentializing tendency in nationalist agendas within which familial and racial criteria define national identity.

Björk's Icelandic nationality is also a means by which she is exoticized in critical reception, which cites her nationality in explanation of her perceived eccentricity and eclectic style. Some representations even draw upon the idea of extraterrestrial otherness, participating in a discourse in which Iceland is seen as "outside" the West: "The clothes, her nearly supernatural face and accent leaves the impression that Björk is an alien, just landed on our planet"[15] (Simonart 1995: 6).

The themes highlighted in this analysis of Björk's reception are a means of interpreting Björk's artistic output, but at the same time they expose audiences to, and help maintain particular ideas about, Iceland and the North. These themes are central to other contemporary representations of Icelandic identity. For example, the discourse around Björk shares striking similarities with official characterizations of Iceland, as illustrated by the quotation below which is taken from a tourist board website:

> Much of Iceland is still taking shape before your very eyes — raw, dramatic landscapes born from volcanic eruptions and carved out by glaciers. Other parts have hardly changed since the first Viking settlers saw them more than 1,100 years ago. You'll experience wilderness and wildlife, energy and total calm, within easy reach wherever you stay, even on day trips. (Visticeland.com n.d.)

Both reflect ideas of contrasts and extremes, dynamic processes of renewal, Viking heritage and exploration, and rural wilderness. Perhaps then, Björk's Icelandic origin is significant only to the extent that it supplies a lexicon of headline-friendly metaphors and a framework within which experience of her music is enriched by associations with ideas of the North. It tells us about imaginations of the North and of Iceland. Yet, as the opening quotation makes clear, nationalist sentiment is an explicit part of Björk's consciousness and has shaped her output.

Nationalist Sentiment in Björk's Artistic Output

During the 1990s, Björk explicitly represented herself as a patriotic Icelander, whose nationality had influenced her music, and whose compositional ambition was to create an "Icelandic" music. In *Family Tree* (2002), the self-documentation of Björk's career up to 2001, Björk provides an insight into the elements comprising this style and her "re-invention" of Icelandic music by providing a taxonomy for her songs:

> <<Roots>>: Where we come from, the ancient things in us – in my case, stubbornness and patriotism; enthusiasm for Iceland, the culture and the natural physical environment; old-woman melodies and indigenous punk rock; my voice...
>
> <<Beats>>: Our craving for modern times – in my case, the desire to unite with the new and unknown, the alien and taboo by merging my voice with foreign electronic beats. With this experience, I could then try to develop a peculiarly "Icelandic" electronic rhythm...
>
> <<Strings>>: Our struggle with education and all things academic – in my case, ten years of classical music training

where I was force-fed German composers then spent the next fifteen battling them: if we were going to invent a new Icelandic modern musical language then where did Brahms and Beethoven come into it? After all these years, string arrangements have enabled me to unite my musical universe with the academic one.

<<Words>>: How we use words to tell stories about different emotional states... (Liner notes to *Family Tree* 2002).

Björk's rhetoric reflects common components of nationalist constructions of identity and belonging. Most strikingly, the language of the category "roots" expresses a territorialism in which the people are part of, and sustained by, the land ("the natural physical environment"); furthermore, that land is presented as continuous with the idea of the nation, thereby presenting the nation as pre-political and given by nature. She references Iceland's literary heritage, thereby showing her continuity with that tradition of storytelling, reinflected with a modern emphasis upon the expression of individualized emotional states. Björk also identifies tensions in Icelandic national and musical identity between the modern and traditional, and between foreign and Icelandic, which she explores through the use of indigenous popular and folk musical forms, and through engagement with foreign and "academic" musics.

Björk's nationalist sentiment found its first expression in Iceland's punk scene in the 1970s and 80s, which was perceived by many of the people involved in it to be about reclaiming Icelandic identity from an older, conservative generation. With the few radio and television channels in Iceland controlled by the State, and the historical dominance of the pop scene in Iceland by Anglophone pop, there were few opportunities for alternatives. Punk's arrival in Iceland in the late 1970s coincided with a quest for an Icelandic musical and social identity, as Björk described:

> The problem that had yet to be solved, when punk happened in Iceland, was to define what it was to be Icelandic. It was a question of not forgetting about nature, how important that is. Not forgetting about the mythology that we have that is very strong in our culture. I think all of it went together in quite an explosive pot. (*Inside Björk*, dir. Walker 2003)

Some of the features referred to by Björk in the quotation above are apparent in her early career. For example, the very name Kukl (sorcery) connects with the idea of (indigenous) paganism as communicated though the sagas, in contrast to "foreign" Christian beliefs. Furthermore, many of the bands Björk worked with prior to her solo career were associated with Íslenska Ásatrúarfélagið (the old pagan Norse religion) via the involvement of Hilmar Örn Hilmarsson, then the chief goði (head pagan): namely, Þeyr (1980–83), the Elgar Sisters (1984–6) and various projects with ex-Sugarcubes musician Einar Örn Benediktsson.[16] The narratives of Björk's lyrics with the Sugarcubes (as told by Björk in interviews) are reminiscent of fairytales and folklore, and their often surreal imagery references Icelandic tropes of the sea, harbours, explosions ('Tidalwave'), ice and glaciers ('Water': both from *Here Today, Tomorrow, Next Week!*); ships, mountains and valleys ('Walkabout' from *Stick Around for Joy*); and demons, angels and gods (the latter of which "do not exist" according to 'Deus' from *Life's Too Good*).

Some writers claim links between the sound materials of Icelandic folk music and Björk's compositional style. Marsh and West claim that Björk incorporates "various native Icelandic influences, such as the vocal technique, a combination of speech and singing, used to narrate the sagas from the twelfth and thirteenth centuries" (Marsh and West 2003: 193). Their argument was supported by Hilmar Örn Hilmarsson who claimed that the roots of Icelandic music lie in the Viking age, and are related to the metrical structure of the poetry of that era (*Screaming Masterpiece*, dir. Magnússon 2005). Yet, there is little evidence for such links: the phrasing and metrical structures of Björk's music have more in common with contemporary rock and pop than with skaldic or eddaic poetry. Björk's only direct engagement with Icelandic musical traditions is found in her performances of the folk song 'Vísur Vatnsenda-Rósu', originally recorded by Björk for Hector Zazou's album *Songs of the Cold Seas* (1995).

In writing *Homogenic* Björk contacted musicologist and DJ Ásmundur Jónsson in an explicit attempt to identify an Icelandic musical tradition she could incorporate into her music to convey her nationalist sentiments. However, the search proved ill-founded: "I really wanted to discover what Icelandic music is, and if there is such a thing. And in a way, there really isn't" (Björk cited in Van Meter 1997). Iceland's musical heritage is weak in comparison with its famed literary history. Two main forms of music appear to have been practised prior to the twentieth century. The first was the Icelandic song form, kvæðaskapur, which consists of metrical epic poems (rímur), the earliest texts of which derive from poetry of the Viking Age. These ballads use alliteration and rhyme, with complex metaphors and would have been sung unaccompanied, although they fell out of common usage in the mid-nineteenth century (Steingrímsson 2000). The second main form of music was religious. As an officially Christian nation since c.1000 AD, hymn singing was one aspect of Icelandic musical life. The hymns were first based on protestant German hymns, and later written by Icelanders (for example, Hallgrímur Pétursson 1614–74) and featured two distinctive musical attributes: first, parallel movement between voices in which two or more lines follow the same melodic contour separated by an interval of a fourth, fifth or octave, and which typically has a stark, empty sound, and second, the augmented fourth of the Lydian mode, which sounds more yearning in character than the now more familiar major mode. The practice of singing in two-part parallel movement (tvísöngur) appears to have been one of the most dominant Icelandic vocal forms between the fourteenth and twentieth centuries, and is found both in Icelandic oral folk practice and religious settings (Ingólfsson 2003). These indigenous musical forms died out during the nineteenth century due to the influence of the church and harmonium, and the introduction of Western European diatonic harmony, and, later, three and four-part vocal styles and keyboard skills (Cronshaw 1999; Faulkner 2005). The result was a "vocal cleansing" in which old musical forms were silenced, while, by contrast, ancient literary forms, the Icelandic sagas, were used to forge Icelandic national identity. In the first part of the twentieth century organizations and collections were initiated to preserve and revitalize some of these musical traditions, the influence of which can be heard in the music of twentieth-century Icelandic composer Jón Leifs (for example, *25 Icelandic Folk Songs*, published 1928).

Despite Björk's claim that she didn't find an "Icelandic" music, there is some similarity to Icelandic folk traditions in the voicing of instrumental parts in her arrangements, and her melodic and modal style. For example, the empty, monastic-like sound of the strings in the introduction to 'Jóga', and parts of 'Hunter' from *Homogenic* is the result of two-part parallel movement in fifths, which is a feature of tvísöngur and Jón Leifs' compositional style,

Nationalism   37

and the Lydian mode is one of the most frequent to feature in her music, as it is in Leifs's.

The influence of Icelandic musical traditions is also evident in symbolic aspects of Björk's music-making. 'Anchor Song' was written during a holiday Björk took in which she cycled between a number of farmstead churches, her aim being to write a song in each using her voice and the organ.[17] Use of organs in the churches built and maintained by farmers positions her within a history of Icelandic religious music-making, and articulates a continuity with Iceland's rural past – a feature found in other contemporary Icelandic pop, such as Apparat Organ Quartet.[18] There is also a symbolic continuity with Icelandic (and a generalized Northern) music through her collaborations with musicians from Iceland, Greenland and Denmark: she deliberately chose to work with Icelandic string players in *Homogenic*, and an Icelandic brass ensemble in *Volta*. In live performance these ensembles serve an explicitly Northern symbolism: for example, the female choir on the *Vespertine* tour wore dresses whose design derived from Greenland's national costume and was referred to as "A choir from Greenland" (in fact, they were a collection of individual singers recruited from auditions held in Greenland where Björk had been holidaying).

These factors contribute to the construction of Björk's Northern "otherness", which is also portrayed by promotional material commissioned by One Little Indian. For example, the documentary *Inside Björk* (dir. Walker 2003) situates Björk as a "northern other" through filming on location in Iceland's most rural and arctic-looking environments, and through voice-overs and interview material which emphasize her connection to (a specifically Icelandic) nature, characterized by "twenty-two hour daylight in the summer and darkness in the winter…and icebergs and eruptions and no trees at all" (Björk, interviewed in *Inside Björk* (dir. Walker 2003)). As others have noted, Björk's identity often draws upon generalized notions of the arctic North, rather than a specifically Icelandic identity (Grimley 2005: 49).

Iceland is one of a number of places that have been perceived as embodying an idea of the North, traced through literature and art from European antiquity to the nineteenth century (Davidson 2005), and is a possible location of Thule – the mythical Northern land alluded to by explorers, philosophers and poets (Kavenna 2005). The choir from Greenland is a good instance of this: Iceland is already for many people a representative of

Northern culture, yet the presence of the choir from Greenland, whose Inuit ethnicity seems to remove them further from Euro-American culture, suggests exoticism – as if Greenland is representative of a more authentic north. Given that Björk's colouring and facial features are more akin to Inuit looks than to those of Icelanders, the choir further aligns Björk with this exoticized Northern identity. Similarly, the throat singing incorporated into *Medúlla* and the music to *Drawing Restraint 9* derives from a game played between women in Greenland, which Tanya "Tagaq" Gillis (from the Nunavut territories of Northern Canada) developed into a performance art. The status of these sounds as a modern interpretation of traditional practices contributes to the construction of a generalized Northern identity.

A distinctively Icelandic identity is conveyed through references to Iceland's literary heritage in Björk's artistic output. Iceland's medieval literature is renowned as the earliest written source of Norse history and mythology. It has three main forms: the Eddas, Norse poems and stories first written down in the thirteenth century but originating in earlier centuries; Skaldic poetry, which commemorated or satirized historical events; and Icelandic sagas, which are prose narratives of the lives and genealogies of Icelanders, and some accounts of historical events.[19] Occasionally in interviews Björk made reference to the tradition of sagas, drawing out her continuity with this cultural heritage within a specifically nationalist context:

> The Danish treated us very badly for the six or seven hundred years we were their colony. For example, the church banned musical dancing. So storytelling became the thing that thrived with us. Storytelling is us. The Icelandic people, we were the ones who wrote down all the sagas. They memorized stories from generation to generation; they could go on for, like, two hours. That's why I believe in old-school songwriting.
> (Doerschuk 1997)

An example of this is the sequence of songs 'Human Behaviour', 'Isobel' and 'Bachelorette' (each on a different album), which narrate the story of a mythical character, Isobel, who symbolizes intuition.[20]

Occasionally Björk's lyrics also reference Iceland's literary heritage. For example, the lyrics "Jump off/your building's on fire", from 'Come to Me' (*Debut* 1993) is a reference to the burning of houses and their occupants in feuds between families in the Icelandic sagas: for instance, in *Njáls Saga* Kári jumps from the house to escape the flames. Björk also rationalized her decision to place the lush 'All is Full of Love' after the distorted sounds of 'Pluto' on *Homogenic* by reference to the Eddic poem *Völuspa* (*The Seeress's Prophecy*, recorded in the *Codex Regius*), in which the beginning and end of the world is described, but in which the world rises again from the sea:

> In Icelandic mythology, you have this saga where the Gods get aggressive and the world explodes and everything dies and then the sun comes up and everything starts all over again. It's ['All Is Full Of Love'] the last track on *Homogenic* after 'Pluto' which stands for death. (Björk cited in Hemingway 2002: 43).

A further connection to Icelandic literature and its nationalist associations can be found in Björk's references to bells. In the music video 'Who is it (Carry my joy on the left, carry my pain on the right)', directed by Engish video artist Dawn Shadforth, Björk wears a dress shaped like a bell, designed by Alexander McQueen (see Figure 4), and is accompanied by children playing hand bells dressed in costumes covered with miniature bells.[21] Although it was not a deliberate reference by the director (Shadforth 2006),[22] the image of a bell, positioned against a barren Icelandic landscape (here, the iconic black sands beneath Hjörleifshöfði, a headland in Iceland), is a theme found in a number of contexts associated with Icelandic nationalism. For example, the nationalist trilogy *Iceland's Bell* (*Íslandsklukkan*, 1943–6), by Halldór Laxness, includes a scene in which "Iceland's only treasure" is cut down from its place at the courthouse at Þingvellir, and broken up to be used in the rebuilding of Copenhagen for the Danish King – a commentary on Iceland's treatment under the Danish, and a scene depicted in the nationalist painter Jóhannes Sveinsson Kjarval's painting of the same name (*Íslandsklukkan*, 1952).[23] These works establish the connotations of bells that give the video its status as a portrayal of nationalist sentiment. Bells also appear elsewhere in Björk's artistic output: for example, the name of the album of jazz standards, *Gling Gló* (1990) is an Icelandic onomatopoeia for the sound of bells (the equivalent of 'Ding Dong' in English); and Björk increasingly used bell-like sounds in her music (celesta, glockenspiel and likembe).

Figure 4: Still image from the music video 'Who Is It (Carry my joy on the left, carry my pain on the right)' (dir. Dawn Shadforth 2004). Dress by Alexander McQueen.

Lastly, Iceland's pagan history, and a more generalized northern identity, is articulated through Björk's celebration of nature, mystery and magic, as in *Vespertine*, and most explicitly in her conception of *Medúlla* as an album expressing a "pagan element . . . that is going back to the roots – before time, or civilization, or religion, or patriotism" ("Lyrics" 1995–2004). In interviews about *Medúlla* Björk used the notion of paganism to articulate a utopian idea of a world in which humans are not divided by religion or nationality. The fact that paganism is used as the symbol of a world prior to the existence of nation-states paradoxically reveals the influence of nationalist enculturation: in the context of Icelandic nationalism, paganism is part of the idealized settlement and Commonwealth period prior to the advent of Christian belief and foreign rule. Association with this idealized period of Icelandic history and identity is further signified by the recurrent motif of travel by ship, referencing Viking ancestry (for example, the title of the 1994 documentary *Vessel*, dir. Stéphane Sednaoui), and references to familial relationships and genealogy – for example, the album title *Family Tree* (2002).

These examples illustrate the way in which some of Björk's artistic practices articulate a continuity with aspects of Iceland's history and mythology. The one aspect of Björk's artistic output that conforms less closely to the trilogy of land, literature and language is the predominant use of the English language in performance and recording of songs. Björk's explicit reasoning for singing in English was that she wanted to communicate to a mass audience who would not understand song lyrics sung in Icelandic. Significantly, once she had attained commercial success in her solo career, Björk's albums frequently included songs in Icelandic, or a combination of Icelandic, English and a made-up, nonsense language.

'Jóga' and the Articulation of Icelandic National Identity

The prime statement of Björk's nationalist sentiment is *Homogenic*, and within that, the music video of the track 'Jóga' (which appeared on *Volumen* in 1999), for which she has claimed an explicit nationalist agenda: "With this song, I really had a sort of National Anthem in mind. Not the National Anthem but certain classic Icelandic songs — very romantic, very proud" ("Björk Family Tree and Greatest Hits: Jóga" 2002). The track's importance for Björk, and for her audience, is evidenced by its many releases: in addition to *Homogenic*, 'Jóga' appears on the *Greatest Hits* album voted for by fans, and on Björk's choice of *Greatest Hits* and the 'Roots' collection (a specific reference to nationalist sentiment), the latter two of which are both on *Family Tree*.

There are strong biographical reasons why *Homogenic* is Björk's most explicitly nationalist album. By the time of *Homogenic*'s release in 1997, Björk had been living in London for five years in order to pursue her solo musical career. But the move had not been without its strains: she and her young son had left family and friends in Iceland. The continued importance of her homeland as a touchstone for her artistic output is attested to by Björk's characterization of her second solo studio album, *Post*, as a letter sent home to friends and family in Iceland. *Homogenic* consisted entirely of material she had written after she had left Iceland, and so was the first opportunity for her songs to fully reflect the impact of her experiences in London. The media's focus on her Icelandic identity also heightened Björk's perception of her national identity, along with the new perspective on her identity that moving to another country provided: "I go to London, and I've never been so Icelandic. When I lived here [Iceland], I didn't even think about it" (Björk cited in McDonnell 1997: 26).

Björk attributed her consciousness of her Icelandic identity during her years in London to her collaboration with what she saw as an "immigrant" community of British musicians: DJ and tabla player Talvin Singh, known for his fusion of Indian classical and Western pop styles, Leila Arab who moved to London from Iran in the late 1970s, jungle DJ Goldie (Clifford Joseph Price) of Jamaican and Scottish descent, and trip-hop DJ and rapper Tricky (Adrian Thaws) whose family came from a variety of ethnic backgrounds:

> Being Icelandic with different baggage from those people led me to ask; what is Icelandic music? Can I just be a girl who grew up in Reykjavík and be proud of it? But still use the drum machine and have something to say in the musical capital of the world today, without making me feel the yokel deep down inside me, the fish factories and dried fish? (Björk interviewed in the album booklet of *LiveBox*, 2003).

Björk's questioning of her identity within a British, multicultural context reflects a more widespread issue raised by cosmopolitanism: namely, tensions between globalization (facilitated by geographical mobility, and digital communications) and the idea of national identity. Björk's description of her response to this situation during the 1990s emphasized her attempt to create a new identity through her artistic output – one that both acknowledged her Icelandic identity (represented by the reference to "dried fish" and their symbolism of a backward, peasant existence), and her cosmopolitanism (its technological modernity represented by reference to "drum machines"). Björk responded to this situation by attempting to create an Icelandic musical identity she could be proud of – a response which indicates the extent to which she was influenced by nationalism during her upbringing in Iceland.

'Jóga' articulates a pre-existing image of Icelandic identity which represents the narratives and histories shared by Icelanders, and in that sense it is an instance of "national" music. The visuals to the music video 'Jóga' (one of seven of Björk's videos directed by Michel Gondry) take up the lyrical narrative of the song: the lyrics speak of "emotional landscapes," while the video cuts between a variety of glacial, coastal and mountainous Icelandic landscapes; the emotional "state of emergency" declared in the lead vocal coincides with panoramic flying shots of mountains, lava fields, volcanic rifts, and sandurs (the braided sands resulting from glacial bursts); and, in the final moments of the music video, the camera's gaze enters Björk's chest to find a heart-shaped island, similar to that of Iceland, where the heart would normally be.[24] These closing moments can be understood as a visual realization of Björk's nationalist sentiments, and of her music's articulation of that attachment: "the music comes more or less from one direction: straight from the heart, because home is where the heart is" (Björk interviewed in van den Berg 1997).

The "state of emergency" referred to in the lyrics can be read as a reference to, and metaphor for, the nation-state of Iceland; it maintains a cultural construction of the landscape in terms of geological processes of renewal, allied to concepts of social and political renewal after independence from Danish rule, and as a reference to a heightened affective state. The personal character of the song's symbolism of "homeland" is evident in its title: 'Jóga' is the nickname of one of Björk's closest Icelandic friends.

Unusually for a pop video, there are neither shots of performance nor a narrative; instead, the visuals take landscape as their subject matter. Travelling camera shots cut between landscapes differentiated by geographical feature (sea, river, estuary, hill, mountain, beach), colour (various hues of red, purple, blue, green, brown, black and white), texture (sand, rocks, pebbles, grass), and distance of the camera from the visual scene (i.e. panoramic versus close-up). Visuals constitute cuts between camera shots moving across geographical features in close-up, juxtaposed with panoramic flying camera shots during the chorus. The two types of camera work are linked by a rising camera shot which takes the camera between the two levels in a single sweeping movement on the final line of the refrain, "push me up to" (0:55–0:57 and 1:52–1:59).

This representation of the Icelandic landscape as pure and raw is a landscape ideology familiar from Icelandic nationalist literature and art: there are no animals or people, other than the cyber-looking Björk, and there are no signs of interventions into the landscape by humans. The close-up shots capturing the textures and colours of moss and lichen-covered rocks (see Figure 5) are strikingly similar to work by Iceland's most revered nationalist painter, Jóhannes Kjarval (see Figure 6).[25] Kjarval was the first Icelandic painter to take the moss and rock of the landscape as his focus; the foreground in his work was given increasing prominence, until the lava fields became independent subject matter. Like other Icelandic artists of the time, Kjarval's paintings depict a landscape before human intervention (including the historic site at Þingvellir), thereby reinforcing the "natural" elision of nation with land, which was so central to the nationalist movement. The importance of Kjarval to Björk's artistic output is also evident in that she titled one of her earliest compositions after him – the track 'Kjarval' from *Björk* (1977) – influenced by a picture which hung above her grandparents' piano ("Always Been Special: An interview with Björk's grandma and grandpa", 1993).

Figures 5 and 6 show the similar filling of the foreground by lichen-covered, rock-strewn landscape in the video 'Jóga' and in a painting by Kjarval. Just as Kjarval's paintings of lava fields prevent the landscape from becoming "background" to a foregrounded human subject, so Gondry's video realization of the track minimizes the foregrounding of Björk as sub-

Figure 5: Still image from the music video 'Jóga' (dir. Michel Gondry 1997).

Nationalism 45

Figure 6: 'Skjaldbreiður' 1957–62 Jóhannes Kjarval © Heirs/Myndstef, 2001.

ject, instead presenting her as part of the landscape represented: Björk's visual presence in the video is confined to the introduction (00:13–00:22) and coda (02:50–3:00); and the visuals equate the landscape with the persona of Björk, and in doing so continues a tradition in which the nation of Iceland is represented as woman (Koestler 1995). Björk's embodiment of landscape is manifested in a number of ways. On each appearance she is motionless like the landscape around her, and flying camera shots which spiral in to a close-up on her provides movement. The effect of this is to make both Björk and the landscape objects of the travelling camera's gaze. Björk's identity with the landscape is further affirmed through her visual appearance: she is first shown lying motionless on a black beach (a synecdoche for Iceland), her white coat stark like snow against the black sand, and she later stands on a mountain top, whereupon the camera enters her chest (a cave hewn from the same rock as the exterior landscape) and circles her island-heart. In neither case does she lip synch to the vocals. Furthermore, her treatment using computer graphics creates a cyber-look akin to the treatment of the landscape. Thus, her visual presence as subject is eroded in favour of the landscape, which prevents the landscape from becoming "background".

This erosion of the subject (Björk) also occurs through musical characteristics of the track. The foregrounding of traditionally background material (landscape) in the visual scene finds its aural equivalent in the bridge section of this strophic (verse-chorus) track, where percussive material previously and subsequently heard as "background" to the lead vocal, becomes the object of auditory attention. Furthermore, the multi-tracked vocals which occur at the coda of the track (02:42), disrupt the unitary persona implied by the lead vocal, and undermine the tendency to hear the singing voice as emanating from the image of Björk within the video; here she is subject matter (landscape), not subjectivity.

Yet the persona of Björk cannot be escaped, particularly in the auditory track where it is implied by the lead vocal, and where synchronization between camera movement and aspects of musical phrasing and rhythm place the persona's embodiment in the camera's gaze. Having zoomed in on Björk lying on the beach during the video's opening travelling shot, the close-ups, which follow, can be experienced as if seen through Björk's eyes, whose voice we hear as first person narrator. Similarly, the coincidence of upward swoop of the camera to the panoramic shots, and the greater musical activity of the transition from refrain to chorus, bind auditory and visual scenes together as the subjectivity of a single virtual persona. The focus on landscape, to the exclusion of all else, then, is Björk's, and not just ours, the viewer's. These devices align Björk with the landscape, allowing her to simultaneously embody it (through her visual identification as part of the landscape), and to be a separate persona whose viewpoint is absorbed in it (through the alignment of the singing voice with the camera's gaze).

Björk attributed the nationalist character of the music of *Homogenic* to her use of strings and to the character of the beats. The "patriotic" character of the strings can be attributed to associations with the Icelandic folk song tradition of tvísöngur: the string writing in the verse is characterized by parallel step-wise movement in fifths, which has an empty sound (see Figure 7). These musical materials also have a religious association, which is

Nationalism 47

Figure 7: Parallel movement in fifths in the string arrangement of the first verse of 'Jóga' (*Homogenic* 1997).

heightened by the reduced vibrato in these sections (a performance style associated with early European sacred music), compared to its increased use in the chorus.

The beats in 'Jóga' are aligned with the idea of seismic energy, and can to some extent be heard as mimetic of ideas of the "raw", volcanic landscape. The percussive materials are foregrounded in the bridge section (1:20–1:40). The sounds are distorted, suggesting raw power, by virtue of distortion's status as sound, which exceeds its means of reproduction. Furthermore, these musical materials coincide with a computer-generated animation showing tectonic plates splitting apart. The percussive sounds that enter in the first verse are progressively filtered, giving the effect of an object occluded to various degrees, and therefore of a sound source moving in relation to both the listener and lead vocal, the latter of which is positioned centrally within the mix.

These percussive materials can be heard as mimetic of Iceland's seismic activity, and therefore its geological "heart". Björk's statement that "The electronic beats [on *Homogenic*] are the rhythm, the heartbeat" is made manifest in the visuals, which show rocks pulsating as if each is a heart pumping blood. The idea of the seismically active landscape as the heart of the nation is presaged in Iceland's political rhetoric: in 1994 the Prime Minister described Þingvellir as a "sacred place" where the "heart of the Icelandic nation beats".[26] Þingvellir is symbolically the heart of Iceland both because of its historical status as the site of the Alþingi, and due to its geographical location at the point of displacement of the Eurasian and North American tectonic plates, which run north-east / south-west through the centre of the island, and whose action is the source of Iceland's geological activity. Thus, the music video 'Jóga' maintains a cultural construction of the

Icelandic nation as raw landscape, and reaffirms nationalist sentiment through the equivalence it draws between Iceland's social and cultural history and its landscape. Besides the character of the string writing and beats, the song's expressive impact can also be attributed to the sense of restraint and flow arising from the contrast between the sparse texture of the verse material and the more lyrical chorus, and the deletion/addition of beats and bars from/to the normative phrase structure. The verses are thin in texture, by virtue of the "empty" sound of the parallel movement, and the step-wise movement of this and the vocal melody. The chorus material is thicker, with a more varied rhythmic character to the violin and vocal lines and their larger intervallic leaps. The lyrical violin line is characterized by large interval leaps between phrases, via which alternate phrases are placed in different octave registers. The resultant effect of snatched breathing or bowing which this creates is heightened by the addition of a beat at the end of each pair of the four lines of lyrics of the chorus, suggesting something tripping up over itself (see Figure 8). The effect within the context of the whole track is of a series of emotional outbursts – a feature heightened by the change to wordless singing with the entry of the second voice. The repeating vocal figure, high in the chest register, fades in with a long reverberation time, as if coming from a vast distance, before it fades out at the re-entry of the lead vocal; acoustically evoking the vast distances of the mountainous landscapes.

Thus, 'Jóga', and *Homogenic* of which it is part, communicate an image of Iceland as a nation proud of, and shaped by its natural landscape; a land of extremes in which the modern and the ancient sit alongside one another, in which the landscape is a metaphor for nationalist renewal, and in which its people are inextricably part of and emotionally connected with that unity of land and nation.

Subsequent albums develop the exploration of identity begun on *Homogenic* through reference to an idealized time pre and post-nationalism, in *Medúlla* and *Volta* respectively. The collaborations with musicians from a wide range of musical cultures on *Volta* enact social and cultural integration, but without expressing nationalist sentiment: *Volta* reflected her frustration at Iceland's political and economic stance, leading her to declare that she was "a bit exhausted with nationalism" (Barton 2007: 9). However, Björk's own statements about her intentions and ideas are often contradictory, and this is no

Nationalism 49

Figure 8: Vocal and violin parts from the chorus of 'Jóga' (*Homogenic* 1997).

exception since one of the tracks on *Volta* is titled 'Declare Independence', the video of which (the seventh directed by Michel Gondry) features Björk exhorting a collective to independence. The national flags of Greenland and the Faroe Islands appear as arm badges on the factory-style boiler suits, and give the track an explicit nationalist specificity, since, unlike Iceland, both remain Danish territories. Interestingly, this does not reflect a conscious political motivation during the compositional process: "Declare Independence is a song I wrote with Mark Bell... We wanted to make a rave track and it ended up being about the Faroe Islands fighting for independence. I'm not sure how that happened" (Björk 2007). In live performances during the *Volta* tour Björk dedicated the track to other "oppressed" peoples, most notoriously to Tibet at the end of a performance of the song in Shanghai, China, in 2008.

Conclusion

Björk's artistic output is shaped in relation to the global imagination of Iceland and her enculturation within nationalist sentiment. This analysis shows that understanding the cultural context of her work's production and reception helps explain her work's thematic content and style. Prior to her solo career the groups of which she was a part expressed nationalist sentiment through punk's stylistic rejection of Anglo-American pop and its associated corporate culture, and through references to Icelandic pagan mythology. During her solo career and move away from Iceland, her nationalist sentiment found expression through artistic work which eulogized the Icelandic landscape; the analysis of the music video 'Jóga' illustrates some of the ways in which it did so. This Icelandic identity consists of continuity with Viking ancestry (through genealogy and ethnic essentialism), paganism and the Saga tradition, and the idea of Iceland as a nation defined in terms of its rural landscape, yet one that is distinctly modern.

One consequence of Björk's success has been a much greater awareness of Iceland among other nations – something which some Icelanders see as raising Iceland's international importance and therefore facilitating pride in the Icelandic nation. In a survey conducted by the Icelandic newspaper *Fréttablaðið* in 2006, Björk was voted the third most important living Icelander, coming after former president, Vigdís Finnbogadóttir, and former Prime Minister, Davið Oddsson. Author of the novel *101 Reykjavík* (1996), Hallgrímur Helgason, commented that:

> My generation was brought up feeling that we were out of place, a nation of losers, too small and provincial. I mean, we didn't even have beer until 1989 and the first Icelandic pizza was baked in 1990. In my youth the word 'red wine' had an exotic ring to it, a bit like 'balsamic vinegar' has here today. We really didn't feel proud of our country. But now everything has changed. All thanks to Björk, I guess. We've gained our self-esteem and our self-respect, a generation has grown up that is more internationally thinking. (Jackson 2004)

This has brought Björk government recognition for her work: in 2000 the Prime Minister Davið Oddsson recommended to parliament that she be given the uninhabited island of Ellidaey by way of a "royalty payment" after she expressed interest in buying it as a home: a government spokesman justified this on the grounds that "Bjork is a very well-known person in the world, especially in the music world. She's also an active player in the social life of Iceland... She is very focused on promoting her mother country. Knowledge of Iceland has risen dramatically since she began her successful career as a musician" (Procenko 2000).

However, from the perspective of some Icelanders, Björk's representation of Iceland plays into regressive stereotypes of Icelanders as stuck in the Middle Ages in their superstitious beliefs (the idea that Icelanders believe in trolls and fairies), as surviving on a rural economy, and peasant practices (such as eating puffin and whale). The eccentricities, which some foreign media perceive in Björk and attribute to her Icelandic identity, are particular to her rather than to Icelanders as a nation, many of whom view her behaviours as equally bizarre. Overwhelming ignorance of Iceland, and global imagination of Iceland in terms of the mythical north, means that Björk, the most famous of Icelanders, comes to stand for all Icelanders.

Björk's awareness of the ethnocentrism apparent in her exoticization by the media, and her protestations at the cultural stereotyping she and other Icelandic musicians receive,[27] has not stopped her own artistic output and promotional material playing into such interpretations. Continuity with Iceland's literary heritage, pagan belief system, musical traditions, and landscape are used to claim an authenticity for Björk's music that functions well within the music industry, in which links to place are often used as a marketing device, and as the basis for claims to sincerity (Whiteley, Bennett et al. 2004). It also draws upon ideas of the North, which endow Björk's artist output with relevance for audiences ignorant of the specifically Icelandic cultural references in her work. The geographical identity of her work is variously Icelandic, Nordic and Arctic, dependent upon the particular aspect of the work under consideration, and the preoccupations of her audience. Björk has not been as vociferous in dispelling myths surrounding Iceland as perhaps some would like, partly perhaps due to this commercial utility, partly in the interests of the entertainment value such material provides, and partly because such myths are treated by Björk as part of a cultural heritage to be respected, and with which the imagination should be allowed creative freedom.

This analysis of the global imagination of Iceland reveals a tension in contemporary Icelandic identity: tensions between traditional conceptions of Icelandic identity as rural, traditional and tied to the land, versus Iceland's current position as an industrial, urban, modern state; tensions between the bounded, homogenous and isolationist Iceland so central to nationalist imaginings of Iceland, and Iceland's desire to be seen as a nation equal to that of other European nations, and part of a globalized world; tensions between internationalization and interaction, versus preservation of Icelandic culture. The way these oppositions have shaped Björk's output can be seen both in her explicit patriotism and her attempts to unify these apparent conflicts through her artistic output. Returning to the liner notes of *Family Tree*, she ends her taxonomy of songs with what is perhaps the most explicit statement of her artistic aesthetic:

> To bring together <<Roots>>, <<Beats>>, <<Strings>> and <<Words>> to unite all these opposing systems is to be a medium between disparate worlds trying to unite history, the present and the environment, into a song, on the radio, in a possible moment of utopia...

From the perspective of post-colonial Iceland this unification addresses itself to oppositions within contemporary Icelandic consciousness as well as to generalized tensions relevant within a globalized world. The remainder of this book explores in detail the notion of unity as played out in her artistic output, starting with two important themes which form the focus of the next two chapters: namely, ideas of the natural and the technological and the extent to which they are compatible.

3 Nature

One of the most firmly established associations framing the reception of Björk's music is that between Björk and nature. Björk's attachment to nature has been well documented (*Bravo Profile*, dir. Walker 1997; Marsh and West 2003) and the reception of her music is unfailing in its tendency to hear the music and to understand Björk herself in terms of attributes of the natural world. This prevailing mode of reception reflects a problematic aesthetic in which composition is seen as having been inspired by nature and expressive of it; "problematic" because it posits a real and unmediated nature which music mimics. This chapter is less concerned with how Björk's music imitates physical sounds of nature, and more with understanding the idea of nature that her artistic output constructs.[1] In other words, nature is understood here as a set of value-laden concepts, and this chapter explores the way in which Björk's artistic output contributes to these. In particular, I focus on the way in which her output presents a unification of the human and the natural, and the salience of this idea within the contemporary cultural context of her work's production and reception.

Nature and the Natural in Artistic Expression

> I think I manage to separate pretty well my more academic, clever side which goes more into arrangements and when I'm in the studio editing and chopping up stuff, but my voice...I've always tried to not think about it, it's the most...it's nature or it stands for the things in me I don't understand. In most of my records it's my vocal, that's how I write my songs: so I just go for a walk in nature for a while and out comes a song that I don't understand. And I'll sing it in one take and not really analyse it, and then afterwards I can spend five billion hours on the arrangement and that's where I'm being maybe more clever or more technical or professional, if you want.
> (Björk 2002)

Björk situates her creative practice as a spontaneous force that is part of the natural world. In doing so she brings together two common ideas of nature: nature as the natural world (of landscape and animals), and nature as "the natural" and instinctual, constructed in opposition to technology and training. The idea that Björk's voice and creativity arose from nature is communicated through accounts of her recording outdoors and by documentary footage which shows Björk composing in rural locations, such as in the *Bravo Profile* (dir. Walker 1997). But the aspect of Björk's artistic output most salient to beliefs about the "natural" character of her music is her singing voice. Her compositional practice of using vocal improvisation while outdoors draws upon and reaffirms beliefs in the "naturalism" of the voice as the source of her music. Like other pop vocalists her voice sounds untutored, which suggests that she, and her music, are unsullied by human or technological artifice: the noisy breaths, explosive consonants, shrieks, howls and guttural explosions are the opposite of trained (classical) vocal styles. Her manner of performance also rejects some of the constraints of technological mediation: she frequently performs bare-foot, and moves around the recording or performance space using a hand-held microphone. Her wordless singing, and her transitions from language to wordless sounds at structural and expressive climaxes of songs, emphasize the pre-linguistic character of the singing voice. The clearest articulation of this view of the voice as "primal nature" is the album *Medúlla*, made almost exclusively from vocal materials. Furthermore, in the promotional documentary, *Inside Björk* (dir. Walker 2003), she explicitly attributes her vocal style to her experience of Icelandic nature during her childhood:

> Iceland probably affected a lot how I sing because I did spend a lot of time as a kid in nature. The way I sang would just form itself. It was definitely not influenced by other singers. Just walking outside to school, or maybe in blizzards, it just kind of like happened, and you would walk and there'd be no wind and you could be all quiet and whispery and you could sneak down next to the moss and maybe sing a verse, and then you would stand up and run to a hill and sing a chorus. You'd have to do that quite loudly because the weather was strong.

These rather whimsical statements position her at one with nature, as an artist whose creativity is untouched by commercialism.[2] The idea of nature articulated by Björk also reflects long-standing notions of nature as a source of consolation. The origin of the idea of nature as a source of comfort can be traced to nineteenth-century Romantic literature, and to Icelandic nationalist sentiment that glorified the pagan beliefs of the early settlers in opposition to organized religion, which was associated with Iceland's years as a colony. Thus, Björk stated that:

> Compared to America, or even Europe, God isn't a big part of our lives here [Iceland]. I don't know anyone here who goes to church when he's had a rough divorce or is going through depression or something. We go out into nature instead. Nature is our chapel. (Gunnarsson 2004)

These ideas (of nature as solace, of the composer as inspired by and expressive of nature, of music as springing forth from nature, unsullied by artifice or by commerce) are tropes familiar from nineteenth-century European constructions of musical creativity still current today. Their relevance to Björk is unsurprising, given her exposure to these ideas through her schooling, day-to-day life, her exposure to nationalist literature and art in Iceland, and the extent to which the authentic author image functions within the structure of the contemporary music industry. But, taken alone these would only indicate her manifestation of generalized ideas about nature. In fact, Björk's artistic output articulates ideas of nature marked by the specific socio-historical circumstances of their production in late-twentieth-century Iceland. This is manifest in three ways: the specificity of the natural world evoked, the elision of the Icelandic nation with its landscape, and Björk's personification of the natural world in her artistic output, which embodies the conceptual unification of human and nature apparent throughout her work. The idea of nature articulated in Björk's output is shaped by contemporary tensions between nationalist imaginings of Iceland, and its industrial, capitalist modernity.

Icelandic Nature in Contemporary Icelandic Consciousness

The specific idea of nature referenced in Björk's music differs with each recording project: the sea (plus boats and travel) is referenced in the lyrics and visual material of *Debut* (1993), rural and volcanic landscapes (mountains, rocks, forests, volcanoes) on *Post* (1995) and *Homogenic* (1997), winter landscapes (glacier, twilight, mountain) on *Vespertine* (2001), the body (bone, blood, heart, kidneys, lungs) on *Medúlla* (2004), and the sea, earth and the human body on *Volta* (2007). With the exception of references to the human body, these themes are familiar from nationalist depictions of Iceland's rural landscape in art and literature of the nineteenth and early twentieth centuries, which, as discussed in the previous chapter, tie ideas of nature to ideas of the nation-state. The romantic view of Icelandic nature remains a salient feature of Icelandic artistic consciousness at the beginning of the twenty-first century (Kvaran and Kristjánsdóttir 2001).[3]

The idea that nature represented the rural nation-states became most central when it was most problematic, namely, with the growth of cities, depopulation of the countryside, and the consequent change in lifestyles that occurred in Iceland in the first part of the twentieth century. Iceland's relatively late industrialization, in comparison to its neighbours, meant that a utilitarian view of nature did not emerge until the early twentieth century (Jóhannesson 2005).

Central to these ideas of nature is a tension between country and city life and the nostalgia of city dwellers for a supposedly lost innocence and simplicity. In late-nineteenth-century England, for example, the depopulation of the countryside and the growth of modern suburban sprawl emphasized this divide for intellectuals at the time, and found expression in the music of composers such as Elgar (Riley 2002). Björk's artistic output can be understood as a response to the sudden shift from rural to urban life that occurred in Iceland during the twentieth century. In this respect her work forms part of a larger artistic response by Icelanders to this experience: for example, in poetry after the 1970s declarations of love for the city sit alongside an image of urban alienation in which people have lost touch with nature (Þorvaldsson 2006: 492). Many of the lyrics of Björk's songs emphasize the antagonistic relationship between city and nature, and align Björk with Iceland's rural landscape in opposition to urban environments that are often depicted as unhealthy and isolating (for example, 'Crying' from *Post* in 1995) or frightening (for example, 'Play Dead' from *Debut* in 1993).[4] Some of the clearest manifestations of this idea can be found in the music videos directed by Michel Gondry, which picture Björk within natural landscapes. For example, 'Human Behaviour', 'Isobel' and 'Bachelorette' form a trilogy about a character's move from nature to city and back again. In 'Isobel' (dir. Gondry 1995) pebbles turn into skyscrapers and outcrops of light-bulbs flourish on the forest floor – playing out ideas about the relationship between the urban and the rural. This trilogy is particularly important because it represents an idea central to Björk's conception of nature; namely, the idea of nature and the natural as instinct that needs to be preserved.

The idea of what constituted Icelandic nature was particularly contentious at the end of the twentieth and start of the twenty-first century, amid debates surrounding exploitation of Iceland's natural resources. The increased harnessing of geothermal energy as a source of hot-water and heating is largely uncontroversial, but the impact of other environmental projects was the subject of public debate and protest: these included the development of an Icelandic medical database by a genomics company in 1996, the renewal of whale hunting in 2006, the privatization of marine life via fishing quotas, and the building of a hydro-electric plant at Kárahnjúkar in East Iceland (providing energy to a US-owned aluminium smelter at Reyðarfjörður), which when it opened in 2007 flooded a highland wilderness. Björk and her parents were involved separately in challenging the latter development.[5]

During the 1990s environmental politics came to the fore in Iceland through the debates over whether the North East interior should be preserved as a National Park or developed as a hydro-electric power station, and arguments between "dark nature protectionists" who wanted to preserve the barren character of the Icelandic interior, and "green protectionists" who wanted to plant forests to stop soil erosion, and "restore" native forests which they claimed had been destroyed by Icelandic ancestors (Jóhannesson 2005). Nationalist discourse informs many of these arguments: the idea that the land should be protected is based on claims that it constitutes an important part of Icelandic identity, and because Iceland has an international duty (to protect a last surviving European wilderness, or to plant trees to help reduce carbon dioxide in the earth's atmosphere). For example, speaking at the *Stop the Dams* gig held in Iceland in 2006, Björk remarked: "It [Kárahnjúkar] is the largest untouched area in Europe and I feel it is my duty to speak out not only as an Icelander but as a European" (DeMuth 2006). The rest of this chapter considers the extent to which this idea of nature shapes Björk's artistic output, and how it responds to the tensions between nationalist conceptions of Icelandic nature and Iceland's current situation as a modern, industrialized nation within a global context. I first consider representations of the physical natural world (volcanic and winter landscapes, and the sea) before considering the animal world, because it is in the representation of landscape that Björk's articulation of a specifically Icelandic version of nature is most apparent.

The Physical Natural World: Fire, Ice and Water

Volcanic Landscapes

Björk's idea of nature is equated with the country of Iceland and her celebration of nature is an articulation of her pride in her nation-state: "I'm very proud of being an Icelander. Because of the country itself – the mountains, the waterfalls and the colours" (Ryming 1993). As the previous chapter discussed, these topographical features form an important part of Icelandic nationalist literature, painting and music, in which the (wild) rural landscape of the highlands came to be seen as coterminous with the nation-state. The most explicit manifestation of this ideology in Björk's artistic output is *Homogenic*, released in 1997 (three years after the celebration of Iceland's fiftieth year as a Republic, which Björk participated in): "*Homogenic* is Iceland, my native country, my home" (van den Berg 1997):

> ...when I did this album I was like, 'What am I made of?' And I'm from Iceland, I'm born '65. Iceland is full of fucking ruptures, very raw lava. I'd wake up in the morning and have a walk by the ocean and scream and sing. There's snow blizzards and people might die because the weather's terrible – all these kind of things. I wanted to get closer to what that is, because Icelandic music doesn't really exist. (Björk cited in Fern 1997: 124)

This interview extract juxtaposes a number of ideas central to understanding the significance of the idea of nature to Björk's music: it suggests a continuity between Björk's creativity and the natural world; it identifies Iceland with its volcanic landscape and extreme weather conditions; and illustrates Björk's self-identification with this ideological image of the Icelandic nation: she asks "What am I made of?", and the video 'Jóga' literally reveals her to be made of Iceland's rock (see Chapter 2). Furthermore, Björk claims to be inventing a specifically "Icelandic" music, where none previously existed. Closer analysis of her music reveals the extent to which her musical articulation of this idea of nature draws upon, and transforms, previous musical practices.

The lyrics of *Homogenic* reference the animals, hunters, volcanoes and glaciers of Iceland's rural landscape ideology, but Björk's vision for the album also extended to the mimetic character of the instrumental sounds. The main instrumental palette of *Homogenic* is strings, which referenced for Björk Icelandic classical orchestral music, and large, distorted and un-pitched beats, which for her are mimetic of the geologically active landscape, "like eruptions" (Björk cited in Fern 1997):

> I wanted the beats to be almost distorted; imagine if there was Icelandic techno. Iceland is one of the youngest countries geographically, it's still in the making. So the sounds would be still in the making. (Björk cited in Micallef 1997)

The discourse of a country "in the making" here also references the idea of post-colonial Iceland forging a new identity.

The mimetic character of the beats can be attributed in large part to their timbre: they often have a high degree of distortion and filtering. When sounds are distorted it is because there is more energy than can be recorded or re-produced, thereby invoking the idea of an excess of power. "Noise" also signifies the natural (i.e. "raw") sounds of nature rather than the "musical" sounds produced by control of culture. Hence, in this context, distortion signifies the power and rawness of the natural world.

Moreover, a consequence of filtering is that it can suggest the movement of a sound source in space. For example, between the first and second verse of 'Jóga' on *Greatest Hits* from the *Family Tree* collection (1:11–1:18) the beats are filtered (see Figure 9). Given that higher frequencies disperse further in the environment than lower frequencies, changing the spectral shape of a noise creates the impression of changing the distance of the sound source from the listener. In this example, the effect of a swept filter suggests that the sound source is moving in relation to the listener; the large, powerful forces from which the sound emanates are in motion and embody the movement of tectonic plates, or the "beats in the making" to which Björk refers above. The characteristics of real-world sounds, such as frequency, amplitude and waveform, tend to vary over time, thus, the modulation in frequency also has the effect of suggesting a natural (i.e. real-world) source.

In addition to the affordances of these timbres, or perhaps because of them, these percussive sounds have a history of association with the representation of Iceland's geology. Björk follows in a nationalist musical tradition exemplified by Jón Leifs, whose compositions Björk remarked "animated eruptions and lava in sound" (Ross 2004). Leifs' programmatic compositions

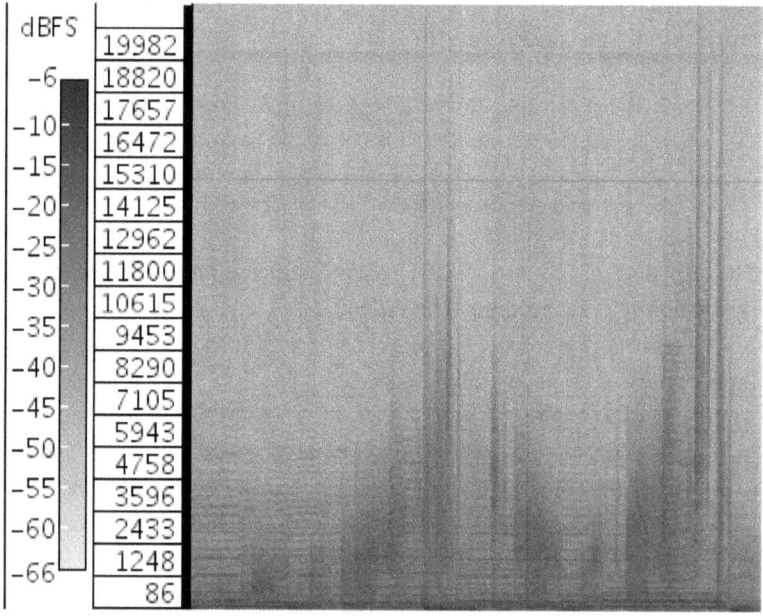

Figure 9: Spectrogram of 'Jóga' (*Family Tree: Greatest Hits* 2002), showing the use of swept filter (1:11-1:18). Peaks in the graph show the presence of higher frequencies.

took as their subject matter the Icelandic rural landscape, and the sagas. His Symphonic Poems, *Geysir* op.51 (1961), *Hekla* op.52 (1961), *Dettifoss* op.57 (1964) and *Hafis* op.63 (1965), are named after Iceland's most famed landscape features: an erupting hot-spring, a volcano, a waterfall and an ice drift. The scores of both *Hekla* and *Geysir* indicate use of an off-stage percussion section, while in *Hekla*, whose subject matter is the volcano of that name, the positioning of the extended percussion section (including chains, anvils and sirens) changes during the performance, the effect of which, like that of the filtering of beats in *Homogenic*, suggests the movement of large ("raw") sound sources.

Winter Landscapes

A second version of the rural landscape that appears in Björk's solo artistic output is the winter snowscape expressed on *Vespertine*, and a track originally intended for inclusion on *Vespertine*, but delayed by the commissioning of a music box for its performance – 'Vökuró' from *Medúlla*. The lyrics of 'Völkuró' reference a specifically Nordic version of nature: "snow", "dusk", "earth", "grass", "spring", "hill", "root", "nesting", "cold", "firmament", "night", "lily white". This same lyrical theme appears in the album *Vespertine*: for example, 'Aurora' mentions "glacier", "shine", "twilight", "sparkle", "mountain", and "snow", and 'Pagan Poetry' refers to "dark currents", "black lilies totally ripe", and "hibernation". Words referring to body parts (fingers, mouth, hair), the night (dark, twilight, sleep) and senses (smell, touch, stroke) are just as frequent on *Vespertine* as those referring to winter landscapes, and can be interpreted as the expression of a heightened internalized world as a result of being indoors cocooned from the long winter night and harsh weather.

Much of the wintry quality of these tracks arises from the inclusion of instruments characterized by a percussive sound and limited frequency range: harp, celesta, and music box. For Björk these sounds are part of her construction of the virtual world of *Vespertine*, which "means things that come out in the dark and shine": "all the noises on the album are trying to be winter-like, or frozen, like the harp and the swan and the music boxes. And celesta, of course, being an ultimate winter instrument" (Björk interviewed on CDNow August 2001 ('About & About: Vespertine" 1995–2007)).

In addition to the cultural associations these sounds might have with winter, they also embody material characteristics of ice: objects that are small and hard, like ice, emit high frequency sounds when struck. Indeed, Björk described *Vespertine* as "see-through like a crystal" ("Björk Family Tree & Greatest Hits: It's in our hands" 2002), reaffirming cultural associations between ice and glass or diamonds, and embodied in the Perspex design of music boxes Björk commissioned from the Porter Music Box company.[6] Björk's preoccupation with achieving the sound of winter even extended to the use of samples of real-world sounds: the sound of boots crunching through snow used as the beat of 'Aurora', cracking ice into microphones as the source for microbeats, and asking Matmos to use "the sound of little buds on a branch of pussy willow bursting open" as a final decorative layer of micro-beats added to tracks, as they described on the documentary *Miniscule* (dir. Gestsdóttir 2001).

Visual symbols of this wintry landscape abounded in performance on the *Vespertine* tour. For example, in *Vespertine Live at Royal Opera House* (dir. Barnard 2001) video screens showed frozen Nordic landscapes, and images of germinating life; white feathers/snowflakes fell during 'Frosti' while Björk sat at the Perspex music box; and Björk's dress worn in the first half was textured, white and off one shoulder, giving the impression of her body emerging from snow.

Grimley argues that *Vespertine* references an interiorized Nordic landscape through its acoustic evocation of wide-open spaces alongside the creation of intimacy via the album's production (Grimley 2005). The wide registral space of 'Hidden Place' is sparsely filled, and there is a lack of musical movement suggesting unchanging continuity, which is a compositional device found in representations of the natural world in art music (Johnson 1999). By contrast, the positioning and treatment of sounds in the mix creates smaller virtual acoustic environments and acoustic intimacy between the listener and Björk. For example, the voice and micro-beats are recorded very close to the microphone and placed at the front of the mix, positioning the listener close to the singer within the virtual space of the recording. Thus, the treatment of sounds in *Vespertine* evokes an intimate virtual space consistent with the lyrical imagery which references winter landscapes, but experienced from inside the home (or imagination) rather than experienced outside.

The Sea

Björk's first solo studio album is marked by references to boats and the sea: four of *Debut*'s eleven songs mention the sea, and a model sailing ship appears in the cover art for the album, and in the background of the music video 'Venus as a Boy' (dir. Muller, 1993), as well as later videos (for example, 'Possibly Maybe' (dir. Sednaoui, 1996). The partly autobiographical 'There's More To Life Than This' talks of a harbour, boats, and island; and in 'Violently Happy' she tip-toes "down to the shore/stand by the ocean/ make it roar at me/and I roar back". And in the 'Anchor Song' Björk sings: "I live by the ocean/and during the night/I dive into it/down to the bottom/ underneath all currents/and drop my anchor/this is where I'm staying/this is my home." However, reference to the sea in Björk's music is more than simply a reflection of her physical surroundings, because it symbolizes a number of different ideas within the context of her artistic output. Björk explained her preoccupation with the sea and with ships as a product of her Icelandic upbringing and identity ("It's a combination of things being born on a small island and always having the ocean [sic]. It makes your head function completely differently") and articulated ideas of nature as solace, of her continuity with the natural world (the sea as her mother), and of the sense of identity, belonging and freedom which the ocean symbolized for her:

> I had a really wild upbringing, which I think is the best upbringing anyone could have. My home was by the sea. If I walked down to the sea and sat down by the shore, I was home. That's my mother, the ocean. Nothing can go wrong. I love swimming, another hippie thing. My mum says it's because I'm a water sign. And the sense of space and boats. I'm obsessed with boats. It's freedom. (Savage 1995)

One feature of Björk's characterization of the sea is its representation as a maternal character, represented in the quotation above by the slippage between the sea as her mother, and mention of her own biological mother. This symbolism emphasizes continuity between humans and nature. For example, the music video 'Nature is Ancient' (dir. Lynn Fox 2002), directly aligns the lyrical theme of the title with the sea and gestation. The visual treatment shows stylized reproduction processes of crustacean-like marine life amid floating amoeba-like particles, culminating in the growth of a human foetus within a transparent sack that floats within this fluid environment.[7] The magical character of this fertilization and gestation process is signalled at the very start of the track by the sound of small bells, typically associated with the benign supernatural, and which continue to accompany the visuals of marine life. The track ends with a similar, although less reverberant, sound that coincides with a camera shot of the foetus' face, affirming its magical qualities.

The symbolism of the sea as a source of life, and as a primal, ancient force is given further expression on *Medúlla*. 'Oceania', which Björk performed at the opening ceremony of the Olympic Games in Athens in 2004, is written

> ...from the point of view of the ocean that surrounds all the land and watches over the humans to see how they are doing after millions of years of evolution. It sees no borders, different races or religion which has always been at the core of these games. ("Björk & Medúlla & Oceania & Olympics" 2004)

Björk embodies the persona of the sea both in her performance of 'Oceania', and in the promotional material surrounding it. The lyrics, written by Sjón, are sung in the first person, which is reinforced by visual material which positions the singer, Björk, as the sea and the source of life: the colours and textures of the dress she wore mimicked the sea, and in a grand gesture, billowing blue material gradually unravelled across the Olympic arena as though it were water (see Figure 10); the video for the track features Björk sparkling with scales as if underwater, while around and above her, and from her hands, dart sea creatures; and promotional photographs show Björk as part of the sea floor, her hair encrusted with shells. The powerful character of this persona is realized musically in the three fermatas (held notes) that feature towards the end of each verse of 'Oceania', which interrupt the music's pulse and heightens expectations of resolution.[8]

A second symbolism of the sea in Björk's artistic output is its signification of Icelandic belonging and freedom, through its association with boats and travel. The idea that the sea represents both belonging and freedom may seem contradictory, but within imaginings of Icelandic history the sea is simultaneously the boundary that defines the Icelandic nation and keeps it distinct from other nations; it represents the Viking ancestry of Icelanders

Figure 10: Performance of 'Oceania', opening ceremony of the Athens Olympic Games. © Mick Hutson/Redferns, 2004. Dress by Sophia Kokosalaki.

through Nordic Viking migration, and is the means through which Icelandic people overcame their island isolationism by travelling to Europe and North America. Ships may well have taken on extra importance with the recording and release of *Debut*, when Björk had left Iceland to pursue her solo career in England. But ships also appear in *Volta* (2007): the sounds of water and ships connect individual tracks on *Volta*, most strikingly when 'Earth Intruders' segues into 'Wanderlust' via a symphony for fog horns, ship engines, and the sound of waves; and the track 'Wanderlust' is an explicit declaration of the ocean as simultaneously providing a sense of belonging but with the freedom of unfamiliarity: "I feel at home whenever/the unknown surrounds me/I receive its embrace/aboard my floating house."

As discussed in Chapter 2, Björk's conception of her Icelandic identity is complex: her artistic output is patriotically nationalist, yet forges a new, technologically modern identity for Iceland; and while she perceives herself to be Icelandic she has simultaneously tried to reconcile this with her cosmopolitan existence in which she has travelled the world, and lived overseas. Thus, the obsession with the sea and ships articulates her personal restlessness and desire to engage with other cultures, and Iceland's global context, through the symbolism which migration by sea has within Icelandic consciousness. With *Volta* (2007) Björk addresses ideas about the meeting of different cultures, including conflicts over land and religion: the idea of global travel and encounters with other cultures is signified by the presence of music from a wide variety of cultures, and the sounds of water and ships act as the acoustic "glue" between individual tracks. The sea, then, is used as a utopian symbol of humankind understood as a single entity, and emphasizes commonalities between people from different cultures. Thus, the recurrence of the trope of the sea in Björk's work has two aspects. First, it expresses her (Icelandic) island identity, but in a way which symbolizes a global context of freedom and travel rather than isolationism; and second, it communicates an idea of nature as the ancient source of life, and therefore symbolizes a mythic, primordial commonality amongst all peoples. Having considered ideas of the physical landscape in Björk's artistic output, I turn now to the idea of nature implicit in her representations of the animal world.

The Animal World

> Ever since I was a child I have always loved the way David Attenborough looked at humans, as if they were an animal species. I have this romantic idea that I am an animal, because I don't think humans are any different from animals.
> (Björk 2001)

The most recurrent animal motif in the visual material accompanying Björk's music during her solo career is the bear. In both 'Hunter' from *Homogenic*, and 'Cover Me' from *Post*, Björk is a hunter, and bears and/or hunters appear in the music videos of 'Human Behaviour', 'Violently Happy' and 'Hunter'. The music video 'Human Behaviour' (dir. Gondry 1993) is an animated tale of predator and prey. The video shows a hunter pursuing a large, brown (toy) bear in the forest at night. Björk, who is both narrator and a character in the story, flees from the bear, which makes numerous attempts to catch her (even driving a car at one point). Eventually she ends up in the bear's stomach. Indeed, the title, along with the lyrics, suggests a perspective on humans as seen from the position of an animal or alien, as Björk described: "'Human

Behaviour' is an animal's point of view on humans. And the animals are definitely supposed to win in the end" ("Lyrics" 1995–2004).

In later music videos, the bear functions as a symbol of strength. For example, Björk's visual image of 'Army of Me' (dir. Gondry 1995) was of herself as a polar bear, with the strength yet warmth that she imagines them to embody.[9] The striking video treatment of 'Hunter' (dir. White 1997) is a single camera shot of Björk singing, bald and naked from the shoulders up, during which she morphs into a cybernetic polar bear: as she moves, bear-like characteristics continually emerge and retreat. The design firm Me Company, who directed and produced the video, described the bear as "a literal symbol of strength, ferocity, self-determination and the North, a pioneering roaming spirit" ("Lyrics" 1995–2004). It constructs Björk as "Northern" rather than Icelandic because polar bears are not indigenous to Iceland. The polar bear's symbolism of strength is reinforced by musical characteristics of the track: the use of the snare drum, with its history of use in military contexts, and the bolero-like bass ostinato played by the cellos.[10] Significantly, both 'Hunter' and 'Army of Me' are musically and rhythmically characterized by references to power and strength. The lyrics to 'Army of Me' are a call for the person addressed to stop feeling sorry for themselves and to "get on with it", while 'Hunter' expresses some of the tension in Björk's role at this time, as the musical creator who had to create in order to keep others in work: as director Paul White remarked, the music video 'Hunter' "is about a woman who allows the animal within to take over when necessary. The provider – in a cold world" ("Lyrics" 1995–2004).

In addition to the bear, Björk has associated herself with the swan, a bird indigenous to Iceland and therefore another expression of Nordic nature as well as a complex symbol in European culture as a whole. The swan appears on the cover art for *Vespertine*, where it is superimposed over an image of Björk in a state of erotic rapture, and was the basis of the infamous dress Björk wore to the Oscars ceremony in 2001. In Nordic cultures the swan is a symbol of female grace and beauty and therefore a representation of Björk's feminine persona on *Vespertine* (2001). In Greek mythology Zeus took the form of the swan in order to seduce Leda, and two swans with necks entwined symbolize lovers: both may reference the sensuality of Björk's relationship with Matthew Barney which was credited as the autobiographical source of the subject matter of *Vespertine*. The swan can also be interpreted in the context of her battles with director Lars von Trier, and the sentiments expressed in the track 'Unison' (*Vespertine* 2001) which she attributed to her battle for authorial control over the music of *Dancer in the Dark*. In Germanic myth the warrior goddesses, the Valkyries, had the power to transform into swans, sometimes appearing in human form without their plumage: the Valkyrie Kara flew over the battlefield where her lover Helgi fought in war and sang a song so soothing that the enemy no longer wished to fight – a sentiment similar to that expressed by Björk. Lastly, given that she famously declared her role in *Dancer in the Dark* to be her last foray into acting, the swan dress can also be interpreted as a reference to Björk's "swansong".

Therefore, personification of animals is another means by which Björk embodies the natural world through her visual image, and like the representations of the physical world in Björk's work, the version of nature which is represented often has Nordic, arctic, or Icelandic symbolism.

Personification of Nature: Expressing the Continuity between Humans and the Natural World

These examples illustrate two main points. First, the kinds of animals and landscapes that appear in Björk's artistic output are associated with arctic environments of the North, and in the case of references to the physical world, manifest an Icelandic rural landscape ideology. Second, the natural world is personified by Björk through the visual material which accompanies her music, comprising sets and costume in performance, promotional photo shoots for use in magazine features, cover art, and music videos. Björk's embodiment of the animal and physical natural world is particularly interesting, because it developed over the course of her solo career. In Björk's appearances with the Sugarcubes some of the same visual tropes appear as occur later in her solo career: for example, the music video of 'Birthday' (dir. Jóhannesdóttir 1987) features a volcanic crater, shots of erupting volcanoes and flowing lava, and a black raven. However, Björk's visual image is juxtaposed with these features rather than embodying them as she does in later visual material.[11] The lyrics of songs from the beginning of Björk's solo career often identify the singing voice with an observer of the natural world: the lyrics of *Debut* and *Post* express an affinity with the natural world by observing 'Human Behaviour' from the perspective of an alien or animal; she goes "home" to the sea in 'Anchor Song' from *Debut* released in 1993, and lives at the top of a mountain in 'Hyper-ballad' from *Post* in 1995. By contrast, on later albums Björk embodies the natural world: she sings "I'm a fountain of blood in the shape of a girl", "I'm a tree that grows hearts" on 'Bachelorette' from *Homogenic* in 1997, and "one breath away from mother oceania/your nimble feet make prints in my sands" on 'Oceania' from *Medúlla* in 2004 (written respectively by and with the poet Sjón). Thus in later lyrics and visual material she personifies the natural world rather than simply observing it.

One consequence of Björk's embodiment of nature is that she is authenticated as a performer: Björk's personification of nature through lyrics and visuals, and the positioning of her compositional practices within rural contexts, suggests artistry unsullied by commerce – part of the romantic ideology which helps construct her as author and which pervades reception of popular music (Ahonen 2006). Simultaneous with this, her preoccupation with, and personification of, nature reflects the idea of continuity between humans and nature that characterizes the animist belief system which forms part of Iceland's history. Norse paganism was characterized by the notion that everything was alive: humans, like animals, plants and rocks, were seen as being part of nature, rather than separate from it. Thus, Björk's embodiment of the natural world articulates the idea of continuity between humans and the natural world, and reflects a specifically Icelandic sense of religiosity. The filtering of this animist view of the natural world into Icelandic culture may explain Björk's embodiment of nature through her artistic output.

Conclusion: The Idea of 'Nature' in Björk's Artistic Output

Björk's musical practices and beliefs signal the centrality of rural nature to her Icelandic identity, and position her creativity as a "natural" phenomenon. The natural physical world personified by Björk has two main aspects: the animal world, of bears, birds and humans, and the physical world, of land and sea. Referring to published interviews Björk had given, Marsh and West argued that "Björk's connection to nature extends to her homeland, Iceland, and arises from Björk's descriptions of Iceland's geographical and social characteristics" (Marsh and West 2003: 182). I have shown that the connection to nature is articulated through musical and visual devices, some of which are inherited from nationalist art and music, and which share common conceptions of the identity between the natural physical environment of Iceland, and the nation-state of Iceland.

Björk's representation of nature is particularly significant in two ways. First, many of the representations of nature in Björk's output feature Iceland's "wild" landscape, which the tourist version of Iceland promotes as providing a powerful experience of wilderness and natural beauty.[12] By emphasizing the beauty of Iceland's highland "heartland", Björk maintained the dark protectionist version of Icelandic nature at a time when it was contested. Furthermore, through her participation in events aimed at influencing environmental politics in Iceland, she contributed to a discourse emphasizing Iceland's international duty to protect its land. This discourse is particularly powerful because it enables Iceland's environmental difficulties (its barren landscape) and late modernization to be re-imagined as strengths that could make an important contribution to Europe and the world, thereby enhancing Icelandic pride. However, by equating the highland wilderness with Icelandic national identity Björk potentially contributed to a situation in which threats to Icelandic nature could be interpreted as threats to the Icelandic nation.

Second, Björk's artistic output expresses an idea of the natural world that is continuous with the human, and redolent of animist thinking, partly through the thematic content of her work, and partly through her personification of nature. In addition to the connection to Icelandic tradition and mythology this represents, this idea of continuity challenges the view of nature as a "resource" to be exploited for commercial gain. Advocates for the development of Iceland's natural resources conceptualize the environment as a resource that can be parcelled up and privatized, and in which inhabitants are separate from nature. This modernist worldview and the associated environmental debates, such as those surrounding the hydroelectric development of Iceland's wilderness areas, are characterized by a radical separation of society and nature. This utilitarian discourse is at odds with the idea that "Humans are an integral part of a larger context, a context that allows no radical distinction between *habitus* and habitat" (Pálsson 1995: 164), which has a long history in Iceland. By making manifest the continuity between humans and the natural world, by unifying them in her artistic output, Björk articulates a different perspective on this separation – albeit one which reaffirms nationalist constructions of Icelandic identity.

One problem this creates is an apparent incompatibility between two aspects of contemporary Icelandic identity: nature, tradition and the rural, versus technology, modernity and the urban. Furthermore, Björk's artistic output represents something of a contradiction that until now I have chosen to ignore: while it articulates ideas of nature, this expression is achieved through distinctly technological means. The next chapter examines the extent to which the idea of continuity between humans and the natural world is extended to embrace the technological realm in Björk's artistic output.

4 Technology

For the character Selma whom Björk plays in the film *Dancer in the Dark* (2000), the soundtrack of which she also wrote, the rhythmic regularities of machines and other everyday sounds are a means of transition into musical numbers and thereby into a fantasy world. For example, in one scene, a night shift on the factory floor turns into a pastiche of a Hollywood musical dance sequence. In the context of a musical-film, such as *Dancer in the Dark*, the use of machines serves as a convenient (and conventional) means of incorporating musical numbers into the diegesis (the fictional world of the film). However, the use of machine-sounds cannot be attributed solely to pragmatism since related themes appear elsewhere in Björk's output: the sounds of machines are used as musical materials (for example, telephone ring tones appear in 'Possibly Maybe' from *Post* in 1995); the lyrics of her songs place technology in the realm of the natural (for example, technologies have been "waiting in mountains for the right moment" in the track 'The Modern Things', also from *Post*); her music videos exploit the visual boundaries between organism and machine (for example, 'All is Full of Love', dir. Cunningham 1999); and she argued passionately against the view that technology is inhuman. Thus, the idea of technology appears to hold a special place in Björk's artistic output.

Other writers have argued that Björk's output dismantles a long established dichotomy between nature and technology. In 1997 Van Meter succinctly summed up what is still seen as Björk's main thematic trope – the idea of the relationship between techno (and the technological) and nature: "Call it techno-nature. Or natural techno. Acoustic strings and programmed machines. Voila! Icelandic music! Björk music!" (Van Meter 1997). Marsh and West argue that the cover art depicting cyber-style graphics and organic forms, and performance of material from *Homogenic* emphasize the continuity between the natural and the technological[1] (Marsh and West 2003: 193). The influence of electronic dance music, and the opposition between technology and nature it helped express, differentiated her solo career (from 1993 onwards) from the guitar-based bands of her earlier collaborations.

Therefore, this chapter is not primarily about the way that music technology is used to create Björk's music, a topic considered later; instead, it investigates the idea of technology manifest in Björk's artistic output, the musical devices used to evoke it, and the broader cultural implications of this aspect of her music.

Electronic Dance Music and Representations of the Technological

Euro-American culture in the twentieth and twenty-first centuries tends to associate technology with a worldview of progress and scientific achievement. This idea of the technological bears the legacy of the nineteenth- and early twentieth-century distinction between the mechanical and organic; a distinction that emerged with perceptions that human labour was being replaced by self-determining machines. Hence, popular conceptions of technology are linked to an idea of the mechanical as routine activity lacking consciousness, and opposed to the organic.

In popular music, the "technological" has long been associated with electronic sound sources (Frith 1986), and popular music reception and production is marked by cultural anxieties about the relationship between humans and technology, as illustrated in Timothy Taylor's analysis of US popular music after the Second World War (Taylor 2001). The most significant expression of this idea is the work of German band Kraftwerk, whom Björk cites as an explicit influence. Their use of the vocoder to technologize the human voice, together with deliberately synthetic timbres and beat patterns, convey emotional flatness and present what Ian Biddle has described as "emptied out (nomadic) subjectivites" (Biddle 2004: 92). In broad terms, the idea of technology and technological progress is elided with the use and sound of electronic technology in music, and the presence of electronic dance patterns within Euro-American popular music culture. Through an elision of technology with modernity, and modernity with industrialization, the synthesized sounds and beat patterns of electronic music have come to be associated with the industrial and mechanical.

This elision between the beats of electronic dance music and ideas of the technological is evident in Björk's statements on the topic, and in critical reception of her music (which reflects a deeply-held conceptual opposition between the beat base of her music and her lyrical vocal melodies).[2] In an interview with the experimental composer Karlheinz Stockhausen in 1996 Björk remarked:

> I think that in popular music today people are trying to come to terms with the fact that they are living with all of these machines, and trying to combine machines and humans and trying to marry them in a happy marriage: trying to be fiercely optimistic about it. . . . But everything is with those regular rhythms and learning to love them, but still be human, still be all gritty and organic. (Bjork 1996)

In this remark, Björk proceeds from discussing the way in which humans relate to the technological developments of industrialization in contemporary culture, to talking about how contemporary musicians were using "regular rhythms": she equates musical beats themselves, not just the technologies which produced them, with the idea of the technological. The significance of this is that if we want to understand the ideas about technology articulated through Björk's music, then we need to analyse the treatment of beats in her output – those electronically manipulated constituents of dance music which have become signifiers of the technological (as the genre term "techno" denotes). I begin by considering three aspects of beats in her music: the relationship between Björk's vocal style and the metrical framework of electronic dance music in *Debut* from 1993 and *Post* from 1995; mimesis of natural sounds in *Homogenic*, released in 1997; and the naturalization of technology through the use of micro-beats in *Selmasongs* (2000), *Dancer in the Dark* (dir. Lars von Trier 2000), *Vespertine* (2001), and through vocal sounds in *Medúlla* (2004). I then consider the extent to which Björk's treatment of the technological challenges popular beliefs about the relationship between nature and technology in the context of feminist and Icelandic nationalist agendas.

The Human Subject Trapped within the Grid

One of the dominant characterizations of Björk's early solo compositional style is its innovative juxtaposition of dance beats and vocals. Björk's integration of the electronic dance beats of house with lyrical vocals and fairly traditional song forms was an innovative combination within the context of early 1990s electronic dance music, in which female vocals were more often fragmented, processed and anonymized. Moreover, Björk's vocal performance displayed an extreme expressive freedom from the beat, as can be heard in 'Big Time Sensuality'.

'Big Time Sensuality', written by Björk and producer Nellee Hooper, and released on *Debut* in 1993, is one of three singles by Björk to have reached Number One in the *Billboard*'s United States Hot Dance Club Play list. The track is in contrasting verse-chorus form, with a tempo of 120bpm. The instrumental material consists of layers of looped and sequenced material against which Björk's vocals anticipate the beat in a performance style typical of popular musics. However, the rhythmic relationship between vocals and percussive track is further loosened by other factors. First, the initial entry of the voice anticipates the third crotchet beat in the second bar, rather than coinciding with the first bar of the four-bar phrase structure as might be expected. Subsequent entries of the voice are similarly unpredictable: the 16-bar verse consists of four four-bar units of rhythmic material within which there are four vocal entries, but these do not coincide, and the vocal avoids crotchet downbeats throughout the verse. So, for example, the second vocal phrase is delayed a half beat after the downbeat of the second unit, the third phrase begins with an upbeat to the third unit, and the fourth phrase also starts with an upbeat, but at the end of the first bar of the fourth unit (see Figure 11). The pitch structure also contributes to this dislocation: the instrumental and vocal material is based on a chord of E, but whereas the step-wise movement of the vocal line hovers around a descending figure from G sharp to the E tonic, the instrumental material plays with the flattened fifth scale degree. The resultant effect is of a vocal line that is not tied to the sequenced and looped instrumental material.

The chorus (which begins with the lyric "It takes courage") is more firmly wedded to the rhythmic pattern of the instrumental material: each vocal phrase at the beginning of the chorus begins on the third beat of the bar, and is characterized by rising melodic contours which sound each note of the chord in turn. Although the vocal line of the chorus is initially synchronized with the percussion and bass, the large interval leaps, and anticipation of the beat in the final half of each chorus loosens the relationship once again. The vocal ad-libbing that occurs after each chorus also introduces an

76 Björk

Figure 11: Bass and vocal of verse from 'Big Time Sensuality' (*Debut* 1993).

improvised element, which is in direct contrast to the sequenced instrumental material.

This loose relationship between vocals and electronic dance materials is characteristic of Björk's early solo music. A similar dislocation between voice and instrumental accompaniment can be heard emerging in later tracks by the Sugarcubes, such as 'Lucky Night' released in 1992 on *Stick Around for Joy*. If the beats of electronic dance music represent the rigidity and mechanistic attributes of technology, then part of Björk's musical appeal is the way her voice embodies a joyful freedom within this environment; what Björk's collaborator Guy Sigsworth (keyboardist and co-writer of some of Björk's songs) referred to as the feeling of "the unforgiving pulse of the machine and the human resisting it" (Sigsworth 2006). Björk's style on *Debut* and *Post* reconfigures the relationship between human and technology by using her voice in a way which works with the technological, but which is not subservient to it. In her subsequent solo studio album, *Homogenic*, different techniques make manifest a reconceived relationship between the technological and the natural.

Mimesis of Natural Sounds

One of the most distinctive developments in Björk's musical style from *Homogenic* on is her "naturalization" of electronic beats. I previously discussed the "volcanic" character of beats on *Homogenic*; a second example is the use of beats mimetic of the sounds of the human body and of water, as illustrated by the track 'Nature is Ancient', originating from 1997, and which appears on the 'Beats' compilation of the *Family Tree* box-set.

The music video 'Nature is Ancient' (dir. Lynn Fox 2002) shows fictionalized processes of fertilization and gestation within a marine-like, amniotic environment. Significantly, the first shot of life (the sack-like organism within which the foetus develops) coincides with the entrance of industrial-style beats, thereby suturing shots of the foetus to the beat, and aligning the "technological" with the "natural". Within this, the beats play an important role in drawing equivalence between the idea of nature, the sea and the source of all life on earth, because the conventional timbres of kick drum, snare and hi-hat are replaced with sounds suggesting an organic source. The track is based on a two-bar rhythmic loop of what sounds like a heart beat heard through a stethoscope: the sound has a high degree of white noise, with the upper frequencies filtered out, and a regular rhythm consisting of two events, the second longer than the first because it anticipates the beat. These two beats are heard as a single entity due to the sharp cut-off after the second beat, and the spatialization of each two-beat entity that places it alternately left and right in the mix. A muffled bass thud, similarly filtered, provides a syncopated rhythmic character to the second bar of each two-bar loop, alternating between the pitches of E flat and D flat. This beat and bass material is placed up front in the mix, and the virtual space of the recording is given depth by the faint sounds of twinkling bells that have been treated with delays. A new bass line with a more pitched quality enters with the vocals in the first verse of the two-part strophic structure of the track, accompanied by a repeated chirp, characteristic of the sounds used in underwater echo-location. These timbres and attack characteristics are similar to the acoustic properties of organic sounds heard through water, or another sound-dampening substance. Together with synchronization between the visual and sonic elements of the video, this treatment of beats unifies the technological and the natural.

With *Vespertine*, the mimetic character of beats in Björk's music took a more literal turn, aided by the new possibilities of digital sampling techniques, and the concept for the soundtrack to *Dancer in the Dark* which was predicated on using sounds from the diegesis as transitions into musical numbers. Hence *Vespertine*'s beats were constructed using everyday and "natural" sound sources such as ice cracking, and footsteps in snow (for example, 'Aurora' in *Vespertine*).

In *Medúlla*, the naturalization of beats was achieved by using vocal materials: the majority of sounds, even those mimicking instruments, are created by the human voice, partly to encapsulate an idea of the primal and pre-technological, according to Björk (*The Inner of Deep Part of an Animal or Plant Structure*, dir. Gestsdóttir 2004). The use of voices only (symbolic of the "natural"), and the absence of beats from seven of the fourteen tracks indicates that Björk's compositional aesthetic was shaped in reaction to the idea of technology as non-organic, and as a marker of ideas of modernity and technological progress. In many tracks, bass and percussion material takes the form of electronic dance beats produced using vocals: the opening of 'Triumph of a Heart' uses short looped performances from human beat-boxers to create kick drum, tom-tom, hi-hat, and a vocal loop in the higher register which sounds like an electronic guitar treated with an effects pedal. The result is a rich texture, with enormous rhythmic vitality. While on the one hand this replication of electronic dance beats using vocal materials seems utterly perverse, it is another technique through which Björk integrates material symbolic of the technological with auditory, lyrical and visual signifiers of the natural.

Micro-beats

With *Vespertine*, *Selmasongs*, and *Dancer in the Dark*, all written within the same period, a new strategy is evident in the treatment of the "technological": the blips and clicks of micro-beats replace, or are placed alongside, the more usual synthesized sounds of electronic dance music. Micro-sonic computer music, a genre involving digital processing, live performance with laptops, and influenced by electronica, minimalism, computer music, and improvisation, developed outside institutional frameworks and was influenced by both techno and twentieth-century Western art music (Thomson 2003). But until Björk's use of it micro-sound had been the reserve of avant-garde and underground musicians. Because these sounds are sometimes produced by using computer malfunctions this music is often called "glitch" or "clicks and cuts" (after the series of compilations on the Mille Plateaux label). Micro-sound is particularly interesting for its subversion of many of the ideas traditionally associated with digital technology, three of which I consider here.

Making Technology Visible/Audible

One characteristic of digital technology is its apparent invisibility. Yet, the adoption of digital technologies in the public domain appears to have coincided with an interest in making technologies visible, and, in the case of music, audible. This idea lay behind the video realization of 'Hunter' (dir. White 1997), which plays with the visual transformation of Björk from human to cyber-bear, as Alistair Beattle of ME company (the design firm that produced and directed the video) recalled:

> We were interested in making the technology very visible, but also playing with translucency and transparency, soft boundaries. The irony of the digital age is that, as technology gets more invisible, people are more interested in being able to see it again, as in Apple Computer's iMac, with its translucent blues and milky plastics that simultaneously tease and reveal. ("Björk Family Tree and Greatest Hits: Hunter" 2002)[3]

Mitchell Whitelaw has argued that much of the work in experimental electronic audio which occurred at the turn of the millennium was concerned with materializing the technology which underlay it (Whitelaw 2003). He points out that the discourse of audio culture draws upon the language of physical matter: in micro-sound the material reference is the "particle", just as in granular sound synthesis it is the "grain". Furthermore, micro-sound lends itself to this description by virtue of the use of the click as the smallest sound imaginable.

Most significantly, the click is a glitch in the workings of otherwise "transparent" sound technology produced when the needle's contact with the vinyl is interrupted by a dust particle, or as the laser reading the surface of the CD is interrupted. Similar techniques include the use of tape hiss, digital aliasing (produced by low-fidelity sampling), and audible edits (sharp clicks produced by discontinuities in the digital waveform) (Whitelaw 2001). Both Björk, and her collaborator, Guy Sigsworth were influenced in the mid 1990s by the music of German producer Oval (Markus Popp) whose music is characterized by the sound of CDs skipping, set against a 'dirty' ambient sound. Although CD scratching had been used previously, it was only in the late 1990s that it became more widespread. The "audibility" of digital technology (that is, its exploitation as sound material, not just as a means of sound production) in some of Björk's music can be understood as a positive embrace of the technological realm and its symbolism of the modern.

Miniaturization and Intimacy

A second feature of micro-sound that is explored through Björk's music is the miniaturization it implies. The concept behind the use of micro-beats in *Vespertine* was that they should give the impression of something small which had been magnified. This idea is further realized through other media associated with the album, such as the title and filming of the documentary *Miniscule* (dir. Gestsdóttir 2001), whose credits and title sequence show the camera's gaze entering a miniature world. The phenomenon of miniaturization, exemplified in dolls houses for example, suggests that the world of everyday objects can open up and reveal a secret life, and creates an "other world and time which negates change and the flux of lived reality" (Stewart 1984: 65). Thus, the theme of miniaturization in *Vespertine* is another expression of the utopian sentiment expressed in the music's lyrics and sound materials ("heavenly" choirs and harp-like sounds).

The use of micro-beats as heard on *Vespertine* is also an innovative development of spatialization of the rock drum kit. Allan Moore argues that there has been a gradual change in the treatment of percussion within the mix (Moore 2005): the production aesthetic of the 1960s and early 70s treated the drum kit as a unitary, multi-timbre sound-source, by locating it centrally, and behind other instrumental sources within the virtual "sound box" of the mix; with the use of drum machines from the late 1970s the distinctive timbres of the different drums are heightened and each is located separately in the mix. Micro-sound, as heard on *Vespertine*, takes this progression one step further by replacing traditional and synthesized drum sounds with digitized sound samples taken from non-instrumental sources and distributing them across the sound box. The use of micro-sound also avoids some of the quantization and hierarchical patterning typical of electronic dance music because percussive sounds are treated as texture as well as rhythm.

In *Vespertine* a single sound object can appear in a number of different locations in the virtual space of the mix, and can even move within the mix. For example, in 'Unison' small fluttering sounds enter top left and middle right in the mix (3:50–4:20). These have a very similar timbre and texture, but have different rhythmic patterns, giving them a distinct identity as two separate sound sources; the rhythmic patterns are so fast and irregular that they are textural rather than rhythmic and it is easier to hear them as continuously varied rhythmic patterns, rather than as looped samples. As a consequence, the sounds are more akin to those produced by a living organism (the scurrying of small insects) than by an electrical or mechanical sound source, although they retain both associations. Elsewhere, what sounds like a single sound source, due to similarity of timbre and location, moves across the virtual space of the recording. For example, in the introduction of 'It's Not Up To You', a one-bar rhythmic loop characterized by high frequency noise seems to move between the upper left and far left of the mix. The syncopated character of this rhythmic loop is heightened by the sudden contrast with a sound on the far right – a single sound with a clearer pitch centre which enters immediately after the original sound on the far left on the delayed third beat and fourth beat of the bar. An even clearer example is what sounds like the flicking of a deck of cards which travels from left to right in the virtual space of 'Hidden Place' (1:54). These techniques result in beats that are mobile and organic.

The timbral characteristics of these beats also suggest miniaturization: the beats tend to consist of high frequency sounds, which in the real world are emitted by small sound sources; the extremely rapid rhythms, and their mobility within the virtual space of the recording, also suggest sound sources with low physical mass. Lastly, some of these micro-beats are placed in front of other sound sources within the mix, positioning them close to the listener. For example, on 'Cocoon' a rhythmic loop based on what sounds like a vinyl click is first placed in front of the vocal (0:08–0:30) before a second vocal treatment enters slightly in front of the click (0:30 onwards). The effect of such treatments is to create a virtual sound space in which the listener is placed in a position of intimacy with the virtual sound sources.

The treatment of other elements within the mix helps create a distinct virtual space for each recording. For example, *Vespertine* is given depth by inclusion of a large string section and choir treated with reverb and placed at the back of the mix, and sounds are filtered to remove higher frequencies and reduce the attack portion of the signal, as though heard through another substance: both 'Hidden Place' and 'Cocoon' open with muffled bass sounds as though coming from outside a space occupied by the listener and Björk's voice. A further aspect that contributes to the creation of intimacy is the treatment of the celesta, which was recorded with the microphone close, and is placed forward in the mix. As Guy Sigsworth remarked, this made it "the confessional instrument that's right next to the singer" (Sigsworth 2006), rather than the distant instrument heard in nineteenth-century orchestral music.

In sum, the treatment of sounds and their placement within the mix create a virtual space consistent with the numerous lyrical references to intimacy throughout *Vespertine*. It may be no coincidence that this miniaturization in sound coincides with the miniaturization of digital technologies, Björk's acquisition of a laptop for composing (which enabled her to work alone as well as with a sound engineer), and a recuperative period in her life when she retreated from the media. Miniaturization and intimacy in *Vespertine* placed technology on a human scale, and brought it into the private rather than the public realm.

Technology and the Irrational

A third aspect of micro-sound explored in Björk's music is the use of the unpredictabilities of technology. For example, the track 'Unison' uses a sample from 'Aero Deck' from *Systemisch* by Oval released in 1996, the sounds of which were produced by scratching CDs and subsequently sampling and looping the skipping that resulted when played. Glitch is widely seen as an "aesthetics of failure" which offers a critique of digital technology and its political economy (Stuart 2003; Thomson 2003). Another instance of this aesthetic is the embrace of accidents or failures of intended compositional techniques as used by Björk's collaborators. For instance, producer Matthew Herbert reclaimed the errors and accidents which occurred during compositional processes as part of his "Personal Contract for the Composition of Music (Incorporating the Manifesto of Mistakes)" (Herbert 2005); and Guy Sigsworth, co-writer of songs on *Homogenic* and *Vespertine*, explored the accidental within his music: "I think with any new technology, you're always looking for the errors or the flaws or the idiosyncrasies of the thing, the accidental properties that might turn out to be features" (Sigsworth interviewed in Inglis (2001: 194–5)). This emphasis on the errors of technology is particularly noteworthy as a response to environments of increasing technological sophistication.

In a similar vein Björk presented her inclusion of micro-sound as a challenge to stereotypic conceptions of technology as rational, and opposed to the human and natural. Commenting on use of the sample from 'Aero Deck' by Oval she remarked:

> ...it's sort of conquering the fact that most people think that technology is cold because it has no mystery, and it's very calculated. . . . So when you take technology and use the areas where it breaks, where it's faulty, you're entering a mystery zone where you can't control it. It's reacting more like an animal or a person to you, and you have to react with it. (Björk interviewed in CDNow August 2001 ("Cocoon Special" 2001))

Use of the music box in her music fulfils a similar aesthetic function; despite being a mechanical musical source the music box has many inconsistencies, such as small timing variations, and a tempo which changes as the spring winds down, both of which are at odds with the rhythmic quantization typical of studio-based pop (Flint 2001: 78–9). Technology is, by definition, systematic, and yet in *Vespertine* a technological sound source, the music box, is exploited for its non-systematic character. It is the very unpredictability of such mechanical sources that humanizes them.

A similar reasoning underlies some of the unusual instrumental timbres in Björk's music, which frequently features early keyboard instruments such as clavichords, harpsichords, and even the Regal, a late-medieval portable organ, which Guy Sigsworth used on the tour of *Post* (nicknamed by the other musicians the 'Duck organ' due to its reed-like tone). Influenced by the recordings of early music historian David Munrow, Sigsworth heard in these early instruments "a broken tone, compared to the instruments that they so obviously evolved into" (Sigsworth 2006). In this instance, musical instruments, which are after all just as "technological" as computers and compact disks, were exploited for their fragility.

Exploration of the irrationality of technology, instanced in Björk's music through use of microsound and exploitation of the failures of technology, is not a new phenomenon: machines have long been associated with magic and the supernatural. In one dominant cultural narrative of Western culture, belief in science and technology has superseded belief in magic as the explanation of the unknown; indeed, magic has been positioned as the obstacle to "progress" towards rationality. Jonathan Sterne's analysis of discourse and artifacts surrounding the development of sound reproduction technologies in the late nineteenth and early twentieth centuries has shown how they "represented the promise of science, rationality, and industry and the power of the white man to co-opt and supersede domains of life that were previously considered to be magical" (Sterne 2003: 9). Yet for many people the workings of technology remain mysterious and therefore form part of the unknown. One way people have historically responded to their uncertainty is by attributing magical qualities to technology. Thus, the metaphor of magic is strikingly frequent in contemporary popular discussions about information technology (Kaarst-Brown and Robey 1999), and many of the associations of Björk's music with magic can be understood in this context.

Magic and mystery is an important reference in Björk's music for the film *Dancer in the Dark* and in *Selmasongs* and *Vespertine*, written concurrently. The evocation of "magic" appears as a metaphor within discourse about compositional strategies using digital technologies in Björk's music: for example, describing the way he liked to explore the possibilities of sound technologies, Guy Sigsworth explained: "It's how you get the mystery into digital, the ghost in the machine factor" (Inglis 2001). *Vespertine* makes explicit reference to magic through its lyrics and use of music box and celesta. Although musical automata, music boxes, player pianos, and eventually the gramophone, came to be seen as threatening within European culture (because they produced human-like sentiment through mechanical means and therefore questioned what it meant to be human), there was a moment during the Enlightenment era when musical automata were considered wondrous (Abbate 2001). This historical legacy, plus the association with nostalgia for childhood innocence, means that the music box is connected with magical attributes deriving from its perceived mysterious and autonomous ability to generate music. These associations are reinforced throughout *Vespertine* by coincidence of the sound of the music box with lyrical references to magic: there are references to secrets, codes and ciphers on 'Pagan Poetry', and the words "mystery of my flesh" on the track 'Sun in My Mouth' coincide with a repeated celesta figure (1:40). Further references to mysticism and magic occur throughout the album: for example, "He invents a charm that makes him invisible" in 'Hidden Place'; and in 'Its Not Up To You', Björk recites the recipe for the perfect day as though it were a potion: "How do I master the perfect day/ Six glasses of water/Seven phonecalls."

The consequence of focusing on technology's "magical" character is that it undermines the idea of technology as systematic and rational. This is made manifest in *Dancer in the Dark* in which the rhythmic regularities of machines provide a means of transition into musical numbers, and into the fantasy world which music represents for the character Selma. As Daniel Grimley points out, the magical character of this transition is marked at its first occurrence, at the start of the song 'Cvalda', through a variety of materials historically associated with magic: the pitched material begins with a circular whole-tone figure based on C – a scale associated with enchantment in nineteenth-century European art music; and the swooping strings, "twinkly" percussion (for example, the celesta), and flute glissandi are instrumental signifiers of the exotic (Grimley 2005: 41).

Musical Practice and Musical Idea

In sum, many of the techniques used in Björk's music counter the cultural symbolism of technology as systematic, rational, and invulnerable. This has two consequences.

First, treatment of technology as irrational and vulnerable undermines technologically determinist views, which argue that technology is an oppressive, controlling force structuring modern life and music. This approach is evident in the aesthetic strategies adopted by Björk, whose rhetoric emphasized the idea that music technologies were neutral tools and that any values a technology might appear to bring to a project were due to human users and not determined solely by the technology:[4]

> Machines are just tools, and in that way a synthesizer or a sequencer is no colder than a guitar or a flute. People tend to treat newly invented things as enemies, as a threat to their security. But it's a question of how you use them. (Björk cited in Berry 1998)

The practices used by Björk and her collaborators reveal compositional decisions mediated by the relationship between particular attributes of the technology and uses made of it: the material possibilities offered by the technology are used in ways determined by the individual, sometimes counter to apparently prescribed uses. Hence, Björk's musical practices undermine the notion that technology controls the individual.

The second consequence of the compositional practices described here is the way that they unite the inorganic (technology) and organic (human). In electronic dance music the view of the technological as self-determining and lacking in consciousness is often expressed through treatment and perception of the beats of electronic dance music (particularly techno) as mechanical, systematic and lacking in qualities considered definitional of organisms, such as unpredictability, interaction, emotion, and individuality. By contrast, Björk's music naturalizes beats through the freedom of her voice from the mechanical "grid" of the metrical frame, mimesis of organic sounds (through timbre, scale, positioning and movement), and by exploiting those aspects of machines associated with magic. Thus, much of Björk's compositional style can be understood as a critical response to popular belief in a binary opposition between the natural and the technological.

One question this raises is the exact character of the compatibility between technology and nature implied by Björk's artistic output. The work that addresses the relationship between technology and nature most directly is the music video 'All is Full of Love' (dir. Cunningham 1999), which shows two cyborgs embracing, and assembled by robotic machinery; the backlit, clinically white surroundings, industrial robotics, and reference to the fictional Yamtaijika Corporation create a futuristic setting, within which the cyborgs appear sensual and vulnerable. However, I first consider the idea of technology embodied in the song 'Scatterheart' from the musical film *Dancer in the Dark*, which presents a much darker, and, arguably more conventional vision of the relationship between humans and technology.

Fantasy and Reality in 'Scatterheart' from Dancer in the Dark *(dir. Lars von Trier 2000)*

One strain of thought in Euro-American culture understands technology to be potentially tyrannical, and *Dancer in the Dark* articulates some of these anxieties. In this musical-film machines and technology are one aspect of an oppressive North American culture: Selma's experience as a factory worker enacts the idea that mechanization threatens human subjectivity. But within the narrative this negative construction of technology is transformed by its integration into the music imagined by Selma. For the character Selma, played by Björk, diegetic sounds are a way into pleasure and an escape from the harsh realities of life as a single parent and factory worker. Every number is musically initiated by an auditory feature of Selma's environment – the first three of which are rhythmic patterns created by machinery. The first number 'Cvalda' emerges from the sound of the pressing machine into a pastiche of a Hollywood dance number, and ends when the machine malfunctions and stops. The lyrics of this song make this connection clear: "Clatter, crash, clack!/Racket, bang, thump!/Rattle, clang, crack, thud, whack, bam!/ It's music! Now dance!". 'I've Seen It All' starts and ends with the sound of train wheels bumping over the track. 'Scatterheart' is accompanied by the sounds of the needle clicking at the end of a playing record, the slap of a rope against a flagpole, and the drip of water from a pipe into a stream, and is particularly significant because it foregrounds sound reproduction technology.

When Selma confronts her neighbour Bill and asks him to return the money he has stolen from her, the silently revolving turntable is the first thing the hand-held camera focuses on before revealing Bill seated at a desk and Selma in the doorway. The turntable, with its dirty ambient hiss barely audible, is a precursor of the murder which follows by virtue of the historical association between phonograph technology, death and female transgression: one of the earliest imagined uses for recording technology was as a means to preserve the voices of the dead, and numerous early commentators make reference to the phonograph as "raising the voices of the dead" (Sterne 2003); and within classic cinema of the 1930s the phonograph was a shorthand for female wrongdoing (Robertson Wojcik 2001: 441–4).[5]

After the murder Selma sits down (1:08:36), and the sound of the record still turning becomes louder with the cut from a close-up shot of the side of Selma's head to the record player (1:08:53) followed by a camera movement back to the side of Selma's head. Because this camera shot focuses on her ear (obscured by her hair) it signals the link between the sound of the vinyl click and Selma's auditory imagination. The vinyl click itself has a regular rhythmic character giving rise to a clear sense of 3/4 time. With the sound of a celesta the camera cuts to a birds-eye view of Selma in the room, signalling the change to a fantasy sequence (1:09:06) and the musical number begins in earnest.

The sound of the needle skipping in the groove at the end of the record becomes the rhythmic basis of 'Scatterheart'. The introductory section of the song alludes to lullabies, both in the instrumentation (the child-like associations of the music box sound produced by the celesta) and lyrics ("Black night is falling/The sun is gone to bed/The innocent are dreaming/ As you should sleepyhead/Sleepyhead"). The lyrics and music of 'Scatterheart' reinterpret the bloodied body of Bill shown lying on the ground as sleeping rather than dead, allowing him to awake and forgive Selma in her musical fantasy. At the same time, Selma's auditory fantasy substitutes for the lack of music from the record player, allowing it to literally raise the voice (and in this case the body) of the dead.

In addition, the mechanistic and rational attributes of the playback equipment become transformed in the song through exploration of its unpredictable qualities: although the sound of the needle on the revolving record is regular, the quiet pops and clicks (the sound of malfunctioning equipment) become micro-beats in this redemptive song; and there is a playful looping (audible edits) of the music box sample so that the third beat of each of the first bars is an obvious repetition, as if the needle has skipped back across the record (see Figure 12). In the context of the cinematic shift to the realm of fantasy, this repetition foregrounds the time-altering attributes of recording technology:[6] repetition, attributable here to the diegetic source of a stuck needle, offers a literal looping of a fragment of time, just as at the macro-level Selma's fantasy, which takes the form of the musical number, halts the progress of the linear narrative which will bring about Selma's eventual death. If machines are the sound of oppression and harsh reality, then the transformation of the sounds of technology in Selma's 'Scatterheat' are a redemptive transformation of, and an escape from, harsh reality into musical fantasy, and the breakdown of the rationality of machines becomes a source of spontaneity and creativity.

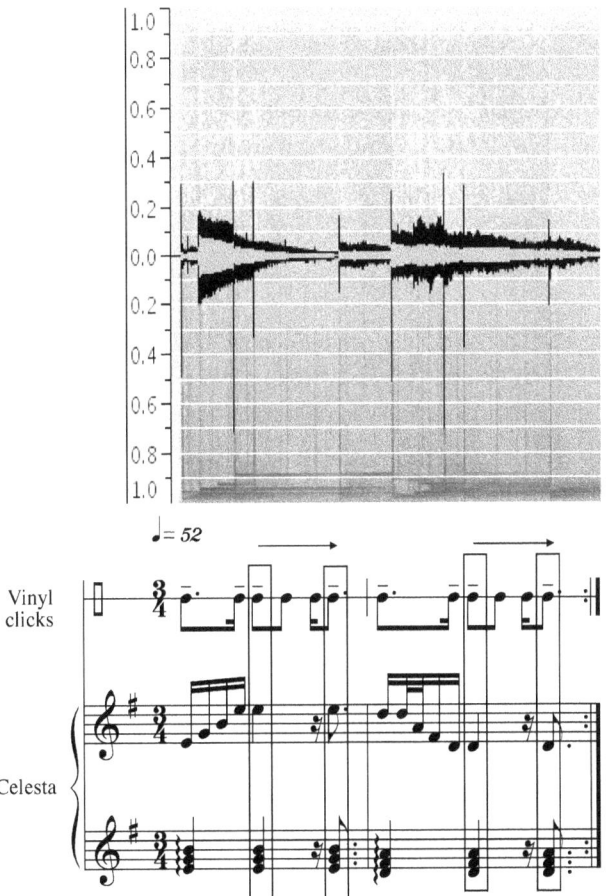

Figure 12: Celesta and vinyl scratch in the introduction to 'Scatterheart' (*Dancer in the Dark*, and *Selmasongs*, 2000). The second of each pair of boxed events can be heard as the repetition produced by a needle stuck in a groove of the vinyl. The image above shows the waveform overview and spectrogram, aligned with the score.

In sum, *Dancer in the Dark* draws upon associations of machinery with oppression and maintains a cultural stereotype of alienated workers in industrialized economies. Selma's transformation of the sounds of machines into the beat-base of her imagined music reconfigures her oppressive environment and offers an optimistic vision of the relationship between human and machine, even if it is of limited power to effect the course of events within the narrative. This optimism is also realized in Björk's solo studio albums and music videos, so it is to one of these that I turn next.

Blurring the Distinction between Organism and Machine in 'All is Full of Love' (dir. Chris Cunningham 1999)

For lyrics which reiterate the idea of "love all around" the sci-fi video treatment of 'All is Full of Love' seems a curious visual interpretation: science fiction is replete with androids and computers that are devoid of emotion, that malfunction with serious consequences, or that pursue aims at odds with those of humans (see, for example, Hal in *2001: A Space Odyssey*, dir. Kubrick 1968). Yet, in this music video a cyborg is lovingly assembled by robotic machinery and shown in an erotic coupling.

The video was intended as a mini-film and was made after the album was realeased from the original version of the track, mixed by Mark "Spike" Stent: Björk's industrial-sounding beats are prominent and the song has a clear sectional structure and separation between elements in the mix, some of which are treated with delays, suggesting a large, reverberant space. The album version was a remix by Howie B, designed to be the "calm after the storm" of 'Pluto', the penultimate track. There is little in the audio-only versions of the track released prior to the music video to suggest a visual realization set in science fiction. However, a futurist, technological aesthetic dominated electronic music culture in the 1990s (Rodgers 2003) which may account for its treatment. The sci-fi setting for the video originated with director Chris Cunningham, but many of its ingredients – the hard, white environment, heavenly and erotic connotations, the idea of love making causing change – originated in the brief given to Cunningham by Björk.[7] The sci-fi setting also makes use of Cunningham's pre-existing fascination with industrial robotics, computer graphics, and the influence of filmic characteristics of the science-fiction film genre. The backlit effects of the white space suggest filmic qualities from the 1970s, and are an explicit reference to Kubrick's *2001: A Space Odyssey*. The influence of another iconic science-fiction film series, *Alien* (in which Cunningham was briefly involved as a model maker), is apparent in the gliding camera shots which move across darkly lit tangles of cable at the beginning and end, and in the white fluids of the cyborgs. The idea of cyborgian subjectivities would also have been familiar to Cunningham through his work with Stanley Kubrick on preparations for the film *AI* (eventually filmed after Kubrick's death by Steven Spielberg). The sci-fi setting allowed Cunningham to be more sexually explicit than would otherwise have been possible.[8] The retro-filmic references in 'All is Full of Love' are characteristic of cyberculture's nostalgia, and part of the track's utopian sentiment: Andrew Calcutt has argued that cyberculture's "desire to reclaim the 'past' and incorporate it into the future is primarily an expression of our feeling of impotence in the face of present-day social problems" (Calcutt 1999: 97).

The form and facial expression of the two cyborg characters are modelled on Björk's,[9] and they lip-synch to Björk's singing voice at various moments, blurring the distinction between human and machine. The fact that the singing voice emanates from the cyborgs is a clear indication of the presence of a cyborgian subjectivity. Steven Shaviro points out that although there is a fixed pulse to the music in this mix, Björk's voice remains detached from it, as if disembodied.[10] Nowhere is this clearer than at the climactic section of the track, when, at the second chorus, the voice of the first android breaks into wordless vocalize: as Carolyn Abbate (Abbate 1999; 2001) has argued, while a musical automaton may sing music provided for it, the improvising voice is symbolic of human autonomy.

Not only are the cyborgs portrayed as conscious, they are also depicted as emotional and sensual. Shots of white liquids flowing over shiny plastic surfaces and joints (produced by reversing film of the props immersed in milk) become more frequent as the track proceeds. Significantly, the only place at which a camera cut coincides exactly with a musical downbeat is at the repeat of the chorus (2:12), the moment from which the cyborgs are shown caressing and kissing. This downbeat is marked musically by a crescendo in the high frequency wash in the soundtrack, and visually by images of white fluids and of the first android shutting its eyes. The camera shot which follows is the longest stationary shot in the video, and shows a striking symmetrical image of the two androids entwined, and tended by the industrial robotic arms, which are also suggestive of restraint and bondage (see Figure 13).

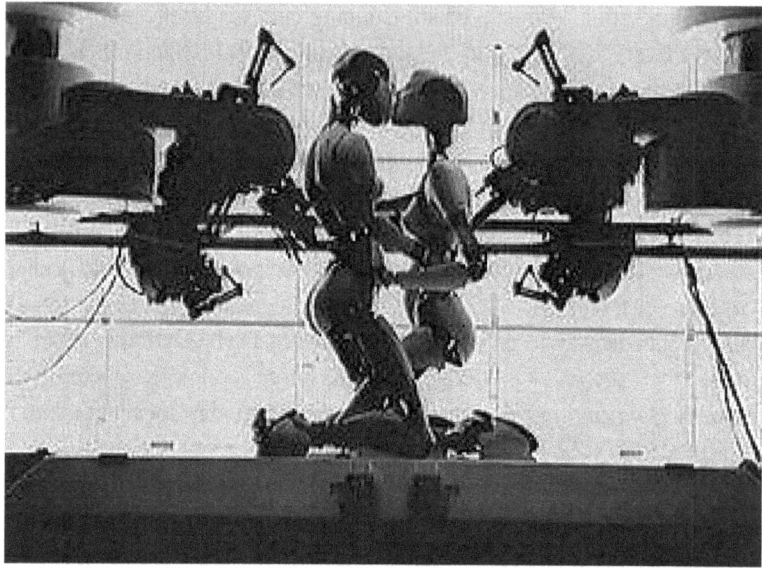

Figure 13: Still image from the music video 'All is Full of Love' (dir. Chris Cunningham 1999).

Music, words and visuals work together here to construct this section as the moment of union, as is revealed when comparing the treatment of the first and second chorus. In the first chorus camera shots alternate rapidly between the two androids, and their fluid-covered robotic parts. Simultaneous with this the vocal lines alternate between the antecedent phrase, aligned by the visuals and lip-synching with the second android ("All is full love"), and the response sung by the first android (see Figure 14). The result is the construction of two separate android subjectivities. By contrast, the single held camera shot of the two androids together presents them as a single entity, in a way that is congruent with the overlapping of the two vocal lines (now repeating the same material: see Figure 15). The break into wordless vocalize at the point of transition from first to second chorus is a literal "going beyond words", beyond rationality into an excess of passion and the sensual.[11] Thus, words, music and visuals embody the moment of union through their form as well as their semantic content.

The most sexually explicit moment occurs at the downbeat of the third chorus, coincidentally the Golden Section of the track – a ratio of propor-

Figure 14: Vocals from 'All is Full of Love' first chorus (video mix by Spike Stent).

Figure 15: Vocals from 'All is Full of Love' second chorus (video mix by Spike Stent).

tions that is found in the geometry of organisms (such as pine cones and sea shells), and has been considered by many the most aesthetically pleasing way of dividing any object.[12] Visually, it is the equivalent of the "money-shot" in pornographic films: in this instance, white fluids flow around one cylindrical protuberance that moves in and out of another. The dark and intermittently lit tangle of cables with which the visuals end also suggests a darker, seamier side to the white heavenly space occupied by the androids. By emphasizing the human characteristics of the cyborgs, the music video affirms the tendency of Björk's music to naturalize symbols of technology.

The second technological presence within the diegesis of the video – the robotic arms which tend to the cyborgs – are similarly construed as sympathetically human-like. These lack a humanoid physical form and their appearance at the start coincides with the entry of distorted unpitched beats. The camera gaze at start and end also has a robotic character by virtue of its restricted movement up and down, thereby endowing the viewer with a similar machine-like subjectivity at these points. The track starts with a synthesized string pad repeating a rocking figure, accompanied by the camera ascending and providing a cross-sectional view of what looks like the dark underbelly of a spaceship or other sci-fi environment. The camera comes to rest on the shot of an android laid on a table, on the downbeat of the four-bar introduction proper, and the robotic arms move inwards towards the silhouetted figure as the bass and percussion track kicks in with a distorted high frequency beat pattern. The lack of clear attack to the bass, and distorted un-pitched sounds of the percussion track suggest a mechanical-electrical sound-source, akin to the "hum" of electricity, and the distorted sounds of poor radio reception. The only other time this beat track is heard in isolation is at the end of the track when the camera pans vertically down back to the darkness it emerged from. Thus, the distorted sounds of the beats are associated with machinery and the non-human, and the song itself is literally set into motion like a piece of musical machinery.

Interactions of the robotic arms with the android are accompanied by sounds traditionally associated with human subjectivity, emotion, and romantic love. Short scalar passages on the clavichord are first heard at the moment protuberances unfurl from the robotic arms and touch the android, the lights flicker on, and the android's eyes open (0:22). Close-up shots of movements of the robotic arms are subsequently paired with these clavichord flourishes: the clavichord fragments in the first two verses each coincide with a shot of the rotation of the robotic arm (0:33, 0:45, 0:55, 1:32). At the chorus (2:29) a clavichord passage coincides with the flickering off of the harsh lighting (a reference to the cliché of the moment of unseen sexual union in numerous Hollywood films), from whence scalar passages saturate the musical texture in improvised fashion. Given that in European and North American culture harp-like glissandi such as this are associated with transcendent emotional states, and changed states of consciousness, the coincidence of clavichord material with shots of robotic machinery, in the context of lyrical references to being loved and taken care of, suggest the robotic operations on the cyborg are benign. A second musical symbol, this time of romantic love, is the use of accordion, which occurs in the chorus and is first heard the moment the second android is seen. Like the clavichord, it functions musically as "filler" between vocal phrases, and has a symbolic association with love and humanity.[13]

In summary, the music video plays on stereotyped notions of robots as unemotional and un-sensual, which therefore heightens the impact of the track's lyrical message: literally the visuals show the technological world to be full of love, and metaphorically the robots stand for the emotionally closed subject addressed by the song's lyrics ("all is full of love/you just ain't receiving/all is full of love/your phone is off the hook/all is full of love/your doors are all shut/all is full of love"). In contrast to earlier fictions based on the idea of the dangers of animating machines, robots and replicants (for example, Ernst Hoffman *Automata*, Mary Shelley *Frankenstein*, the robot in Fritz Lang's *Metropolis*), the cybernetic creatures in 'All is Full of Love' are vulnerable, emotional and sensual, and the robotic machinery which tends to them does so lovingly. According to this perspective, then, if technology stands as a symbolic form of hyper-rationality, its undoing here presents a more benign view of the technological, in which human and machine (organic and inorganic) are united.

Conclusion: The Compatibility of the Technological and the Natural

Björk's artistic output responds to a general cultural anxiety about the relationship between technology and nature: rather than the popular conception of technology as "domination over the natural world" (Pfaffenberger 1988),

Björk's output presents a vision in which technology and nature merge. This is a theme that has wider relevance in the early twenty-first century. During the 1990s the cultural trope of the cyborg became a metaphor for the breakdown of boundaries between the natural and technological, as exhibited in Donna Haraway's seminal analysis of late-twentieth-century US scientific culture (Haraway 1991: 152). Haraway attributes this change to three phenomena: a breakdown of the boundaries between human and animal, the "leaky" distinction between organism and machine made manifest by late-twentieth-century machines which share many attributes with humans, and, lastly, the imprecise boundary between the physical and non-physical, as manifested in the miniaturization and lack of materiality associated with digital technologies (Haraway 2000). This theme also appears in the work of contemporary artists. For example, Rebecca Horn's installation-machines, from the 1980s onwards (for example, *Halbmond des Adlers* 2002), include machinery and animal parts such as feathers or butterfly wings: they start, pause, slow, akin to living creatures rather than mechanical objects, and they move in response to movements of viewers in the gallery, rather than operate in isolation.

As well as having general salience within the shared histories of European and North American cultures, the breakdown of the distinction between the technological and the natural has a specifically Icelandic significance for Björk, as evidenced in her explanations of her compositional style on *Homogenic*:

> ...in Iceland, everything revolves around nature, 24 hours a day. Earthquakes, snowstorms, rain, ice, volcanic eruptions, geysers. . . . Very elementary and uncontrollable. But at the other hand [sic], Iceland is incredibly modern; everything is hi-tech. The number of people owning a computer is as high as nowhere else in the world. That contradiction is also on *Homogenic*. The electronic beats are the rhythm, the heartbeat. The violins create the old-fashioned atmosphere, the colouring. (van den Berg 1997)

Statements by Björk regarding the modernity of her homeland, and those of other Icelandic musicians who have gained international recognition, can be seen as a direct response to portrayals of Icelanders by foreign media as superstitious and (by implication) technologically backward. Thus, *Homogenic* was an attempt to "be truthful about Iceland" in a way which reflected her experience of being "born with raw nature everywhere, but still brought up with computers and technology" and did not consist of caricatured signifiers such as "Viking helmets" (Björk cited in McDonnell 1997). From the perspective of post-colonial Icelandic consciousness there is a balancing act to be achieved as nationalist discourse looks both back to an imagined Golden Age of the Commonwealth era represented in the Sagas, and forward to a future "shaped by Enlightenment values of reason and progress through human efforts to dominate nature" (Brydon 2006: 235–6). In the 1990s this tension was reflected in official rhetoric that represented Iceland's eagerness to embrace new technologies using metaphors of Icelandic mythology drawn from the Sagas. For example, *The Icelandic Government's Vision of the Information Society* from 1995 states: "Iceland is now sailing before a strong, favourable wind into the century of the information society" and "As Icelanders, during the middle ages, explored lands and areas of the ocean far and wide modern Icelanders are desirous of exploring and settling in the new world of the information society" (Henten and Kristensen 2000: 85). By presenting technological modernization as an extension of Iceland's mythological past, the technological and modern are reconciled with the natural and traditional. Björk's statements and compositional decisions articulate the musical solution she found in her solo career to the tensions embodied in Iceland's contemporary national identity: sonic, visual and conceptual unification of the technological with the natural.

A second ramification of the compatibility between technology and nature articulated in Björk's artistic output is its feminization of the technological. The technological worldview associated with industrialized society is gendered masculine: in broad terms gender stereotyping means that although everyone interacts with technology only some technologies are deemed suitable for men or women, and hence women are excluded from gaining an understanding of the principles by which technology operates. Feminist thinking has argued that because men are inventors and distributors of technology they use it to maintain their power over women (Benston 1988; Cockburn and Ormrod 1993). As a female author-figure for her artistic output, the deployment of technology within Björk's music is therefore particularly significant.

Björk's role in the making of her music reflects some of the normative gender roles within contemporary pop: her voice was often her compositional starting point, and in a few tracks beats were created by or with male musicians. However, she displayed (and claimed) increasing agency within the technological realm through credits and interviews, and did so in a way that brought technology into the private, domestic sphere. Björk's position as author-figure for her music means that the potential challenge to normative constructions of gender can be read within a feminist political agenda. For example, Björk used small mobile recording devices in domestic and outdoor settings.[14] Much of *Vespertine* was composed during the filming of *Dancer in the Dark* using a studio in a house shared with her recording engineer and others. Valgeir Sigurðsson, engineer on *Vespertine*, recalled that "she liked that idea of moving the studio into the home rather than being in a studio, . . . part of the concept was to make it almost like going to the bathroom or to make a sandwich" (Sigurðsson 2006). This domestication of electronic music, by sampling sounds from around the home and music-making in home-studios, links music technology with the realm of the feminine.

Moreover, Björk's artistic output during her solo career naturalizes technology rather than technologizes nature. The naturalizing of beats through mimesis of sounds of nature, and through the aesthetics of technological failure undermines a masculinist, technologically determinist worldview. Her voice, representative of the natural and feminine, is rarely technologized throughout, contrary to practices in electronic dance music of the 1990s which often used anonymized female voices against electronic dance beats, or which used the vocoder to give the human voice a cyborg-like quality (as heard in Cher's 'Believe' released in 1998).[15] The sonic background of her music is often made to fit vocally-composed melodies rather than the voice being subservient to the beats, as is more often the case in dance musics. Furthermore, Björk contextualizes microsound within an explicitly expressive setting, counter to its cultural history as a form of post-techno minimalism that arose as part of a prohibition on emotion (Sherburne 2004: 325).

However, Björk's reclaiming of the technological for the feminine can be seen as a reactionary response because it left in place gender categories: in *Vespertine* the feminine is still aligned with the emotional and the private, domestic sphere making her use of technology congruent with Western

European and Northern American gender norms. The extent to which this changed after 2001 is discussed later.

Analysis of Björk's artistic output, and the discourse surrounding it, reveals a unification of the natural and the technological. This is a response to both general cultural anxieties, and tensions within contemporary Icelandic identity. Within the context of Björk's Icelandic upbringing, the unification embodied in her artistic output reconciles the tensions between Iceland's rural landscape ideology and its technological modernity. From this perspective the unification of nature and technology also brings together rural and urban, tradition and modernity, mythology and science. In the next chapter I explore the innovative character of Björk's musical style in more detail, exploring the way in which this idea of unity is realized through sound, and how this changed over the course of her career.

5 Sound

> A song that a two-year old and a granny can sing, that's the tops. That's the ultimate. If you make the most experimental song in the world but it will still be pop, completely simple. (Björk interviewed in Marcus 1996: 215).

Björk's explicit artistic mission during her solo career was to create experimental, yet accessible, popular music. After the eclectic, electronic dance and jazz influenced styles of *Debut* and *Post*, each new studio album brought a change of instrumental palette and concept: from a focus on strings, synthesized beats and Icelandic patriotism in *Homogenic*, to the whispered intimacy, microbeats and celestial sounds of *Vespertine*, to the vocal-only paganism of *Medúlla*, and the "electronic-tribal" beats of *Volta*. Stylistic change was part of what defined Björk as an innovator.

However, Björk's experimentalism during her solo career was perceived by many to be taking her towards a less commercial sound than that of *Debut*. Furthermore, critics claimed that as each new album found a new audience, part of the previous audience was alienated. From this perspective, Björk's dual aspirations of accessibility and experimentalism seem at odds. Popular music is generally linked to saleability, because it is understood as mass mediated music for the general public, and defined in opposition to art music (perceived as the music of a social elite) and traditional music (which is disseminated orally).[1] Experimentation and innovation is therefore inconsistent with commerciality because it introduces uncertainty into the market: salebility is premised on the idea that it is possible to predict what can be sold. Björk's understanding of the term "popular" unharnesses it from the idea of commerciality, while retaining its opposition to art music:

> The meaning of the word [pop] comes from folk, or people. . . . I feel materialism has really distorted that word, and it

has changed its meaning into 'sellable', not 'music of the people, working-class style'. (Björk interviewed in Diva 2007)

According to this argument, "popular music" can be musically experimental, so long as it remains "music of the people", that is (for Björk), modern, urban, mass mediated and anti-elitist.

Björk's aspirations are reflected in her long-term allegiance with Smekkleysa SM SF (Bad Taste Ltd), and her membership of the Sugarcubes. The sound and motivations of the Sugarcubes were the product of two main factors: the demise of post-punk groups Kukl and Peyr whose noisy, experimental sound had previously had success within the alternative music scene outside Iceland, and Smekkleysa's 'Bad Taste' manifesto, which determined to show that contemporary notions of "good taste" (which were complicit with acceptance of corporate culture and capitalist individualism) were the enemy of creativity. The result was pop songs whose light-hearted surface was constantly thrown into doubt by darker undercurrents. Standard song structures and rhythmic patterns, simple chord progressions and melodies, and a familiar indie guitar-based instrumental set up, provided an accessible, kitsch pop sound. But this pop surface was disrupted by the extreme character of Björk's vocal sounds, Einar Örn's seemingly nonsensical interjections, the dissonant instrumental lines, musical pastiche, and absurd and surreal subject matter and imagery. Their energy and spontaneity rejected the constraints of pop and made accessible what otherwise might have been perceived as experimental.

This chapter examines the way in which Björk's dual aspirations of populism and experimentalism are played out in her music by tracing the developments in her musical style. A central component in understanding the character of Björk's music is the recognition that, while her style has undergone many changes over her career, the idea articulated by that sound has remained remarkably consistent: as I will show, just as Björk's thematic tropes merge apparent opposites, so Björk's sonic world is all about creating unity.

Björk's Voice

Björk's vocal style is the most striking characteristic of her music: critics and audiences comment on the expressive range and distinctive timbre of her voice. Her voice was also her main compositional tool, as she explained in an interview at the start of her solo career:

> I never had the ambition to be a singer, I always wanted to make good music. It's like learning shorthand writing. It's not so much that you're into it, but it makes it easier to write anything. That's why I sing. (Björk interviewed in Aston 1993: 42)

Most of Björk's music consists of vocals with an acoustic and/or electronic (synthesized) sonic background. Exceptions to this are her film soundtracks and the occasional instrumental composition.[2]

Björk's voice has an "alternative" character within the context of popular music: her wide range of timbres includes a breathy singing voice, a warm and fuller sound in the mid register, a "belting" vocal style typical in music theatre and pop ballads (in which the chest voice is carried high into the upper register),[3] a head voice, shouting, whispering, and a sound between singing and speaking which often has a child-like quality.[4] The extreme character and variety of these vocal timbres is unusual. Moreover, she uses a wide range of vocal noises (extended vocal techniques): guttural throat growls, shrieks, squeaks and noisy inhalations and expirations. Rapid changes in her vocal tone within and between songs suggest a mercurial shift between emotional extremes. The placement and spacing of syllables and words are particularly idiosyncratic at times, with emphasis given to individual consonants, vowels, or keywords. Occasionally words or syllables are repeated, suggesting a pleasurable savouring of the words, and mangled pronunciation suggests child-like naiveté and an exoticism heightened by the rolled "r"s which characterize her Icelandic accent. Some similarities can be heard to the vocal style of English punk Siouxie Sioux (lead singer of Siouxie and the Banshees and The Creatures) particularly in Björk's earliest recordings with Tappi Tíkarrass, Kukl and the Sugarcubes, although Björk denied being consciously influenced by other singers.

In many respects, Björk's vocal style is directly at odds with the sound generally associated with vocal control. For example, one convention is to draw in breath rapidly and inconspicuously, yet Björk's breathing is often noisy, exacerbated by a high degree of compression,[5] and frequently occurs mid-phrase.[6] The intensity of sound is often inconsistent, suggesting uneven airflow from the lungs and through the vocal folds (the twin membranes stretched across the larynx which are set into vibration by the flow of air from the lungs, producing a pitched sound). Occasionally Björk uses a forceful glottal stop before vowel sounds: this technique is used by untrained singers to conserve breath and produce a more focused tone, but it often results in swoops and wobbles due to the pressure it creates behind the closed larynx. Elsewhere the attack of her vocal entries is breathy, usually a result of airflow being too fast or too pressured, which prevents the vocal folds from coming together completely. Listeners need not be consciously aware of the physical mechanisms giving rise to Björk's vocalizations to hear the sounds as expressing certain kinds of physical and mental state: these vocal sounds imply the same physical cause – an excess of energy, and a lack of control – explaining in some measure the sense of edginess and excitement which many people hear in her vocals.

Unusually for pop, Björk often sings non-lexical vocables (wordless singing) which are commonly mistaken for Icelandic, and which often occur at moments of climax within songs, as on 'Big Time Sensuality' (*Debut*), 'Bachelorette' (*Homogenic*), or 'Pagan Poetry' (*Vespertine*). (This is in addition to singing entire tracks in either English or Icelandic, often dependent on the geographic location of performance.) One practical reason for Björk's wordless singing was that she used her voice to create melodies and structures for her songs, and singing without words enabled her to do this more fluently. She has said that her earliest compositions were wordless, and that only later did she begin to sing a few words in Icelandic or in English, until, by the time of the Sugarcubes, she was singing more lyrics than wordless vocalizations. In this respect, wordless songs, such as 'Amphibian' from Spike Jonze's film *Being John Malkovich* (1999), or 'Öll Birtan' from *Medúlla* (2004), constitute a return to her earlier vocal practices. Words and music were usually composed separately by Björk, who used a variety of techniques to devise lyrics, such as keeping a journal from which she would take self-written prose and poetry when needed, using pre-existing poetry, and writing lyrics with the poet Sjón. The effect on listeners of singing without words is that it can suggest authentic emotional expression: non-lexical singing taps into a common cultural belief in the "natural" and spontaneous character of the singing voice, in contrast to the perceived rationality of language. It further aligns the Björk persona with ideas of the natural outlined previously.[7]

Although Björk's music is perceived to have become more experimental over her solo career, this is not reflected in her vocal style, which was distinctive even in her early teens. Only four years after the release of *Björk* in 1977 (which shares few similarities with her later style), her recordings with the punk-pop band Tappi Tíkarrass reveal her powerful "belt" sound, a half-shouted and half-sung punk vocal style, and a slight catch at the end of notes anticipating the throat growl later used with the Sugarcubes. The unusual instrumental sounds and textures of Kukl, two years later, provided the perfect environment for Björk to extend her range of vocal effects: in Kukl both she and Einar Örn used a punk-like vocal style that was a cross between singing and speaking. In the Sugarcubes the two vocal roles became more distinct from each other, as Björk developed her use of a wider vocal range and sustained singing style.

Björk's use of vocal effects changed further over her solo career: the punk-like shouts and "little-girl" timbre became less frequent, there were fewer extreme vocal contrasts within single tracks, and her vocal tone became fuller. These changes can be illustrated by comparing two performances of the same song, separated by a twenty-year period: Björk's performance of 'Ammæli' on the 1986 Sugarcubes album and her performance from the Sugarcubes' twentieth-anniversary reunion gig held in Reykjavik on 17 November 2006.[8] 'Ammæli', which brought the Sugarcubes international attention when it was released as the English-language single 'Birthday' in 1987,[9] consists of a repeated verse and chorus, and the vocal melody uses notes taken from the underlying chords, a commonly used alternation between chords I and IV in successive bars (chords of C major and F major with added sixth). However, long reverberation added to the 1986 version, and Einar Örn's dissonant trumpet interjections in both, give this otherwise innocent-sounding track a sinister twist. This juxtaposition of simplicity and quirkiness continues in the lyrics, in which the first-person narrative of a five-year-old child describes an erotic attraction towards a man.

The vocal timbre of the 1986 version of 'Ammæli' is more child-like than that of the performance in 2006: the vocal tone is thin, situated in the mouth and nose, and frequently switches mid-phrase between this thin voice, a half-whisper, a squeezed singing tone, and head-voice. The main difference is that whereas in the earlier version the transition between different vocal qualities is fairly smooth, in the later performance there are distinct shifts between vocal timbres. Comparing the first (wordless) chorus in each case (see Figure 16), the later performance uses a belt-style voice with an open throat throughout the first three and a half bars, then switches to head voice for the highest notes of the phrase (the pitches G and A), followed by a whispered G in the octave below. By contrast, the earlier recording includes a change from a thin belt-tone to a breathy tone within each vocal phrase and the highest pitches in the second phrase (bar 4 of Figure 16) are sung in a much breathier head-voice. Furthermore, the treatment of the sustained pitch C which ends each answering phrase is significantly different in the two versions: in the early version the tuning wavers (an expressive effect), whereas in the later performance it is sung as a regular, legato alternation between the pitches C and B. Lastly, the early performance includes a slight squeezed-shriek effect between the first two notes of each vocal phrase, followed by a guttural, pitched throat growl through the second and third note of each phrase.

These vocal noises suggest a voice on the very edge of control, emanating from a (small) physical body which has more energy than can be contained; the vocal style of the later performance also conveys a sense of excess, and edginess, but with less of the instability and child-like vocal quality that characterizes the earlier recording.

This comparison of vocal performances separated by a twenty-year period reveals two important issues regarding Björk's vocal style. First, Björk used a much more extensive range of vocal effects than is typical of commercial artists. Second, her voice did not become more experimental over her career, but she did acquire a richer vocal timbre and sing with greater definition of different types of vocal effect. This change in style is attributable to aesthetic and physical circumstances. The sudden jump in vocal range between 1986 and 1988 (Figure 17) can be attributed to Björk's switch from

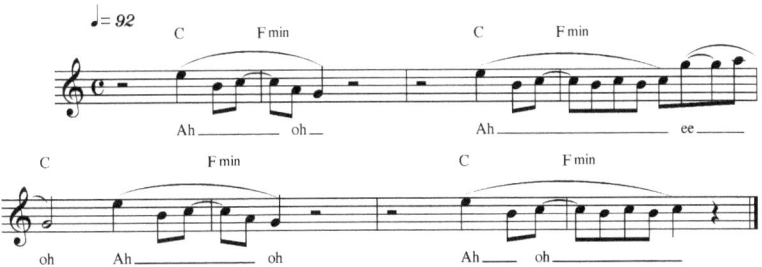

Figure 16: Vocal melody of the chorus from 'Ammæli' (*Life's Too Good*, The Sugarcubes 1988). The rhythms in this example have been quantised.

punk to a more sustained and melodic vocal style suited to the Sugarcubes' indie-pop style. The change in vocal style during her solo career can be traced partly to Björk's complete loss of voice while touring in 1995, and her subsequent adoption of vocal exercises.[10] It may be no coincidence that *Post*, recorded at this time, uses the smallest vocal range of all Björk's studio albums (one and a half octaves): her higher register is absent, as shown in Figure 17, akin to the range she used with Kukl during the 1980s and before its expansion with the Sugarcubes. Björk's two-octave vocal range with the Sugarcubes gradually descended until 1997 after which she started to use her higher register again. The albums in which her voice regains its upper register (*Selmasongs* and *Vespertine*) are the first albums in which she uses less vocal projection; it may be that the theme of internalization which characterized these albums enabled Björk to use a different vocal style, which allowed her to make use of her upper register in a way that was more physically sustainable. Björk also appears to have gained notes in her lower register over the course of her career (which can be heard in the opening vocal phrases of 'Earth Intruders' on *Volta*).[11] This may be driven by aesthetic decisions, improved vocal technique, and the ageing process: although physical maturation of the female vocal apparatus is generally complete by the age of twenty, there is normally a slight descent in vocal register after this age.

Although they contribute to the experimental character of her music, Björk's vocals function to convey emotion, rather than to display (normative) vocal virtuosity. In this respect, Björk differs from other Anglophone contemporary female pop singers. For example, both Maria Carey and Christina Aguilera have huge vocal ranges (reportedly, five octaves in the case of Carey; four octaves in the case of Aguilera), and use vocal effects such as the whistle register (the highest register of the human voice), and melismatic singing (vocal runs sung on a single syllable); but their vocal display has been criticized by listeners who believe it emphasizes the performance at the expense of the emotions believed to have inspired it.

The way in which vocals were recorded and treated also reveals the importance Björk and her recording engineers placed on capturing emotionally expressive performances. Many of Björk's vocals were recorded using a Dictaphone (which Björk often used to capture compositional ideas) or handheld microphone with the mix played over monitors, rather than the more

Sound 107

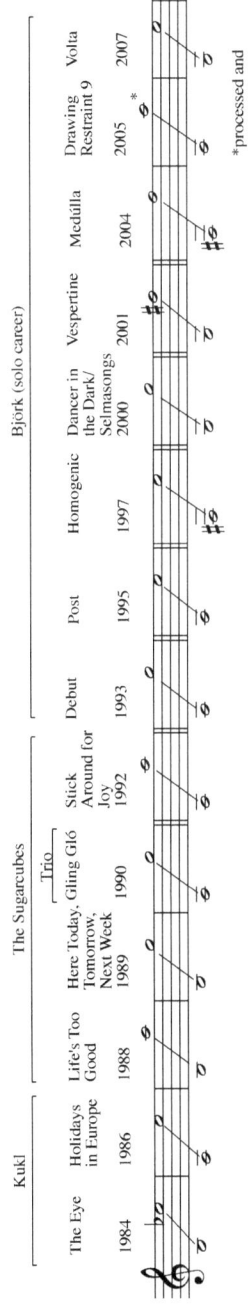

Figure 17: Vocal range by studio and soundtrack albums (1984–2007).

standard practice of using a microphone on a stand within a vocal booth (Stent 2006).[12] Although using a handheld microphone created technical difficulties, such as "spill" from the monitor mix onto the vocal track, this method of recording vocals enabled Björk to move around the recording space while she sang, creating what she perceived to be a more "natural" singing environment.

The emphasis on conveying emotionally expressive performances is evident in the treatment of Björk's voice in recordings. Many tracks contrast obviously technologically mediated vocal sounds with more naturalistic ones, creating a vocal that is constantly changing. This can be heard on 'Earth Intruders', from *Volta*, in which each successive section of the vocal has a completely different sound: the first four lines have been filtered, as though heard through a telephone; the next line ("turmoil, carnage") has a greater amount of reverberation, as though at a distance; and the phrases which end the section use the same filtered sound as heard at the start, but double-tracked so that Björk's voice is heard twice. According to Damian Taylor, recording engineer on *Vespertine* and *Volta*, Björk "knows which vocals she wants where, which ones she wants to be set back, up front, telephoned", remarking that "it's really part of the creative process for her" (Taylor 2006).

The practice of applying different treatments to different vocal phrases is common within contemporary pop tracks, but the recorded sound of Björk's vocals is distinctive for two reasons. First, her vocals lack the continuous use of reverberation heard on many commercial pop recordings. Björk's preference was for a naturalistic recorded sound, with effects used for specific dramatic reasons rather than for cosmetic enhancement, arguing that "when you do it, I think you should go all the way with it and be really obvious with it and not do it just to fix what's wrong" (Björk quoted in Swenson 2004).

An example of this deliberate use of excessive treatments on Björk's recordings can be heard in the album and video mixes of the track. For example, the album mix of 'All is Full of Love' from *Homogenic* by Scottish born producer and musician Howie B (Howard Bernstein) uses a long reverb which results in a wash of sound, suggesting a very large space, suggestive of the "heavenly" environment envisaged by Björk for the track; Mark "Spike" Stent's mix of the same track for the video directed by Chris Cunningham creates the impression of multiple personae within the track (the two cyborgs within the video realization) by differentiating the call and the response phrases of the chorus through changed reverberation and placement in the mix.

A second distinctive feature of the way Björk's voice is recorded is that multiple vocal layers are often created by multi-tracking different vocal performances, rather than using chorus effects (in which the same vocal track is effectively copied and added to the original). The technique used in Björk's tracks results in a more naturalistic and "lo-fi" sound than the hyper-real synchrony characteristic of contemporary mainstream pop (an example of this heightened synchrony can be heard on Christina Aguilera's 'Candyman' from the album *Back to Basics* released in 2006).

Björk's vocal style is an important component of her experimentalism. In the context of the vocal and recording practices of commercial music these effects can seem messy and eccentric, yet these same characteristics are central to perceptions of her as an authentic, emotionally expressive artist because they suggest untutored, anti-commercial and intense emotional expression. Björk's vocal performances therefore simultaneously communicate the ideas of experimentalism and accessibility that she aspired to in her music.

The Relationship between Voice and Sonic Background

Björk's voice is central to the music of her solo career in a way that goes beyond standard voice-accompaniment arrangements in popular genres, and her previous musical collaborations. Because she usually starts by composing melodies using her voice, the beats and sonic background are cut to fit, rather than the usual practice in electronic and dance music in which the voice is made to fit the rhythm of a pre-composed sonic "background". Her voice is set against a sonic background in such a way as to create separation between voice and background through tensions between the pitch content of the vocal melody and the harmony of the instrumental parts, and between her vocal timing and the rhythmic regularities of the instrumental parts. These tensions often dissipate towards the end of individual tracks through processes of textural accumulation through which the voice merges with the other elements present in the track. The consequence of this is the expression of sonic and conceptual unity.

Melodic and Harmonic Characteristics

The distinctiveness of Björk's vocal style is created from a mix of vocal timbres, the way her voice is recorded, or treated in performance, and her unusual note choices within vocal melodies. Melodies were central to the way Björk created songs, hence she said "I will wait patiently for a good melody and usually don't even start with a song unless that has come to me. Then the other half of me can noodle endlessly on arrangements" (Björk interviewed in Kot 2007).

Björk's vocals on the Sugarcubes' albums and her first solo albums were often noted for their angular character: her melodies on these albums tend to use the first, third, and fifth notes from the scale (triadic pitch collections), as heard in the first vocal line of 'Mama' shown in Figure 18. Melodies made from these basic pitches can sound musically simple; hence they contribute to the Sugarcubes' playful pop image, and to perceptions of Björk as child-like. Björk's vocals prior to the Sugarcubes had included melodies with a more lyrical character and which moved by step, as can be heard in the step-wise rising vocal melody which begins 'Siðasta Ég' from *Family Tree* (originally recorded with the Elgar Sisters in the mid 1980s), and prior to that had comprised punk shouts, and short melodic fragments with Kukl; this suggests that it was a stylistic choice to use "simple" melodic materials in the Sugarcubes, rather than her habitual style at the time. Disjunct, or angular, melodies based on triadic material became less frequent over the course of Björk's solo career as she moved towards a more chromatic and harmonically complex style: whereas nine of the eleven tracks on the Sugarcube's *Life's Too Good* and over half the tracks on *Debut*

Figure 18: Vocal melody from 'Mama' (*Life's Too Good*, The Sugarcubes 1988) showing the use of triadic pitches.

contain disjunct triadic melodies, the albums from *Post* onwards are characterized by step-wise melodic movement.

The quirky vocal melodies of Björk's solo career use 'tensions' at the beginning of phrases (notes taken from outside the underlying harmony generally, or the chord specifically). Björk's accompanist and co-writer Guy Sigsworth remarked upon Björk's choice of musically adventurous phrase beginnings during improvisation sessions for *Vespertine*: "rather than go for the note that is already in the chord" Björk would find a pitch which would create a more interesting, if slightly musically riskier melodic effect and "react with adventure" to whatever Sigsworth was playing at the time (Sigsworth 2006). For example, the instrumental backing to the first vocal phrase of 'Possibly Maybe' from *Post* sounds a chord of B major, yet the voice enters on the sharpened fourth degree (E sharp) over a chord of B major (see Figure 19). The voice is therefore in harmonic tension with the accompaniment, complementing the lyrics that suggest emotional tension and doubt. This technique of starting vocal phrases on tensions continued throughout her solo career: the first and second vocal phrases of 'Sun in My Mouth' from *Vespertine* start with the flattened-seventh and flattened ninth scale degrees respectively, over a sustained chord of A major; and the first two vocal phrases of 'Storm' from *Drawing Restraint 9* begin on the second and fourth degrees of the E-minor scale, which forms its pitch centre.

Björk's use of melodic tensions derives from the modal character of her harmonic style (her choice of scale types). Many of Björk's tracks use modes common in popular genres: the Ionian (also known as the major mode), and the "bluesy" Aeolian (minor mode) characterized by the "depressed" sound of the flattened third and sixth scale degrees, and Dorian, which has a less

Figure 19: First vocal phrase of 'Possibly Maybe' (*Post* 1995) showing the sharpened fourth scale degree that starts the phrase.

bright and urgent sound than the Ionian, due to its flattened seventh scale degree. However, Björk's music has a distinctive melodic and harmonic sound due to her use of other less commonly encountered scales: in particular, the Lydian and Phrygian modes. The yearning quality of some of Björk's songs arises from the use of the sharpened fourth degree of the scale (relative to the major scale) which characterizes the Lydian mode, such as in 'Aeroplane' from *Debut*, '5 Years' from *Homogenic* (the e natural shown in Figure 20), 'Possibly, Maybe' from *Post* (shown in Figure 19), and 'Hope' from *Volta*.[13] The raised fourth scale degree is often heard as leaning towards the fifth degree (in the same way the seventh (the "leading tone") leans towards the tonic in the major scale), and creates a sense of wistfulness. It has a historical usage in contexts of innocence combined with desire (for example, a raised fourth occurs on the second syllable ('-ri-') of the word 'Maria' from the song of the same title from Leonard Bernstein's musical *West Side Story*) and so it potentially contributes to perceptions of Björk as passionate and child-like.

Other tracks by Björk shift tonal centre with the introduction of new pitches to the vocal line, which gives them an unstable quality. For example, the first vocal entry of 'Miðvikudags' from *Medúlla* begins with notes from the G major scale, yet immediately introduces the sharpened fourth (C sharp) on the downbeat of the third bar (see Figure 21), shifting the tonal centre to A (Dorian mode).

Björk's use of the Lydian mode in her vocals with the Sugarcubes and her solo career may be attributable to, and is a signifier of, the Icelandic music she was exposed to during her upbringing: Icelandic hymns originating prior to the nineteenth century, and nationalist composers' deliberate integration

Figure 20: Vocal melody of '5 Years' (*Homogenic* 1997).

Figure 21: First vocal entry in 'Miðvikudags' (Medúlla 2004).

of Icelandic traditional music into their works, both frequently used the Lydian mode.

Many of Björk's tracks use the Phrygian mode, which has flattened scale steps two, three, six and seven (as heard in 'Venus as a Boy' from *Debut*, 'Enjoy' from *Post*, 'Where is the Line?' from *Medúlla*, and 'Bath' from *Drawing Restraint 9*). The Phrygian mode (which is distinctive due to its flattened second scale degree) has a historical usage in Western art music which associates it with dark and depressive contexts on the one hand, and with Spanish and Arabic "exoticism" on the other due to its use in flamenco and other Spanish musics (Collins 2006). Its appearance on 'Venus as a Boy' draws on these associations, aided by the lyrics and the Bollywood string sound which suggest erotic exoticism. Philip Tagg (1994) notes that although the Phrygian mode was extremely rare in Anglophone popular music between 1970 and 1990, it became a feature of electronic dance music. This has been attributed to the exposure of musicians and producers (during their adolescence) to 1980s computer games consoles, whose limited sound capabilities favoured melodies using the Phrygian mode (Collins 2006). Björk came into contact with this harmonic palette through her exposure to electronic dance music of the early 1990s, and her work within this vernacular with British dance musicians Graham Massey and Nellee Hooper.

The majority of Björk's music uses harmonic progressions (and voicings) common to pop and rock genres: individual songs use a small number of chords, connected either by close harmonic relationship (on the circle of fifths) or by step-wise scalar movement, and these progressions are usually repeated in subsequent verse and chorus sections. Björk's use of primary chords is illustrated by the track 'Oceania' from *Medúlla*, each verse of which uses repetitions of the same underlying chord progression, comprising B flat minor (chord IV), C minor (chord V) and F minor (chord I). An example of Björk's use of step-wise harmonic movement is heard in 'Possibly Maybe' (*Post*), in which the chorus alternates between B major in the verse, and C sharp minor in the chorus. However, Björk used increasingly complex and chromatic harmonic sequences from *Vespertine* onwards. Tracks on *Medúlla* are much more complex than hitherto, and it may be no coincidence that out of all her studio albums to date *Medúlla* was dubbed the least accessible by the music press.

A final distinctive feature of Björk's harmonic style, heard in her solo career, results from her use of parallel movement within instrumental arrangements. 'Hunter' and 'Jóga' both have a lyrical character, yet the instrumental accompaniment has a stark aural effect produced by the use of parallel fifths. Parallel movement in fourths, fifths and octaves within instrumental ensemble accompaniments is rare within popular music, but is one of the distinctive features of the Icelandic musical tradition of tvisöngur, and the nationalist compositions of Jón Leifs (see, for example, *Twenty-Five Icelandic Folk Songs* 1928).

In sum, Björk's technique of using repeating blocks of closely related chords, common to pop and rock genres, creates an accessible sound, which is distinctive due to its use of unusual modes, and arrangements. Tensions between pitches in her melodies and the harmonies of the accompaniment create separation between voice and sonic background – a characteristic that is also created through rhythmic tensions, which I examine next.

Beats and Timing

Prior to her solo career, the rhythmic character of Björk's musical collaborations was influenced by jazz, punk, rock and pop. However, much of Björk's music during her solo career is beat-based, and influenced by styles of electronic dance music, and it was through this that she came to develop her characteristic dislocation of voice and rhythmic background. Electronic dance music tends to be heard, and created, in terms of a 4/4 time signature, and patterns tend to occur in groups of four at different levels. The influence of both "break-beat driven" (drum 'n' bass, jungle) and "four-on-the-floor" (house, techno) sequencer-derived electronic dance musics can be heard in Björk's music, particularly in the quarter-note bass drum kick and the syncopated eighth-note synthesizer stabs on 'Crying', 'There's More to Life Than This', and 'Big Time Sensuality'. In 'Violently Happy' the filtering and reverb effects on voice and synth pads reference acid house. On *Post* the down-tempo 'Possibly Maybe' is influenced by trip-hop, whereas

Homogenic, Vespertine and *Volta* are influenced by industrial techno, electronica and hiphop.

As well as creating beats herself Björk collaborated with a number of beat-makers, of whom one of the most influential was Mark Bell. Her working relationship with him illustrates the kinds of collaborations she has had with other beat-makers. On *Homogenic, Selmasongs,* and *Medúlla,* he added to, or edited, beats Björk and others had programmed. On other occasions Björk listened to beats he had made, then chose one that she edited to a track (for example 'Wanderlust' from *Volta*). On a few occasions he brought music which she then sang over, resulting in the tracks 'I Go Humble', 'Nature Is Ancient' and 'Declare Independence' ("An interview with Björk" 2007).

The majority of her music is in duple metres, emphasizing the feeling of two beats in a bar often in the form of a programmed rhythmic grid. However, from *Vespertine* this rhythmic grid sometimes became irregular or was absent entirely. Many of the tracks on *Vespertine* lack a clear pulse at the start (for example, 'Unison' and 'An Echo, A Stain'), and the metric grid, if there is one, emerges only later. This is true of even more tracks on *Medúlla*: metre is frequently ambiguous, often due to extreme variations in the expressive timing of the vocal performances (the vocal line often speeds up, slows down and sometimes pauses, making it difficult to discern an underlying pulse, as on 'Show Me Forgiveness', 'Submarine', 'Sonnets/Unrealities XI'); and individual lines seem to inhabit different metres as a consequence of the multitracking of individual vocal parts (for example, 'Ancestors' and 'Desired Constellation'). *Medúlla* marks a distinct move away from the dance-based rhythms that define commercial popular music.[14] Yet this did not mark an abrupt switch to a different style: some tracks on *Medúlla* have, or develop over their course a sense of clear, danceable metre, and the subsequent album, *Volta,* once again includes a much greater preponderance of beat-based tracks: 'Earth Intruders', the first track on the album, starts in a duple metre with the sound of marching.

The beats in Björk's early solo recording projects use sounds typical of electronic dance music; albeit with idiosyncratic additions, such as a timpani sound for the riff on 'Human Behaviour'. However, one of the most innovative aspects of her music from 1997 is the wide palette of timbres in the beats of her music. From *Homogenic* on, many of Björk's recording projects involved a period of "sound collection". In *Homogenic* this phase included listening to Icelandic music in search of the patriotic sound she was after, and trying to make beats that sounded "volcanic" to represent the Icelandic landscape. In *Dancer in the Dark*, *Selmasongs* and *Vespertine* the research phase included finding sound sources in the environment (of the film diegesis or at home) and using them to create percussion sounds. For instance, the beats for *Vespertine* were created from pre-engineered sound sources called up when needed to serve in the place of traditional percussion sounds such as hi-hat and snare (Sigurðsson 2006). The period of collecting vocal sounds for *Medúlla* coincided with Björk's pregnancy with her second child, which meant that she was able to compose even when she felt unable to sing. Having felt confined to a less collaborative phase, due to the restrictions imposed by breastfeeding her young daughter, the next album, *Volta*, included more direct improvisation with other musicians, such as a session in the studio with Timbaland which produced 'Earth Intruders', 'Innocence' and material used on 'Hope' (Stosuy 2007).

I previously showed that the treatment of the beats on *Homogenic*, *Vespertine* and *Medúlla* "naturalizes" their technological symbolism through mimesis of real-world sounds, such as the "volcanic" beats on 'Jóga' and the liquid-like sounds on 'Nature is Ancient'. The distortion on the beats in *Homogenic* signifies the power and rawness of the natural world, while the use of swept filters suggests the movement of a sound source through the virtual environment. A second kind of mimesis performed by Björk's beats is the imitation of small organisms in *Vespertine*. The spatialization of the beats in the mix, their rapidity, and irregularity mimic the movements of insects. For example, the microbeats used in different sections of the same track are slightly varied, and in some tracks their treatment and spatialization in the mix changes throughout, the intention being that "it would feel a bit more organic" (Stent 2006). In the case of *Medúlla*, some tracks began in versions with synthesized beats, but once Björk had made the decision that the whole album should include only vocal sounds some of these parts were rewritten for voice. For example, 'Where is the Line?' initially had electronic beats programmed by Mark Bell, but in order to fit the *a capella* conception of the album, a new version was created using human beat-boxer Rahzel to produce beats with the same rhythmic character as the original (*The Inner or Deep Part of an Animal or Plant Structure*, dir. Gestsdóttir 2004). In *Volta* there is a return to acoustic and anachronistic (early 1990s) synthesized timbres for beats. The variety of timbres used by Björk and her collaborators is more typical of the "intelligent" subgenre of electronica than the mainstream of popular music.

The rhythmic regularity of the programmed "grid" of beats forms part of the sonic background against which Björk's voice moves with remarkable rhythmic freedom. Previously I showed how Björk's vocals play with the grid of beats by anticipating the beat, entering on unexpected beats of the bar, and using different pitch material to the sonic background (see the analysis of 'Big Time Sensuality' in Chapter 4). In sum, Björk's music is characterized by the relationship between the rhythmic flexibility of her vocal performances and the metrically rigid grid of beats which exist together in a kind of tension, just as there is an opposition between the harmony of the sonic background and the tensions introduced by Björk's vocal melodies.

Merging of Voice and Background

Over the course of many of Björk's tracks the separation set up between her voice and the sonic background dissipates, as both are subsumed into the same musical texture. This is achieved through linear processes of musical emergence: the texture gradually thickens as individual sound sources enter or are multi-tracked; rhythmic activity increases as gaps within the metric grid are filled by additional percussive and instrumental lines; the vocal range increases from step-wise movement in the verse to larger intervals in chorus sections; and there is a shift from language (usually English) to wordless singing. Some of these processes can be heard on 'Wanderlust' from *Volta*, and the aptly named 'Unison' from *Vespertine*.

'Wanderlust' consists of a standard two-part structure, with contrasting verse and chorus, and a coda (or "outro") of Morse-code signals. Each verse consists of a four-part structure (A A B A), while the chorus material is repeated twice each time. Each section of the verse adds new material: for example, the first verse begins with Björk singing accompanied by solo trombone, but additional brass entries, high frequency beats, and vocal delays gradually thicken the texture. The contrasting section within the verse ("I have lost my origin, I don't want to find it again") is given momentum by the entry of a heavy and squelchy synthesized bass on the third of each four-beat unit. The chorus accelerates this process of textural thickening each time it appears because it includes sustained brass chords, and a more active bass beat, plus an emphatic synthesized two-note bass figure on the third beat. Each subsequent verse and chorus uses the same material as the first, but with increasing multi-tracking of the voice and brass, and more percussive use of the brass ensemble.

This increasing textural density and complexity has various effects which function to merge the separate elements. First, the multi-tracking of her voice, the use of vocal delays, and placement in different positions (left, right or centre) multiplies her voice; as a consequence it is no longer the unitary and focal object it was at the beginning which enables it to merge with the other instrumental sources. Furthermore, the brass instruments have a melodic and symphonic role at the beginning of the track (playing sustained notes and melodic flourishes), but become increasingly percussive (as in the second repeat of each chorus, for example); by the instrumental repeat of the chorus (at 4:37) the brass provides both sustained (symphonic) material and (beat-like) percussive material, merging acoustic and electronic sound sources and styles. Acoustic and electronic sound sources are also brought together through the layering of percussive brass material and a Morse-code signal in the coda (at 5:16, and derived from the phrase "Wanderlust, relentlessly craving Wanderlust"[15]): the overlaying of the Morse-code sound onto the brass material, which then drops out, creates aural and conceptual continuity between the acoustic and electronic, and between music and real-world sound. There is a final fusion at the very end of the track as the Morse-code signal is overlain by the sounds of the sea, highlighting a continuity between natural and human-made sounds, technology and nature, and recalling the lyrical reference in the first verse to "leaving this harbour" and the track's emergence from the ensemble of foghorns and brass which link 'Wanderlust' to the preceding track 'Earth Intruders'.

Creating "Unity" through Integration of Musical Materials

The initial dislocation and subsequent merging of musical materials highlighted in 'Wanderlust' is an example of a more general process whereby Björk enacts the idea of unity through sound. The link between nature and technology (and its representation through the fusing of acoustic and electronic sources) is a topic I discussed previously, but this analysis of her sound reveals the way in which this theme is embodied in Björk's compositional style. It also offers a way to understand the function of her apparently eclectic style, which brings together diverse collaborators, musical genres, and sound sources:

> Overall I'm always quite interested to unite – to create a whole. . . . I have always felt that by uniting techno and acoustic, the modern and the roots, man and woman, the symphonic and the rhythmic, sound and vision, words and music... I can go on for ever, but I seem to be quite driven by uniting these things . . . (Björk cited in Scrudator 2007)

Similarly, her description of working with other musicians on *Volta* presented it as a process of fusion: she contrasted the solitary process of writing melodies and lyrics, editing on a computer, and arranging instrumental parts, with being "really excited about leaving all that behind and just merging with somebody who is hopefully quite different from me" (Stosuy 2007).

Björk is noted for having brought together different musical styles, but the significance of this is its creation of sonic and conceptual unity between apparently disparate materials and ideas. The merging of electronic and acoustic sources is evident throughout Björk's career, and was one of the distinctive characteristics of her sound from *Debut* onwards. Kukl's *Holidays in Europe* used samples of everyday sounds and other musics to create a collage effect. In addition, the Sugarcubes had included some musical pastiche in a comedic take on pop. However, Björk's integration of different musical styles and everyday sound sources during her solo career has a very different effect. *Debut* and *Post* included jazz covers alongside her own original tracks, which themselves included diverse influences. Her inclusion of different styles is more than stylistic eclecticism: it rejects divisions of genre or musical culture, and can be understood as a means to act out cultural integration through musical sound and practice. In the mid-1990s Björk conceived of her interaction with other musics as an opposition between her voice (which stood for her Icelandic identity) and musical styles she encountered on leaving Iceland. So, for example, she described her work with "English electronic beat-makers Graham Massey and Mark Bell" as "the desire to unite with the new and unknown, the alien and taboo by merging my voice with foreign electronic beats" (liner notes to *Family Tree*, 2002).[16]

Ten years later Björk's conception of this unification of cultures took a more encompassing form, partly as a result of living in the United States during the occupation of Iraq: the combination of sounds on *Volta* articulates the idea that humankind is a single "tribe", contrary to the divisions she perceived were wrought by organized religion (Powell 2007).

However, Björk's collaborations with non-Western musicians present a difficulty – namely the idea that her eclecticism is a form of musical colonialism. This was an issue Björk was evidently aware of, given the frequency with which she voiced her desire to avoid appropriation and exploitation of other musicians, and which she attributed to her own experience of exoticization by foreign media. For example, when she composed the soundtrack for *Drawing Restraint 9*, a film set on a Japanese whaling ship, she wanted her representation of Japanese culture to "treat it as an equal" without using clichéd musical signifiers of Japan.[17] Furthermore, Björk's remarks on this topic abound with the idea of "collaboration", which attempts to deflect potential perceptions of exploitation and appropriation. This is a difficulty experienced by many international musicians, for whom collaborations often involve power and wealth inequalities.[18]

Björk explains her collaborations as being driven by a desire to work with talented musicians (attested to by the range of musicians she works with), rather than the desire to create a "hybrid" style. Her attempts to avoid exploitation are evidenced to some extent by her treatment of musical material. For example, Inuk throat singer Tanya "Tagaq" Gillis appears on a number of tracks on *Medúlla* and *Drawing Restraint 9*. Tagaq's own performances of throat singing remove it from its original context as a game played between two Inuit females, and Björk similarly uses it as musical material free from its original context. However, its treatment within these albums is such that it retains its identity while forming part of a larger compositional texture: the intro and outro of the first track on *Medúlla*, 'The Pleasure is All Mine', presents relatively long segments of Tagaq's singing which do not fit the underlying phrase or metrical structure, thereby preserving the internal coherence and independence of her material.[19] Arguably, the sonic character of the different musical sources as they appear in Björk's music and the presence of other performers within Björk's recorded and live performances is a means by which Björk's ideas of unifying musical (and national and ethnic) cultures is realized through her artistic output as a reflection of a cosmopolitan existence: "To be in the moment, to be a 2008 person, it's more of an international affair, especially sonically. You hear the radio in a taxi, and go to an Indian restaurant and hear Indian music. You're hearing everything. I think you can still be from where you are, and be truthful about that, but you are still a person of the world" (Björk cited in Westwood 2008).

Another type of unification that occurs in Björk's music is that between music as sound art, and the auditory world of everyday life. From the beginning of Björk's career real-world sounds were incorporated into her music: Kukl's albums include the sounds of nature (for example, the transition from the sounds of a rainstorm to the percussive sounds of shakers, rattles and drums, and back again on 'Handa Tjolla' from *The Eye*), and travel (the airplane flight noises which open and close *Holidays in Europe*); *Debut* also includes the sounds of various environments (voices and music inside a club on 'There's More to Life Than This', street noises in 'Like Someone in Love', and tropical beach noises in 'Aeroplane'). The integration of real-world and musical sounds is more thorough in *Vespertine* and *Selmasongs* in which everyday sounds were sampled to create beats. In *Volta* the sounds of sea travel join one track to another, as if depicting a metaphorical journey, rather than the more literal journey portrayed in *Holidays in Europe*. As a consequence Björk's music is connected with, and shown to be a part of the everyday auditory world, rather than a separate sonic experience hived off from the rest of life (as exemplified by Western classical music heard in concert hall settings, for example). In this regard, the merging of instrumental and vocal music with real-world sounds articulates a unity between music and sound, between popular music and the everyday, which reinforces the status of Björk's sound world as music of "the people".

This analysis of Björk's voice, and the melodic, harmonic, rhythmic and timbral character of her music, reveals that her innovations are found in particular musical features of her music, and in the larger process that they serve: the presentation of sound material which is opposed in some way, but which is united through the musical processes of individual tracks and albums. So, although many aspects of her music are congruent with her aim to write "experimental pop" (the constantly changing and varied combinations of instrumental and stylistic palette, her extended vocal techniques), others, such as her engagement with dance-based styles, and the emphasis on "authentic" emotional expression, and unification of opposites, are more compatible with music industry expectations of singer-songwriters. The questions this raises are how and why her music changed, and what the consequence of this was for her status as a commercial artist.

The Sound and Consequences of Musical Innovation

Björk's music has gone through a number of stylistic shifts, but the most extreme was from the guitar-based alternative rock style of Tappi Tíkarrass, Kukl and the Sugarcubes to the electronic dance-based and jazz-inflected sound of her first solo album, *Debut*. Björk summarized this change in her style:

> I guess as a teenager I wasn't so much interested in what my friends were into. The punk thing: I liked the spirit but the chord structure was pretty boring and the Indie thing for me was totally lame. I did like occasional band [sic] like Associates, Eyeless in Gaza, DAF, Brian Eno and Kate Bush. I guess what these have in common even though they are different is that they were mixing electronics and acoustics, were very rhythm orientated and the musicology [sic] wasn't so square, (c-f-g) more chromatic and unpredictable. And then years passed and suddenly there was 808 State!! I was so excited and so were a lot of people my age that had tolerated the Indie stuff and finally here was something pagan, high energy, electronic and with polyrhythms!! So I started hanging out in clubs in England around 90 [sic] and for me it had all the excitement the Indie scene had lacked. ("An interview with Björk" 2007)

When she started developing her solo ideas in the early 1990s, she took a number of songs arranged for brass quartet to Graham Massey with the idea of adding dance beats to them: "She sent me a lot of tapes of quite earthy stuff, I wouldn't say folk music, but stuff that was very rootsy, and quite a lot of jazz stuff. And I instantly connected with what she was trying to do on that level – of trying to do something that was quite soulful, but with electronic music" (Graham Massey interviewed on *Inside Björk*, dir. Walker 2003). Hence, although the change from the Indie style of the Sugarcubes who disbanded in 1992, to the dance-influenced style of *Debut* in 1993 was dramatic, it was the product of ten years of writing solo material and a deliberate effort to identify and work with the variety of musicians who would together enable her to realize her musical ideas.

By comparison with the stylistic break between the Sugarcubes and her solo career, subsequent changes in Björk's musical style were more gradual. The shift to the electronic dance-influenced style of *Debut* was greeted by some as a sign that she had "sold out", due to the association of electronic music with commerciality, whereas Björk's subsequent changes in style were perceived as a shift towards a less commercial style. The way in which Björk's style became more experimental, and arguably less accessible, is illustrated by comparing song structures across her solo career.

The majority of Björk's tracks with the Sugarcubes and during her solo career use common pop and rock song structures, such as single or two-part strophic forms (in which the same music is repeated for each verse, or verse and chorus), and verse-chorus-bridge structures (in which a contrasting section intervenes before the final repetitions of the chorus). Audiences of pop and rock are familiar with these structures, which provide sufficient repetition for listeners to get to know a song quickly, and to enjoy variations within and between performances and mixes. However, through-composed structures – that is, tracks that avoid clear sectional forms or repetition of blocks of material – become increasingly frequent over her career. Structures which present a series of ideas, rather than repeating blocks of material, are relatively rare within popular music, and tend to occur in genres thought of as more experimental or progressive.[20] These changes in song structure are associated with changes in Björk's compositional process, which I illustrate with three examples, taken from a ten-year period of her career.

Duple Structures in Debut

Debut and *Post* combine characteristics of electronic dance music (the use of synthesizers, drum machines, sequencers and samplers, fast tempo (typically 120–150bpm), and repeating bass drum pattern) with acoustic instruments and voice, and created an innovative eclectic style.[21] Cyclic patterns are a central feature of the majority of Björk's music, but are particularly prominent in her early solo work with programmer Graham Massey and producer Nellee Hooper. These tracks use repeating sequences of instrumental patterns which are multiples of two, four, eight, and sixteen units from the lowest level to the level of the hyper-measure (the longest sequence in a particular track, and often 16 or 32 bars).

'Human Behaviour' is characteristic of this style. The track consists of nine instrumental loops shown in Figure 22, which are muted and un-muted at various points, over which the vocals, and occasional strings, sound. Entrances and exits of these looped sequences delineate the sectional divisions of the track. The melody, heard in the lead vocal, emphasizes the duple structure of the track: the vocal line of each verse repeats two groups of eight bars, which itself consists of four pairs of two-bar phrases. Thus, the structure of the track is heavily influenced by electronic dance music, and its creation through sequencer technology.[22]

Programmed, cyclic beat patterns are used as the basis of many of Björk's later tracks, even those which otherwise avoid repetition (for example, 'An Echo, A Stain' on *Vespertine*), and where the cyclic patterns are made from vocal material, as on *Medúlla*. From 2001 tracks that avoided repetition and clear sectional structures became increasingly common, which contributed to her perceived experimentalism.

Linear Structures in Vespertine

Björk had worked with non-repeating structures as early as Kukl, but the tracks on *Vespertine* which avoid repetition are significant in three respects.[23] First, Björk improvised using pre-existent texts as the source of the lyrics, which, according to co-writer Guy Sigsworth, resulted in a "loosening of the song moulds".[24] The two tracks on *Vespertine* to which this process applied were 'Sun in My Mouth', which takes lines from the poem "I will wade out / til My Thighs are steeped in burning flowers" by US poet e.e. cummings (1894–1962), and 'An Echo, A Stain' created by randomly taking words from the play *Crave* by English playwright Sarah Kane (1971–1999). These texts do not have a strophic structure, and their language is open and evocative, by virtue of idiosyncratic punctuation and juxtaposition of individual words into phrases in unexpected orders. As a consequence the resulting compositions avoid or obscure the repeating sectional structures typical of Björk's previous music.

A second aspect of the sessions with Guy Sigsworth was the use of a sonic "background" against which to improvise. Sigsworth explained how for 'An Echo, A Stain' he prepared "a vocal kind of chord" which they

Sound 125

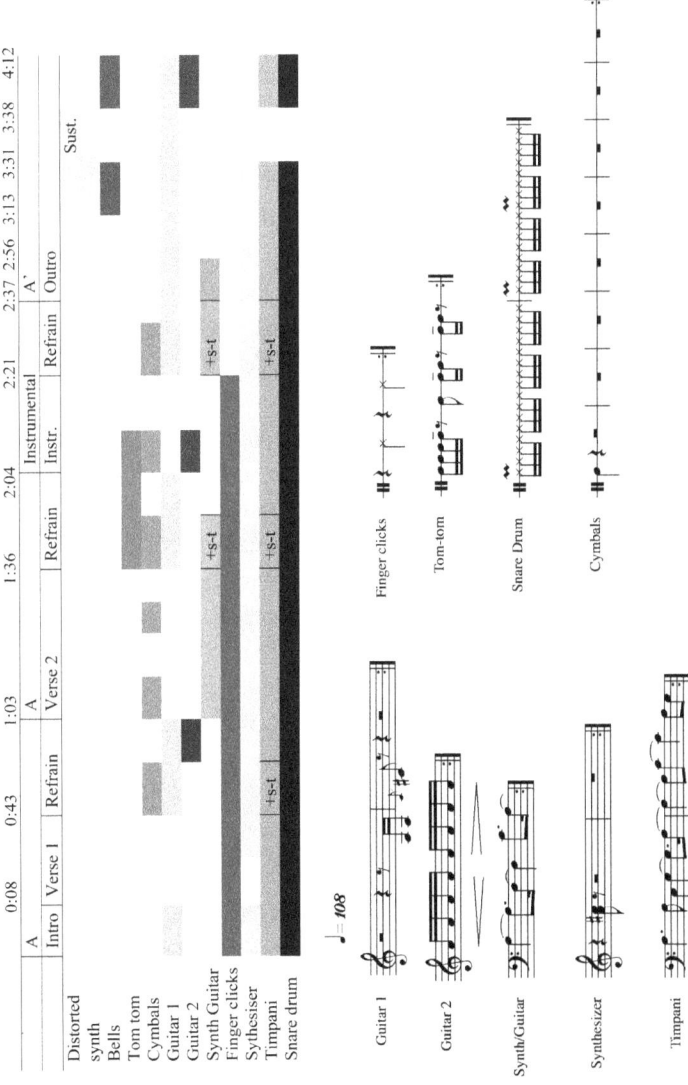

Figure 22: Instrumental loops in 'Human Behaviour' (*Debut* 1993).

improvised against (Sigsworth 2006). This improvisational method leant itself to developing a series of ideas rather than structures involving repetition.

The third significant aspect of Björk's work on these two tracks, which contributed to the avoidance of repetition, was the adoption of Pro-Tools sound editing software. The first of Björk's tracks to use Pro-Tools was a cover of 'The Boho Dance' for a Joni Mitchell Tribute album, which was recorded prior to *Dancer in the Dark* and *Vespertine*, but not released until 2007. The techniques and sound world of this cover version were to prove influential for Björk's later music. Björk had been attracted to the Joni Mitchell song by its trumpet line. To initiate the cover version, Sigsworth recreated the line on a clavichord, processed it at half and double speed (which changed its pitch) and edited it on Pro-Tools.[25] The decision to add instrumental parts by running the tape at half and double speed was a consequence of trying to overcome the limitations of the instrument, and was inspired in part by Holger Czukay, guitarist with the band Can, who had used a similar technique in creating guitar compositions. An additional influence was the track 'Do While' from *Diskont* by Oval, released by Thrill Jockey in 1994, which manipulates a low-register celesta-like sound source – an instrumental source that was to be an important part of the sound world of *Dancer in the Dark* and *Vespertine*. Use of Pro-Tools digital editing from *Vespertine* onwards allowed greater direct control over the fine details of each track, and to use methods of working compatible with the lack of repetition and looser song forms which characterized her next album – *Medúlla*.

Layering of Looped Fragments and the Breakdown of Duple Structures in Medúlla

Medúlla includes tracks that avoid exact repetition (for example, 'Show Me Forgiveness', and the choral piece 'Sonnets/Unrealities XI'). It is also the album that received most criticism for inaccessibility. Duple organization continues to play a role in *Medúlla*: for example, in 'Who Is It?' phrases are organized into groups of twos and fours, and in 'Frosti', composed for music box, duple structures persist in the absence of beat-based percussive material. However, some tracks use cyclic patterns which are performed throughout rather than created by looping a shorter sample, as was the case in *Debut*, reflecting the use of Pro-Tools sound editing, and Björk's desire to capture "performances".[26] For example, the ten-bar introduction to 'The Pleasure is All Mine' begins with a repeating two-bar figure in two parts, both of which are Björk's voice, over which other vocal figures enter. It is evident, from the expressive variations in timing, pitch, dynamics and articulation, and from the varied repetition in bar eight, that this material is performed throughout rather than looped. Other tracks, such as 'Mouth's Cradle' and 'Triumph of a Heart', use the more usual technique in which looped samples of various lengths (here all vocal material) are superimposed, each additional layer filling a gap in the rhythmic structure of the overall sequence, and adding to the textural density.

The superimposition of parts is a particularly important stylistic feature of *Medúlla*, because, more than her previous music, the emphasis is on the horizontal dimension of the music. 'Miðvikudags' illustrates the way in which individual lines are layered but do not fit exactly together, contrary to standard sequencing practices in electronic dance forms. This emphasizes the horizontal dimension of the music: rather than being repeated identically throughout, each cyclic pattern undergoes slight variations; the timing of individual parts is subject to expressive variation; and the grouping and metrical structure of individual lines do not always coincide, thereby avoiding duple structures. Björk described this technique as a partial return to some of her earliest musical experiments aged ten "having two rubbish tape recorders and recording my voice into one, and then recording on the other one, the tape recorder and me, adding a voice on top, and then back, playing with a teaspoon on an ashtray or something" (Björk interviewed in Kennedy 2004). This layering of individual parts, in which each retains its independence, is more akin to practices in folk or art music than in popular genres.

Comparing song structures across Björk's solo career reveals the increased avoidance of repetition, as she explored different compositional techniques. However, this was not an outright change in her style; rather, the new methods she acquired were expressed alongside existing ones in each new album. Hence, *Volta* marked a return to a more accessible style, in which the majority of songs were beat-based, used familiar harmonic progressions, and consisted of one- or two-part strophic forms, with or without the addition of a bridge section.

Björk's experimentalism is also evident in her exploration of the possibilities offered by new audio technologies. For example, she re-released albums in 5.1 surround sound in the collection *Surrounded*; on acquiring a laptop to compose she chose to use sounds which reproduced well over laptop speakers (such as harp, celesta, music boxes, and micro-beats), with the thought that her music was likely to be downloaded and listened to using mobile digital devices (*Miniscule*, dir. Gestsdóttir 2001); a different response to downloading is represented in *Volta* in which tracks are joined by sound material in order to create an identity and narrative for the album as a whole which is different from that heard when individual tracks are downloaded. Furthermore, Björk was the first performer to introduce the Reactable live electronic controller to a mainstream audience, which she and other musicians played on the *Volta* world tour. The Reactable is an electronic synthesizer which has a multi-touch visual interface: cameras underneath the luminous round table-like surface of the instrument track the movements of blocks which the musician moves around, and whose movements and combinations elicit beeps, tones and synth lines.

Many of Björk's innovations enhance rather than decrease the accessibility of her music, but the change to song structure and style arguably did not. The music of *Vespertine, Medúlla* and *Drawing Restraint 9* is musically akin to art music and arguably more elitist than her stated ambition to write experimental but accessible pop suggests. Furthermore, performances on the *Vespertine* tour took place in opera houses and concert halls rather than rock arenas – a consequence not just of the acoustic characteristics of the music which were more suited to smaller interiors, but a result of a more contemplative listening mode envisaged for the music which Björk attributed to her own "craving to go to a concert where I have a comfortable seat and I can enjoy all the little details and nobody is in a hurry and just sit there with your box of chocolates, and then you can go and have a break and talk a little bit, and the pace is very slow" (*Miniscule*, dir. Gestsdóttir 2001). She also participated in a number of art music projects in the late 1990s and early 2000s, including a performance of Schoenberg's *Pierrot Lunaire* in 1996, a recording of *Prayer of the Heart* in 2001, a piece composed for her by John Tavener, and a Carnegie Hall performance of Meredith Monk's *Gotham Lullaby* as part of Meredith Monk's 40th anniversary career celebrations in 2005. Moreover, the music for *Drawing Restraint 9* appeared in an art film which was not on general release.

However, as her music moved further away from a commercial style, so her albums included more humour, thereby undermining the idea that she might be taking herself too seriously and becoming part of an avant-garde, elitist art world. The surrealist humour of the Sugarcubes' music, videos and performances was a precursor to this, but Björk's self-parodies are often overlooked. Sometimes the humour is in the lyrics, as in the track 'Unison' from *Vespertine* in which she describes herself "With a beard and a pipe / And a parrot on each side". But the comedy is also musical: for example, 'Triumph of a Heart' from *Medúlla* features an unusual abrupt change of key from each chorus into each succeeding verse, which is heard as a sudden shift into a higher gear – a common technique used in pop songs to heighten the expressive impact of the final repetitions of the chorus, but here used throughout (see Figure 23). The sequence of abrupt modulations in this track adds to the comical effect of human trombones, beat-boxers, and other extreme vocal effects, and to that of the mock-documentary (*Triumph of a Heart: The Stories behind the Video*, dir. Gestdóttir 2005) and associated music video (dir. Jonze 2005), which features Björk leaving her cat-husband and rural cottage for a wild night in Reykjavík. Humour also attracted Björk to work with Timbaland on *Volta* due to the "physical comedy" she heard

Figure 23: Chord sequence in 'Triumph of a Heart' (*Medúlla* 2004).

in his beats: "he isn't doing gangsta, he's doing pranksta!" (Powell 2007). Humour is therefore a way in which Björk's music remains connected with the everyday.

Conclusion

This analysis of the sound world of Björk's music highlights two main issues. First, her music is characterized by the gradual emergence of textural, metric, and modal structure, and by a diverse instrumental and stylistic palette which individual tracks initially present as opposed in some way, but which are unified over the course of a song. Because these musical and visual materials have associated meanings, musical unification acts out the conceptual unification of apparent opposites: the natural and technological, traditional and modern, rural and urban, myth and science, folk and art, music and sound. Second, the chronology of Björk's solo studio recordings reveals her exploration of new musical techniques and combinations of sounds. The experimentalism of her style is an outcome of her search for new ways to realize her vision of unification.

The achievement of Björk's music is its ability to be experimental within the context of Anglophone popular music, and yet be non-elitist. Her music's engagement with beat-based dance music and its call on the body, its inclusive approach to other cultures and genres, and its ability not to take itself too seriously allows it to retain its connection to popular forms. Furthermore, songs are carefully selected and ordered on albums so that tracks without a clear beat, and which avoid exact repetition, are alongside others with a more commercial character. The emotional core of Björk's music – the expression of unity – is ultimately an accessible idea that connects to everyday concerns, and is channelled through the central focus on Björk's voice and persona. Her music both challenges the listener and simultaneously declares its authenticity. In this respect Björk's experimentalism during her solo career is different from that of the Sugarcubes, whose style did not evolve significantly, and who avoided emotional sentiment: her emphasis on emotional expression and authenticity makes her music more akin to and consonant with music industry norms for singer-songwriters. The next chapter examines the idea of authorship exhibited in Björk's artistic output, and its consequences for perceptions of her music as authentic emotional expression.

6 Emotion

Reviews of Björk's performances and live recordings often focus on the expressive character of her music. Writing in 1993 Simon Reynolds described the way that

> Bjork's singing communicates an ineffable alloy of mixed emotions, a mad jumble of astonishment, elation, rapture, dread, awe. *Debut* is drenched with just this goose-pimple-inducing stuff. The title of 'Violently Happy' captures the Bjork effect perfectly: a gush and rush of euphoria, a tidal wave of oceanic feeling. (Reynolds 1993: 25)

Moreover, these emotions are often heard as the authentic expression of Björk's own emotional life: thus, one reviewer stated that "her lyrics on *Homogenic* contain revelatory emotional confessions" (Herman 1997), while another remarked of *Vespertine* "it's like you've invaded Bjork singing to herself about her fella whilst doing the dishes" (Wade 2001).

Björk's accounts of her artistic motivations also suggest that her music communicates her real-life emotional experiences:

> ...it's my job to be emotional. Doctors cure diseases and shoemakers make shoes. It's my job to go through emotions and describe them to other people. (Björk interviewed in *Nylon*, 14, June/July 2001 ("About & About: Björk" 1995–2007))

At least some of her collaborators shared this idea of emotional communication: describing the way in which Björk took material in its early stages to him in order to establish a sound-world for each recording project, mix engineer Mark "Spike" Stent remarked: "It helps her realise where she's going and it's up to me to try and get into her head and really understand what she's trying to achieve, sonically, musically, emotionally" (Stent 2006). He conceptualized his role as facilitating the realization of her vision and emotional expression, but he also responded to the emotion he perceived in the musical material: "It's not a technical exercise for me and I think that's why B and I work so well together. . . . It's a feeling based thing, it's an emotional reaction to what I'm trying to do." The idea that Björk's music communicates her emotional experiences dominates critical reception of her music, her self-conception of her creativity, and that of many of her collaborators.

Belief in Björk's emotional authenticity reflects one of the most prevalent ideologies of music creation and reception. Authenticity appears in various guises: it is historical, cultural, or ethnographic accuracy; it is truth to the unique and individual self. It is manifested as the expression of true emotions in artistic output through qualities associated with intimacy and immediacy; it is a sincere commitment to one's creativity, evidenced through lack of artifice, connection to the primal, artistic motivations rather than those of fame or money, and by the refusal to court the mainstream.

These ideas shape the discourse surrounding Björk's music. In promotional material Björk is represented as a musician who is able to release the music she wants, supported by a record company which is free from the taint of commerce; an innovative artist who constantly strives for the new; making music as an involuntary and spontaneous act — a way of life rather than work, and one with therapeutic, self-expressive value; connected to nature; and a prodigy who was "born singing". In addition, Björk, her collaborators, and her audience, place emphasis on her artistic integrity: what Taylor (1997: 21–28) terms "authenticity of positionality" (the idea of not being a sell-out), and "authenticity of emotionality". For example, Björk's struggle with Lars von Trier over artistic control of the music to *Dancer in the Dark* was interpreted by Derek Birkett as evidence of her artistic integrity, and proof that she was motivated by art rather than money (Birkett 2006).[1]

Allan Moore (2002) untangles the many ideas of authenticity by asking not "what" is authenticated but "who". Thus, authenticity becomes the idea that the performer speaks the truth about the situation from which he/she comes, or someone for whom the artist speaks.[2] It is therefore singer-songwriters for whom this ideology holds most strongly, and whose subjectivity is heard through their singing voice. (It is no coincidence that critical reception of the Sugarcubes pays less attention to emotional authenticity.) Authenticity is both a marketing tool and a concept musicians and audiences believe in, which therefore shapes the creation and reception of music.

It seems self-evident that the sentiments expressed in Björk's songs are hers. Yet, this interpretation is dependent upon a chain of factors: perceptions of her unified authentic author image (which itself is dependent upon the idea that the artistic output in her name is created by her), the mirroring of biographical events in her work, and material characteristics of it which can be deemed expressive by her audience. This chapter does not attempt to explain the emotional reactions of individual audience members to her music; it explores the means by which the idea of emotional truthfulness is communicated and the relationship between her music's perceived expressive character, thematic content and her biography.

The Authentic Author Image

Björk's perceived authorial agency is central to reception of her music as emotionally authentic. Björk's authorship of her music is both a practical reality, realized in her actions, and the beliefs of herself and those she works with, and an image projected through the various media associated with her artistic output: her name as classification of artistic output; the association of her work with her visual image and voice; the documentaries which show Björk's agency in action. The ideas and images of Björk which are repeated across various media texts enable audiences to form a coherent public image of Björk and it is through this "star-text"[3] that Björk is attributed with agency by audiences (Ahonen 2006: 3).

Björk's "solo" music, like that of most other pop musicians, is the product of collaboration with other musicians and studio engineers, as revealed in interviews and television documentaries where she is shown participating in different stages of production: song writing and recording her vocals, directing other musicians in recording sessions, recording and processing sounds on her portable laptop or in the studio, identifying people she wishes to collaborate with, commissioning videos, being present at and controlling production and post-production processes. This shared authorship of her artistic output is formally symbolized and legislated through credits on her "solo" recordings. She was credited with writing (or co-writing) the majority of her songs and lyrics, but successive solo studio albums reveal her increasing responsibility for other artistic roles: most of the arrangements from *Debut* to *Vespertine* are credited solely, or in joint authorship, by Björk and a variety of other musicians, but from *Medúlla* (2004) Björk is attributed with the arrangements; she is credited with producing, or co-producing, the majority of her tracks from *Homogenic* onwards (1997); and is sole or joint programmer on tracks from *Vespertine* onwards (2001). The only role Björk has not been assigned is that of mix engineer – a role performed by Mark "Spike" Stent in the majority of her tracks from *Post* (1995) onwards.

Björk explained that she acquired studio skills during her career, allowing her to take direct control over more aspects of the music.[4] In contrast, both Derek Birkett (founder of One Little Indian) and Valgeir Sigurðsson (recording engineer) suggested that Björk's increased crediting was a more accurate reflection of her authorship than was previously the case (Birkett 2006; Sigurðsson 2006). Derek Birkett attributed the previous crediting of her recordings to other people to Björk's naiveté and generosity, to attributing too little significance to production credits early in her career, to receiving different advice from people around her, to her own realization that she was producing her own music, and the increasing reticence of other people to claim ownership over her work as she became a more significant artistic figure.

Björk's collaborations with other musicians formed two main types, mentioned previously: collaborations during the writing process (which most frequently involved herself and a recording engineer), and a distinct stage of collaboration with other musicians, which from *Vespertine* onwards she described as "completing" her "almost finished" recording project: "I can make all the skeleton and the song writing, but then when I am almost finished I am curious to get the real virtuosos in the field to add like some sort of acrobatic things" (Björk interviewed on *Vespertine Live at the Royal Opera House*, dir. Barnard 2001). This description simplifies the creative processes involved and generalizes across individual tracks and recording projects, perhaps in an attempt to deflect media portrayals that undermine her role as author of the work in her name.

Documentaries about making and touring Björk's music demonstrate the variety of activities in the recording stage: improvising to a recording or with other musicians live in a studio environment, overdubbing (recording a take of a vocal or instrumental track onto the record), recording performance of improvised or written materials to later cut up and process (for example, the choir sounds on *Medúlla*), and sending a digital version to musicians to add their own material. The resulting "performance" heard on Björk's studio-albums is in many cases an artefact of the compositional assemblage that only ever existed on record. These "recording" sessions also illustrate the lack of a clear divide between composition and recording activities which is symptomatic of most studio music (Zak III 2001).[5]

The collaborative character of Björk's music-making is not unusual within popular music, but its acknowledgment and discussion is fraught with potential difficulty due to the apparent threat it represents to authorial control and the maintenance of a coherent author-image. An exchange on this topic took place between Björk and a member of the *bjork.com 4orum* who asked Björk whether the fact that it was possible to hear the musical contribution of other musicians within tracks in her name meant that she was "copying". Björk's response to this reveals her perception of her authorship ("I write most of my stuff on my own, especially the melodies and the lyrics"), her motivations for collaborating ("I have many months of working like that, but then I always arrive to a point where it seems too indulgent and lonely . . . and I get overexcited about someone I find brilliant and I want to write with her/him"), and the importance of collaborating rather than "immorally" re-creating another musician's sound ("the idea of [Thomas Knak's] music is incredibly distinctive of him . . . but it is actually quite easy to make . . . and I could have so easily just copied it, but never. . . . I contacted him and asked him to be him and it says on the cd 'Thomas Knak' so his work has his signature") ("About & About: Björk" 1995–2007).

Björk attributed her attitude to authorship to her experience of "fronting" the album *Björk*, released when she was eleven years of age.[6] Her subsequent actions testify to this resolve: she and other members of the Sugarcubes resisted attempts to portray Björk as the main creative force in the band (when she only created her vocals); and she did not allow inclusion of covers on the *Greatest Hits* album, despite the fact that 'Its Oh So Quiet', a renamed cover of the song 'Blow a Fuse' by Hans Lang and Bert Reisfeld, was her biggest selling single.

According to Björk, most of her collaborations during her solo career were "done with mutual respect and a lot of enthusiasm and we meet like equals, the unfortunate thing is that because I am quite well known people don't see it as that..." (*bjork.com 4orum* unknown date ("About & About: Björk" 1995–2007)).[7] The "equality" of the collaborations was partly achieved by providing only general briefs. For instance, Björk sent Matmos (US experimental music duo Drew Daniel and M. C. Schmidt) a recording of some music she had written for celesta while she was working on *Dancer in the Dark*, from which, according to them, they produced a track more akin to their own compositions than to hers. She then approached them to work on *Vespertine*, sending them MP3 files of fairly complete tracks including beats which they would add percussive sounds to and send back, and through which they gained a better idea of "what she was looking for" (Matmos interviewed in *Vespertine Live at the Royal Opera House*, dir. Bernard 2001).

In the case of video directors, the character of the collaboration is less prescriptive because she sees herself as musician not visual artist. Speaking of the making of the video for 'Wanderlust' (dir. Encyclopedia Pictura, 2008) she said:

> I mean with certain video directors I will get quite involved in the story board and I'll be there to make sure it's uniting with the song, and there's a connection there. With Encyclopedia Pictura [US film maker duo, Sean Hellfritsch and Isaiah Saxon] they're just so fertile, what you do is just become more a curator, making sure they've got the money they need, the space they need... (Ryzik 2008)

For example, the development of the video treatment for 'Who Is It?' from *Medúlla* started with a very minimal brief from Björk but went through a process of change and refinement to reach the final realization (Shadforth 2006).[8] 'Who Is It?' is one instance in which visual and compositional ideas evolved together, since in this case the Bell-choir version of the track was made at the same time as Björk and Shadforth were working on ideas for the video.

Published interviews with Björk and her collaborators often suggest a great deal of creative freedom for those she works with. For example, harpist Zeena Parkins described her experience of playing parts "that needed to be done", on the one hand, and bringing ideas and creating something new, on the other, as a "very luxurious kind of working situation to be in" (Zeena Parkins interviewed in *Miniscule*, dir. Gestdóttir 2001). However, such statements need to be understood in context: Björk frequently brought in instrumentalists at later stages of production when instrumental parts already existed, as in the case of *Vespertine*.

This working situation is aided by Björk's idiosyncratic style of verbal communication: Björk tended not to use technical terminology, preferring to employ poetic and metaphoric descriptions of her creative ideas. Many of the people she worked with attributed their creative freedom to this manner of communication, as Matmos's experience illustrates:

> I found it very baffling at first, being told to make the music more 'transparent', but eventually I realised that it's sort of a shorthand that points you toward something but doesn't spell it out for you . . . 'primordial', or 'make music with no history', 'make music that's triangular'. It was a fun, respectful recipe rather than a sort of command to make it in three-four time, or just something programmatic. Instead it felt very free and loose and you could do what you like. (Drew Daniel interviewed in *Vespertine Live at the Royal Opera House*, dir. Bernard 2001)

Björk attributed her collaborative working relationships to her background in punk, to the influence of her father's job as leader of the Icelandic Union of Electricians, and to heightened awareness after witnessing what she perceived to be the hierarchical working practices of director Lars von Trier during the making of *Dancer in the Dark*. Giving collaborators a minimal brief, and using poetic descriptions of her ideas may be effective ways of facilitating freedom within collaborations. Nonetheless, as the examples above illustrate, this does not mean that the collaborator can simply do whatever he or she wants.

Derek Birkett argued that Björk is ultimately in control of the music-making process. Recounting Björk's intention behind the collaboration with Timbaland on *Volta* he remarked "it's not a collaboration in the conventional sense where you do what you do, you take it to Timbaland, and Timbaland does what [he does]. What Björk will do is take it to Timbaland, go 'This is what I want to do. You help me do it'" (Birkett 2006). Most artists who work with Timbaland choose to go to him to produce their records because he is known for making hit records with wide appeal. By contrast, Björk asked him to do "something you've never done before" (Birkett 2006), although in this instance it resulted in a jam session from which she took material she later cut up and edited rather than the process originally envisaged. Whatever the commercial perversity of this approach, or its success, it has one important consequence for her authorship: by asking an established artist to enter into unknown territory, both become explorers together; or tactically, the other participant in the process is "wrong-footed" thereby removing some of their control. It is a particular type of collaboration, which Mark "Spike" Stent gives a sound engineer's perspective on: "she gives people a lot of space but ultimately I mean she's collaborating, but it's odd really. It's all about getting people to see her vision, I think. . . . So they'll work on something together and then she'll take it away and completely change it, or use certain elements in different sections, or make different things from it. It's almost like remixing as you write the song" (Stent 2006).

The idea of Björk's authorial "vision" is maintained by her collaborators, who stressed her authorial role: mix engineer Stent positioned himself as facilitator of her "vision" and "emotion",[9] and engineer Valgeir Sigurðsson, who was at an early stage of his career when he worked on *Vespertine*, *Selmasongs* and *Dancer in the Dark*, emphasised Björk's agency.[10] Even in her work with visual artists, the artist positions themselves as realizing Björk's vision: for example, video director Dawn Shadforth recounted the way in which she was given a (characteristically) loose brief for the video 'Who Is It?', but, rather than simply coming back with a completed treatment, the final form of the video was reached through an ongoing collaboration, and the impact of material circumstances (such as the choice of location for the shoot, and of costume, which in turn influenced physical movements and choreography (Shadforth 2006)).[11]

The informants I cite work within a context in which it is politic to project Björk as the authorial vision behind her work, and within a system that privileges interpretation of the creative act as realization of authorial vision, but that does not entail a conspiracy to present Björk as controlling agent when she is not. The foregrounding of Björk's collaborators, through credits, and information hosted on the official Björk website, weakens the Romantic ideology of authorship, and acknowledges its social character, but she is still the controlling force behind the artistic output in her name. The significance of this is that it allows her audience to attribute the perceived emotional character of her work to an expression of Björk's own interior life.

Emotional Expression and Biography

Björk frequently attributed autobiographical meanings to her music in interviews. An unambiguous statement of the autobiographical character of her studio albums appears in her comparison of these to the experience of writing music for the film *Dancer in the Dark*:

> I did three solo albums in a row in the space of five years and they were all about me and they felt quite narcissistic. [With *Dancer in the Dark*] I was ready to give myself over to something else, . . . but I wanted it emotionally to be someone else's. (Björk on VH1.com, 2000 ("About & About: Selmasongs" 1995–2007))

In 1994 Björk described *Debut* as "pieces from my diary or my photo album. They were all about the past", whereas *Post* contained "things from my new diary, my diary of the last two years" (Fay 1994). This is both literally true (Björk kept a diary which she drew on for song lyrics), and a metaphor for her perception that her music revealed something of her life. *Debut* comprised songs she had written over a ten-year period in Iceland and the content reflects Björk's preoccupations as a teenager during that time: 'Big Time Sensuality' was written about a friendship, 'Venus as Boy' was about a lover, and 'Violently Happy' was about the need to substitute another form of thrill-seeking in the absence of someone who previously provided that ("About & About: Debut" 1995–2007). Björk also claimed that the "shy" character of these songs reflected her position as a "beginner" musician at that time, but that with *Post* she expressed a more confident attitude, as can be heard in 'Army of Me', written as a wake-up call to her brother whom she felt had been "out of order" (Björk cited in Hemingway 2002: 40).

The content and tone of *Homogenic* reflects the pressures that Björk was under from 1995 to 1997. For example, she is the 'Hunter', on the track of the same name, who must "bring back the goods", referred to in the lyrics: "that song's about when you have a lot of people that work for you and you sort-of have to write songs or people get unemployed" (Björk cited in Hemingway 2002: 43). Björk described the emotions of *Homogenic* both as those of a persona ("Homogenic is a woman who was put in an impossible situation", *Music News & Reviews*, 22 May 1998 ("Homogenic" 1995–2003)), and as her own, by reference to biographical events, namely working for two years without a break, increased media attention on her private life and the letter bomb and suicide of a fan in September 1996:

> I was on a four-year mission, . . . I wanted action, to have this feeling like I'm risking everything or I'm bored. Then last September [1996] everything exploded. . . . Emotionally, this album is about hitting rock bottom and earning [sic] your way up. (Micallef 1997)

The tone of *Homogenic* is aggressive: she may have hit "rock bottom" but she came out fighting rather than cowering, an idea which is reflected in the album cover, shown in Figure 24:

> When I went to Alexander McQueen, I explained to him the person who wrote these songs – someone who was put into an impossible situation, so impossible that she had to become a warrior. A warrior who had to fight not with weapons, but with love. I had 10 kilos of hair on my head, and special contact lenses and a manicure that prevented me from eating with my fingers, and gaffer tape around my waist and high clogs so I couldn't walk easily. I wanted to put all the emotion of the album into that image. (Björk interviewed in *Chicago Tribune*, 15 May 1998 ("About & About: Björk" 1995–2007))

By contrast with the emotional confrontation on *Homogenic*, *Vespertine* was about the pleasure in domesticity and interiority (album booklet from *LiveBox* 2003): it was a celebration of time alone and in her home (the album was made in evenings after working on the filming of *Dancer in the Dark*) and of her relationship with her partner and future husband, artist Matthew Barney. Whereas she described *Homogenic* as "very emotionally confrontational" *Vespertine* was "the opposite. Very introverted, very quiet and calm and peaceful" (Demby 2001).

Björk's biographical accounts of *Medúlla* and *Volta* provide an explanation of their emotional source and the physical constraints that shaped them. 'The Pleasure is All Mine' was written while at a studio in La Gomera in the

Figure 24: Front cover of *Homogenic* (1997) CD.

Canary Islands, when, for four days, Björk was without fourteen month old Ísadóra for the first time, and was able to spend all her time song writing without the interruptions of childcare. Similarly, 'Submarine' was written after Björk's pregnancy when she felt herself to be emerging from her focus on Ísadóra: "the part of me that writes songs had gone dormant, and this song says it's time to wake it up" (Kennedy 2004). The focus on the body reflected in tracks like 'Triumph of a Heart' was also a consequence of Björk's experience of pregnancy: "After *Vespertine* I was going to do an album with intuition only, no brain please. I was thinking more visceral, flesh and blood, pregnancy... death metal" (Sandall 2004).

Volta involved jamming sessions with other musicians, which she attributed to her desire to work directly with other musicians away from her home environment after a more confined existence due to breastfeeding and caring for Ísadóra (Pareles 2007). This widening of horizons led to a heightened awareness of socio-political circumstances, Björk's reaction to which influenced tracks on *Volta*: colonial power ('Declare Independence' was an expression of Björk's observation of Denmark's rule over Greenland and the Faroe Islands), war in the Middle East ('Hope' included musings on media reactions to a female suicide bomber), natural disasters (the tsunami whose aftermath she witnessed in Banda Aceh, and whose imagery influenced 'Earth Intruders'), and gender and other forms of inequality: "The *Volta* chapter is very much about justice. Justice for women, the female spirit, nature and people in need in general" (Scrudator 2007).

Two issues recur throughout these biographical attributions to Björk's artistic output. First, her music is overwhelmingly positive in tone, as revealed through an analysis of her song lyrics. Lyrics are not wholly responsible for the affective character of music, and in some genres of popular music, and some listening conditions, lyrics are not the focus of attention. However, lyrics are one means by which listeners experience music's emotional character, and in the case of Björk's solo career, attention to the details of their meanings is encouraged by the supply of lyrics on official websites and in booklets (sometimes as autonomous poetry, such as the "Words" booklet from *Family Tree*). The incidence of affect words (such as 'love', 'turmoil' and 'craving') is higher in the lyrics of Björk's studio albums than in other comparative language samples,[12] and significantly more affect words are positive rather than negative. Furthermore, the proportion of lyrics concerned with affect is significantly higher in *Debut* than in *Vespertine*, *Homogenic* or *Post*, and a significantly higher proportion of lyrics in *Medúlla* are optimistic, confirming critical opinion and Björk's description of the character of the latter album.[13]

Björk attributed the positive character of her music to her Icelandic upbringing (this affirmative outlook is immortalized in Icelandic culture through the novels of Halldór Laxness, Iceland's most revered twentieth-century nationalist writer):

> In the first years of my solo career – the period around *Debut* – I wasn't able to record a dark or sad song. You have to know, I was raised hardcore happy. That's something typically Icelandic: to be happy, to feel good, to see everything from the positive side. So it took me a lot of courage to try something moody. On *Debut* it didn't work, on *Post* it did, eventually. 'Possibly Maybe' was my first dark song. (van den Berg 1997)

Prior to 'Possibly Maybe', the only song with what she perceived to be a more negative outlook ('Play Dead') had been written by adopting the persona of the main character from the film *The Young Americans* which the song appeared in, and she recalled: "It was actually fun because the character in the film was suffering and going through hardcore tough times and at the time I was at my happiest. It was quite liberating to sit down after writing a whole album to write from someone else's point of view" ("About & About: Debut" 1995–2007). Statements such as this reinforce audience interpretations of Björk's other songs as representations of her thoughts and feelings.

Björk's artistic responses to negative events reflect her positive attitude. For example, the track chosen by Björk to be the subject of a charity remix album to raise money towards the relief effort after the South East Asian Tsunami in 2004 was 'Army of Me' (*Army of Me-Xes*) whose lyrics speak of self-sufficiency rather than compassion ('Stand up/you've got to manage/I won't sympathize/anymore'). Björk's self-stated refusal to dwell on the negative explains her expressed musical distaste for "suffering artists".[14] It also explains some of the humour in her music. The flamenco guitar and voice song 'So Broken' was written subsequent to Björk learning of the letter bomb sent to her, and the sender's subsequent suicide in 1996. Initially the song was a deliberate over-dramatization of Björk's self-pity, yet in later performance and recording it took on a more conventionally authentic expression of loss.[15]

Second, much of Björk's rhetoric in interviews, and the lyrics of songs from Kukl onwards, are about experiencing life to the full, having intense experiences ("there is as much intense emotion in 'I feel fantastic', as in 'oh, I'm such a martyr!'" (Aston 1996)), and retaining a sense of wonder at the world around her. She described many of her life decisions (such as moving to England prior to *Debut*) as ways she pushed herself, and took risks. This intensity of experience is expressed through the range of emotions between and within albums, and through lyrical references to extreme acts of sensation seeking, such as "jumping off cliffs" – which she also used in interviews as a metaphor for her sense that she had taken artistic risks in her music-making (Björk interviewed on ZTV 1995 ("Post" 1995–2003; "Celebetty: Bjork" 2000; Barton 2007)).

The Sound of Emotional Authenticity

The idea that that there might be ways of analysing the emotion we hear in music seems directly at odds with popular belief which tends to the idea that emotion is spontaneous, ineffable, and beyond reason. However, there is no necessary contradiction between experiencing emotions as ineffable, and attention to technical characteristics of a musical work. Neither does this approach necessarily imply that emotional effects have been deliberately "constructed" by the music's creators.

The authenticity of Björk's emotional expression is evidenced by the "natural" qualities of her voice – namely, a perceived lack of artifice and mediation. For example, one member of an online fan forum responded to the claim that there were "imperfections" in the vocals on *Medúlla*, by remarking:

> I don't think imperfection really describes it. . . . It's more like: she sings naturally, throwing all her emotion into her voice and yet keeping the pitch, and if it cracks, it cracks – that's part of the expression, . . . its very "rawness" seems to touch places inside me other singers can't reach. Her expression is so totally direct – and I sense that authenticity of expression is a lot more important to her than technique of expression. (Posted 24 November 2006 ("4orum" n.d.))

As discussed previously, the lack of obvious vocal training, or adherence to stylistic norms of vocal production embodies the idea of unmediated expression, what the fan in the quotation above refers to as "totally direct" and "authentic" expression. The tendency to hear songs this way is common to the reception of many contemporary singer-songwriters. For example, in 2006, billboard posters for LaMontagne's album and tour *Trouble* announced that "When he opened his mouth, out flew his soul – and beautifully rasping roars of love, life and loss". Such discourse reflects the historical legacy of the author-ideology in which music is received as if it is the direct expression of a composer-author's (private) thoughts and feelings – what Taylor has called "emotional authenticity" (Taylor 1997), and what Allan Moore has identified as "first person authenticity" (Moore 2002).

Audiences hear Björk's music as the direct expression of her emotional life because she is part of the star system, within which the "private life" of a celebrity is an important part of their public persona, communicated by press coverage and prominent entertainment values in newspaper journalism. The historical reasons for this association between stars and interest in their private lives has been traced to the emergence of the film star system in the United States in the twentieth century: the increase in information about film stars' lives outside the roles they played in films occurred because only by knowing something about the "private" lives of stars could the star persona exist separate from the different roles the star played in film (deCordova 1991).

In addition, material aspects of artistic production support the star persona. In cinema film, close-up camera shots allow a close view of the actor's face and draw the spectator's attention to the actor's looks rather than his or her role. A similar argument has been made for the role of the microphone in maintaining the star persona in popular music by creating intimacy between listener and musician (Frith 1996: 187–89). Use of the microphone made certain kinds of sounds audible in performance for the first time, and gave rise to the recorded sound of emotional intimacy. The intimacy made possible by the microphone is the recorded manifestation of the idea that the singer communicates sincerely felt emotions, unmediated, to the listener, and recording techniques, such as reverb, delays, filters, and overdubbing, help "stage" voices, which are, as Serge Lacasse terms it, the "aural index" of the singer's persona and represented emotions (Lacasse 2005).

Björk's critical reception suggests that the most extreme realization of emotional intimacy in her output is the album *Vespertine*, described as "a work of dazzling sonic design and almost claustrophobic emotional intimacy" (Ross 2004). According to Björk:

> the key to what we were looking for was taking something that was very, very, very, very tiny and magnifying it up to big and it sort of gave you a sensation that you'd been told a secret – the same way as if you see a picture of a cell in the body magnified very big you sort of get this feeling that you are being trusted for some inside information. (*Miniscule*, dir. Gestsdóttir 2001).

The videos explore this idea of intimacy through striking close-up camera shots of Björk's face and naked body: the music video 'Pagan Poetry' shows dramatic body piercing, and the video of 'Hidden Place' shows a continuous movement of fluids out of and into Björk's mouth, nose and eyes, embodying the metaphor of the body as container (of self and of emotions). The confessional nature of some of the lyrics places the listener in a position of psychological intimacy with the singer. The cover art to *Vespertine* also announces the theme of intimacy: Björk is featured in black and white, shading her eyes, lips slightly parted in an unmistakeably erotic pose (see Figure 25). Production of the album realizes this same theme through creation of intimacy between sound sources (primarily the voice) and the listener.

The production of an intimate sound in a recording has a psychoacoustic basis in the amount of reflected sound, and the relative loudness of sounds within the mix. First, in the real-world (as opposed to the virtual world of recordings) the amount of reverb (reflected sound in which there

Figure 25: Front cover of *Vespertine* (2001) CD.

is no discontinuous repeat of the original sound) differs according to the proximity of a sound source to reflective surfaces: the closer a sound source to reflective surfaces, the more continuous the reverb will sound; the further away a sound source from the reflective surface, the greater delay there will be between original and reflection, and the reflected sound will be heard as an echo rather than reverberation. The amount of sound coming direct from the sound source relative to reflected sound also differs according to the position of the listener in relation to the source of the sound: when the listener is close to the sound source he or she will hear a larger proportion of direct sound than reflected sound. Thus, sounds recorded close to a microphone contain more of the recorded signal direct from the source and less reflected sound (reverb), suggesting the listener is in close proximity to the sound source. Second, in the real-world the relative amplitude of sounds specifies their proximity to the listener: hence, sounds which are louder in the mix in a recording tend to be heard as being nearer the listener than sounds which are quieter. Thus, manipulation of these elements in the recording and production process can specify varieties of physical space (size and type), the position of the sound source within that space, and the proximity of the sound source to the listener. These in turn influence the emotional character of a recording, because they specify a location and physical relationship between listener and sound source.

The virtual spaces suggested by individual tracks on *Vespertine* are often quite large, resulting from a high degree of reflected sound on large orchestral and choral forces. However, two characteristics suggest intimacy. First, her voice is often highly compressed, and recorded close to the microphone with a dry acoustic, suggesting the listener is in close proximity to Björk: for example, the vocals on 'An Echo, A Stain' are almost whispered yet they are loud even in the presence of the orchestral forces, and on 'Pagan Poetry' Björk's unaccompanied voice on the phrase "I love him/I love him" sounds shockingly exposed after the lush orchestration which preceded it, and unprocessed in comparison to treatment of the vocals elsewhere. Second, the relative loudness of micro-beats (brief, high-frequency non-pitched sounds used in a percussive role), and their lack of reverberation, places them close to the listener.

An extreme example of this intimacy is the track 'Cocoon', written by Björk and Thomas Knak, and mixed by Mark "Spike" Stent. In this track the lead vocal is recorded close to the microphone, with seemingly little treatment, placing the listener in close proximity to the singing voice. The vocal tone is a timbrally unstable whisper: in places the melody is barely sustained and on the verge of becoming an un-pitched whisper. It is as though the listener is being told a secret, appropriate to the intimacy of the lyrics ("When I wake up the second time in his arms/gorgeousness: he's still inside me!!!"). Treatments of the voice in this track include taking the treble off the vocal delays to give more "depth" to the voice, and using a harmonizer in the return of the main section to make the vocal appear "wider", which is tucked behind the main vocal track. This contrasts with the dry sound that returns with the next section (at 2:34).

However, it is not simply the treatment of the voice that suggests intimacy. 'Cocoon' comprises four additional kinds of instrumental materials, the placement and timbre of which create the character of this virtual space. The track consists of two alternating sections: A sections outlining the A flat major tonic with added seventh, consisting of two sung, and one instrumental statement of a four-bar phrase; and B sections of eight bars length, outlining a chord of B flat minor (see Figure 26). The track starts with a two-bar loop of a short rising figure (repeated throughout the introduction and the A sections) which suggests a large sound source (because of the relatively low pitch) heard through a dampening material (the absence of attack and the sustained character of the sound suggests that the higher frequencies have been muffled, rather than an instrument dampened). The same sound source is heard in a higher register later in the track, where it has a more metallic quality. The remainder of musical material consists of a kick drum loop (two quaver kicks on the first beat of each bar – a second, brighter kick drum sound enters in the B section), (synthesized) vinyl clicks, and two different loops of stick sound, used to differentiate sections. The vinyl sound, which is the main rhythmic feature, has been treated with delays that can be heard in the background crossing over and creating the illusion of depth. (Again there are at least two different loops used, which correspond to the two types of section.) The consequence of these treatments is that the virtual acoustic environment of the recording is spacious, but Björk's voice emanates from an enclosed space within which the listener too is located – the "cocoon" of the title.

Timing		0:30			1:15	1:45			2:30	3:00	3:15			3:46
Section	Intro	A			B	A			B	A´	A			Outro
Bars	8	12			8	12			8		8			10
		4	4	4		4	4	4			4	2'	2	

Figure 26: Formal scheme of 'Cocoon' (*Vespertine* 2001) showing the structural interruption three minutes into the track.

The introverted, heightened state expressed by the track is also communicated through the form of the song. The song comprises alternating sections, framed by intro and outro, but the third repetition of the A section twice comes to a halt: on its third occurrence the A section (3:00) begins in the absence of instrumental material, and does not complete a full statement; the true recapitulation of the A section starts shortly after (3:15), but the vocal line of this also becomes static with repetition of the lyric 'From a mouth' (3:32) (see Figure 27). One way of hearing these disruptions of the song form is as "hesitation", as though the singer has become distracted by her narrative, and is dwelling instead on one thought in particular: the lyric "Who would have known?" at the false recapitulation, and the phrase "from a mouth" at the second "interruption". The repetition of "from a mouth" draws attention to the idea of the mouth, and to a heightened sensuality.

Treatment of Björk's voice, and its placement within the virtual space of the recording, create acoustic, and therefore psychological intimacy between singer and listener, maintaining a reception practice in which her voice is heard as expressing her emotions – but to an unprecedented and, for some, uncomfortable degree.

Conclusion: Person and Persona

Björk's artistic output is bound up with attributions of authenticity to a "real" Björk perceived to lie behind the star-text. In this respect Björk's promotion and reception is similar to that of other star musicians. I have developed this idea by showing how production, together with promotion and reception practices, sustains perceptions of emotional authenticity. Furthermore, Björk's artistic output has a distinctive emotional identity characterized by emotional extremes (highs and lows, confrontation and reflection), and what critics

Figure 27: Sketch of 'Cocoon' (*Vespertine* 2001) showing "hesitation" at the words "From a mouth" (3:15–4:08).

referred to as its "oceanic" character – the experience of boundlessness, of being immersed in and at one with the world.[16]

Björk's own characterization of the emotional character of her work points to a desire for fusion, describing happiness as when you're in a position when you can create either music or communicate with the people you love. And it's so strong that it's the same on the outside as it is on the inside... or same passion is maybe a better word... and then it's sort of, it's even... the flow is very even. And then I feel very very happy. ("Interview on Japanese TV" 2002)

She also described herself as "a very emotional being; I want there to be a real fusion, not just connecting at the surface level" (Ingólfsson 2005: 17). Björk's expressed desire is to achieve a state of unity in which there is no difference between notions of inside and outside the self. This is particularly significant given that unification is central to the conceptual content and musical processes of her artistic output. Given the positive valence of her artistic output, this is an optimistic vision of unity: "trying to unite history, the present and the environment into a song, on the radio, in a possible moment of utopia..." (liner notes to *Family Tree* 2002).

Given the centrality of emotional authenticity to musical reception, surprisingly little scholarly attention has been given to analysis of the relationship between artistic biography and its mediation through popular music. Perhaps the domain seems tainted by uncritical mappings of artistic biography to music that have characterized some elements of the popular press and earlier biographical studies of musicians. Nonetheless, biographical readings remain an important way in which many audiences and musicians understand musical creativity, even if we do not fully understand whether or how artistic creation is mediated by biographical experience.

Despite Björk's readiness to supply biographical readings of her music, there are a number of problems with thinking of song as the expression of authorial thoughts and feelings. For instance, listeners' interpretations of the biographical meanings of Björk's music are often inaccurate: she notes that although her songs might have particular meanings for her (friendships, her relationship with her work, a country, or a hobby), listeners most often interpret them in terms of romantic relationships (Toop and Björk 2002). For example, one reviewer states of 'I Know Who You Are', from *Volta*, that "Björk celebrates her lover's body before aging and death takes its toll: 'Let's celebrate now/All this flesh on our bones/Let me push you up against me tightly/And enjoy every bit of you'" (Pattison 2007). Yet Björk has described the song as an ode to her daughter. This is significant not because it shows that biographical interpretations are sometimes inaccurate, but because it shows the illusory character of the direct access that music is supposed to afford. Whatever its autobiographical source, music is sufficiently non-discursive that it has a more generalizable appeal. So, while listeners can choose to hear Björk's music in terms of its autobiographical character, this does not limit its meanings.

An alternative to biographical readings is the idea that music can offer a virtual subject for the listener to identify with which is other than the singer-songwriter, composer or performing artist (Cumming 2000; Kramer 2001; Dibben 2006). For instance, according to Kramer, subjectivity is represented in song and is personified by the figure of the composer, performer, a dramatic character, or some imaginary other which the listener attempts to fill, and through these means comes to experience themselves and the world around them in terms of particular cultural narratives. One such narrative is that of romantic love through which audiences engage in fantasies arising from a sentimental, fatalistic view of sexual relationships, and which "provide people with the means to articulate the feelings associated with being in love" (Frith 1996: 164).

The idea of the virtual persona offers an additional way to understand the relationship between Björk the real person, composer and singer of the songs, and the character or persona who is the subject of the song. In the case of Björk as the author of her music this takes a rather literal form in that she associates each of her albums with a particular persona, as the three extracts from interviews below illustrate:

> For every album I've done there's been one character that does the albums. And then there'll be separate other little characters that are the songs. The *Debut* character from the photograph, from the cover, sort of a very shy, slightly polite kind of newcomer. And I think that's how I felt. The character that represents *Post* is kind of that wide eyed girl from the country still but she's been in the city for a while at that point and is consuming the city and the city's consuming her. (*Inside Björk*, dir. Walker 2003)

> *Homogenic* was very much about a person that's put into an impossible situation and a lot of lot of pressure. I would work

> everyday for like sixteen hours: I think I had 2 days off in
> [19]93, 1 day off in [19]94, that's including weekends and
> Christmas and everything, and I was doing kind of fifty things
> a day. And then you give and you give and you give and you
> give and then you feel you can't, you haven't got anything
> more to give. The *Homogenic* character becomes like a warrior and not a warrior with weapons who wants to fight back but somebody who wants to fight with love. (*Inside Björk*, dir. Walker 2003)
>
> I think the character that made *Vespertine* was a lady in waiting who would play music in her living room. Quite elegant, slightly decadent lady, who had studied musical instruments and had a music box in her lap and then she would sing on top of it. (*Vespertine Live at the Royal Opera House*, dir. Barnard 2001).

The idea of a performer acting out different personas for different recording projects is not unusual (similar accounts have been given by other performers, such as Madonna and David Bowie), but Björk connects these different personas with autobiographical events. Thus, there is an elusive connection between the characters featured in the albums and songs, and Björk's own identity. One way of understanding this is to view Björk's music as an indirect mediation of her biographical experiences. As she herself has argued, there is a difference between the star persona constructed and communicated through her artistic output and the discourse surrounding it, and her self-identity: "this hullabaloo is not about you, it's about that person you've created" (Björk cited in Deevoy 1994).

Much of the discourse surrounding her music encourages listeners to receive the music as if it offered up the "real" Björk's affective life, yet this is only one way to understand the music in her name, albeit one with powerful commercial utility. The ability to access Björk's psyche which her music appears to offer is not necessarily experiencing Björk as she experiences her life, but experiencing some aspect of an emotional world and a (virtual) subjectivity arising from the confluence of three factors: the listener, the discourse surrounding the music, and musical sound.

From a broader perspective, the emotional authenticity which Björk's music appears to offer audiences, and which she herself attributed to her music, can be understood as a response to the social alienation produced under modernity (Moore 2002). It is this striving for the authentic on the part of audiences and musicians alike, which is such a powerful aspect of music's appeal. The dependence of authenticity upon apparent access to the "real" person behind the star persona results in media pressure on celebrities to give ever more personal information in interviews, and to access the personal lives of stars and their families. (For example, Björk attributed her infamous assault on a journalist in 1996 to what she perceived as an invasive attempt to interview her son.) The author-cult is also implicated in the extreme reactions and obsessions exhibited by some fans: because the mediated personas of stars are so ubiquitous, their images circulating in the public domain, and their private lives the subject of gossipy journalism, it can feel as though we know them intimately (Gledhill 1991: 214–15). In the case of Björk, the potential for this intimacy is realized through her mediated public presence in images, journalistic reporting, and "behind the scenes" style documentaries,[17] and through the emotional intimacy of some of her recordings and performances.

There is a melancholy moment in the documentary *Miniscule* that reveals something of Björk's struggle with the sometimes-incompatible demands of public figure and private individual, and her attempt to reconcile these tensions through her artistic output:

> I think for people like me who end up in this kind of job, people who make music, and I'm sure it's in other professions too, but the reason why you go into it at first is that you want to give. It really is that naïve. . . . But that's what drives you, is you want to give something of you. And I guess with people who have similar job as I have [sic] it gets misunderstood . . . . And so you kind of get confused and start giving things that maybe nobody wants, or the media will ask you for things that is nobody's business. And then you stop giving what you wanted to give in the first place. But there is still . . . a part of me that has hope and wants to give and communicate something that is quite private, but it has nothing to do with my everyday life still. It is still this bubble, this kind of fantasy fairytale bubble. (*Miniscule*, dir. Gestsdóttir 2001)

7 Contribution

Impact and Significance

Björk is notoriously difficult to categorize: she is a performer, an actress, a composer of film-music, a singer-songwriter, a producer of collaborative works; she is positioned within popular music but has musical and artistic tastes beyond those of pop genres. She has also been recognized for her achievements within different artistic worlds: she has been nominated for or won awards for different genres ("alternative", "pop" and "world music"), media (albums, singles, music videos, film), and roles (vocalist, composer, actress).

If the resulting collage is a confusing one, then a vision of the artistic identity Björk would like us to see can be found in those aspects of her artistic output which are explicitly self-defining, such as the Björk-chosen *Greatest Hits* released in 2002, other releases within the *Family Tree* box set, and the work she refused to release, requested be deleted, or otherwise suppressed. For instance, she refused permission to release the recording of her performance of Schoenberg's *Pierrot Lunaire*, and she allowed release of the piece written for her by John Tavener, *Prayer of the Heart*, as part of his birthday compilation *A Portrait: John Tavener* (2004), but only on condition that there would be no advertising of her involvement on it. Similarly, the album of jazz covers, *Gling Gló* released in 1990, is not marketed or advertised anywhere in the world, because Björk does not want it to be, even though were it advertised it would potentially be a highly lucrative release (according to Derek Birkett it sells more than one hundred thousand copies per year in the absence of marketing). By limiting access to some of her past work Björk attempted to shape public perception of her artistic identity and to project a coherent vision of her work.[1]

So what then *is* the artistic identity that Björk would have us see? By omitting her performances of compositions by others from *The Family Tree* collection, and her self-chosen *Greatest Hits*, and by suppressing her performances of work created by other people, she presented herself as a creative artist rather than solely a performer. Hence, she protested strongly against her record company's wish to include the cover song 'It's Oh So Quiet' on her *Greatest Hits* compilation:

> ...for a couple of months, I was like, 'Why the f*ck did I do 10 years of entering the unknown and having this feeling of being a pioneer?' . . . when you go blindfolded into the unknown and you've been on a mission that the world needs new music and you've experimented with all sorts of people and have this excellent adventure – doing that for 10 years and sitting down with the record company people and they say, 'Oh, forget about everything you've ever done. The only thing that's worth anything is "It's Oh So Quiet."' You just go, 'What?!' I didn't work like a lunatic and wave the flag and the trumpet, with this fierce belief for all this time, to have that song be the only result. (Björk interviewed in Lagambina 2002)

The preceding chapters have examined the detail of Björk's self-perceived artistic vision, and the extent to which it is manifested in her artistic output. The central theme revealed by my analysis, which has achieved increasing definition through her solo career, is the enactment of unity. This encompasses four main ideas.

First, the subject matter of Björk's artistic output from the 1990s is overwhelmingly concerned with the relationship between nature and technology. Her artistic output expresses a unity of the natural and technological, thereby resolving their tension as binary opposites, and it does this through particular technical means: visual representations show the compatibility of the natural and technological, the sounds of beats (which are conceived by her as symbolic of the technological and modern) are "naturalized" by reference to organic processes and substances, acoustic and synthesized sound sources are brought together, and she uses her voice in a way which resists the metric grid of beats. In Chapters 2 through 4 I argued that this unification resolved a tension in the cultural consciousness of industrialized nations of the twentieth and twenty-first centuries. More specifically, it addressed a conflict within contemporary Icelandic consciousness between the historical foundations of Iceland's claim to independence – its trinity of land, language and literature – and its situation at the end of the twentieth and beginning of the twenty-first century as an independent nation-state with an urban, and increasingly industrial economy, trying to position itself on an equal basis with other nations in a globalized world. The unification of nature and technology expressed in Björk's work articulates a fusion between the related concepts of the rural and urban, traditional and modern, showing that these apparent opposites are compatible. Although this issue has relevance for all industrialized nations, it has a specifically Icelandic pertinence. Its origin in Björk's artistic output can be attributed to her musical and intellectual development in the 1980s, during which Iceland's alternative popular music scene became identified with the search for a new and affirming sense of Icelandic identity. Furthermore, it has particular salience amid debates in contemporary environmental politics in which Iceland's industrialization is seen as a threat to an important component of national identity – the natural landscape.

Second, Björk's use of sound materials unifies the world of everyday and musical sound. This is one way in which the unification of the natural and technological is expressed sonically, as noted above, but it also embodies a unification of musical artistic expression with the world of everyday sound, thereby contributing to the symbolic unification of art (and the elite it is often associated with) and life (of the masses). One innovative aspect of Björk's music is the way it brings together three types of sound material: real-world (everyday) sounds, acoustic (instrumental) sounds, and electronic (synthesized) sounds. The process of unification enacted within individual tracks dispenses with divisions between music and the everyday auditory world, as well as between nature and technology.

Third, the stylistic diversity exhibited in her music refuses to recognize genre divisions, thereby expressing the unity of musical worlds. Her collaborations cross boundaries between art music (through her work with composer John Tavener, conductor Kent Nagano and performance artist Meredith Monk), world music (through collaborations with Malian kora player Toumani Diabaté, Congolese electric likembé ensemble Konono No 1, and Inuk throat singer Tagaq), and within sub-genres of popular music (for example, British electronica musicians Graham Massey, Mark Bell and Matthew Herbert, US hiphop and r&b producer Timbaland, progressive rock drummer and vocalist Robert

Wyatt, noise rock drummer Brian Chippendale, and experimental percussionist Chris Corsano). Only a handful of other international artists (such as Damon Albarn or the Kronos Quartet) have achieved anything like this creative freedom in their musical collaborations.

Björk's artistic output communicates this vision of creative freedom and unity of musical worlds through the sound and conceptual content of her artistic output, which changed together with the new musical techniques she developed to communicate her ideas. On her earlier solo albums, *Debut* and *Post*, she brought together apparently disparate musical worlds through the inclusion of covers of jazz standards, as well as through the then unusual combination of melodic and soulful vocals, unusual acoustic instruments, and the rhythms and instrumental palette of electronic dance music. In subsequent albums this creative freedom was expressed through the variety of sound sources and styles within tracks, rather than inclusion of covers. The centrality of stylistic diversity to Björk's self-identity is affirmed by her choice of music on her *Family Tree* compilation, which brings together material explicitly influenced by a variety of genres: Icelandic punk, English electronic beat-makers, her classical training, and Iceland's musical and literary heritage. As discussed previously, disparate musical materials, and the collaborators they are sometimes made and performed by, signify different musical cultures, which are often musically unified over the course of individual tracks, or sit alongside one another in an equal relationship. This musical unity articulates a conceptual unity between musical genres and therefore the social worlds they are associated with. Whereas Björk initially conceived of this as a fusion of her Icelandic identity with "foreign" elements, later albums, particularly *Volta*, articulate a unity between different cultures (a quest for a "universal tribal beat" (Williamson 2007)). This fusion of musical cultures avoids idealizing the local "authentic" expression of folk culture, or condemning the global as inauthentic or resulting in a bland mass culture; instead it communicates the idea that music (and the world it represents) can embrace diversity.

Fourth, Björk's vision of unity is embodied in her visual persona and communicated through all the artistic media at her disposal: music, cover art, promotional photographs, videos, concert sets, her clothing, and even titles[2] articulate her ideas to an extent which goes beyond the practices of many other artists. This unity of media embodies the very fusion her work expresses. For example, the music video 'Jóga' depicts Björk as part of and made from the Icelandic landscape she eulogizes in the track. As well as articulating Björk's patriotic sentiment at that time, this video exemplifies the central vision and method of Björk's artistic output — the idea of oneness with the world: there is no distinction between Björk's inside and the outside world represented in the video. Most significantly, Björk's embodiment of her ideas through her appearance (as sea, ice, bear, fire) is a visual representation of the "oceanic" state her music engenders: a state of infinite boundlessness and unity.

Two aspects of Björk's expression of unity are examined further: the economic and social relationships within which this vision was realized, and the political ramifications of this utopian ideal.

Artistic Innovation in the Context of the Music Industry

The identity suggested by Björk's self-presentation is in some respects more akin to that of performance artists Meredith Monk and Laurie Anderson, both of whom she is reported to admire hugely, than to female pop artists. Yet where Björk differs from these musicians is in her positioning within the world of pop rather than art music; Björk integrates the avant-garde into the populist by bringing in collaborators from disparate artistic fields in a deliberate attempt to communicate to a mass audience. Speaking in 2003 she remarked that she was

> doing music for the everyday person. Like I could've so easily gone and become a composer and done some avant-garde music in some corner for the chosen eleven and half person. But I've never wanted to do that. (*Inside Björk*, dir. Walker 2003)

Yet there is an evident tension between her experimental aesthetic, realized as an increased tendency towards a more art-oriented musical style in *Vespertine, Medúlla* and *Drawing Restraint 9*, and her desire to communicate to a wide audience, as illustrated through her continued reflection on this topic: "I keep having conversations in my head: should I keep trying to communicate with the common heart, or shouldn't I?" (Lester 2007).

Björk's explicit aim to create "innovative" music for "the everyday person" is one of her music's most interesting attributes, because musical experimentation is at odds with much of the music that receives mainstream exposure and economic success. Björk's boundary crossing is problematic from the perspective of commercial success. Sales of Björk's later albums have been smaller in some territories than *Debut* and *Post*: the former was certified double platinum in 1994, and the latter platinum in 1996 by the British Phonographic Industry, but to date her other albums have reached no higher than Gold in the UK. Nonetheless, each recording project had a few territories where it sold particularly well: for example, *Medúlla* sold well in France, Italy, Spain and Japan,[3] but not as well in previously successful territories. However, each new project is buffered to some extent by sales of Björk's back catalogue: although each new album had relatively small sales for an international artist (*circa* two million copies), the back catalogue sold disproportionately well when each new album was released (Birkett 2006): both *Debut* and *Post* were certified Platinum in the United States in 2001 attesting to their continued sales ("Gold & Platinum" 2006).

An important factor, which facilitated Björk's artistic innovations, was the relationship with her record company, One Little Indian. As an independent record label, One Little Indian operates outside the major labels (multinational companies who own their distribution channels) that currently account for approximately three quarters of the music market. Despite offers from major record labels early in her career, Björk stayed with One Little Indian due to her loyalty towards Derek Birkett who had backed her first solo album and the artistic freedom she had in that relationship.[4] For example, Björk agreed to a *Greatest Hits* album only after negotiating release of a separate album of her own choice of Greatest Hits, plus a retrospective. Perhaps most infamously, Björk's desire for artistic control led to a brief halt to work on the film *Dancer in the Dark* while she, director Lars von Trier, and their respective managers renegotiated the terms under which she would work on the music for the film, so that she would have greater control over the editing of the soundtrack.

Derek Birkett and Björk met through their participation in anarcho-punk collectives in the 1980s, and shared counter-cultural values. These values shaped the relationship between Björk and One Little Indian, and between One Little Indian and other record companies, as illustrated by their reluctance to enter into joint ventures (recordings or films) with other companies.[5] Björk's control over her artistic output is further instituted in the licensing arrangements between One Little Indian and the major overseas distributors of Björk's artistic output. According to Derek Birkett, the licensing is such that overseas companies follow the lead of One Little Indian: Björk produces an album with the support of the One Little Indian team who packages and releases it, and it is then handed to Warners in North America and Universal in Europe who are licensed to put it out in the exact same way. According to Derek Birkett, "all Björk has to do is control me and then the whole world [of distributors] is controlled and follows suit" (Birkett 2006). In the rare instances that an overseas company refuses to release material, the position of One Little Indian as an independent label enables them to do things that might otherwise be precluded. An example of this is the Archive DVD series: *Björk: The Television Archive* and *Björk: The Live Archive*, which were eventually released through Wellhart, when contractual obligations of the companies licensed to distribute overseas prevented release in the normal way. Both Björk and Derek Birkett stated their belief in interviews that her artistic innovations were possible because with One Little Indian she was able to release the music she wanted, and undertake artistically elaborate tours even when not commercially viable to do so. Examples of this were her refusal to repeat successful formulas, choosing instead to tread new ground with each new album; her reported reluctance to perform crowd-pleasing dance hits such as 'Big Time Sensuality' at gigs; her engagement with experimental artistic styles; and the consistency with which she avoided the easiest or cheapest artistic option (for example, she delayed getting a human beat-boxer to work on *Medúlla*, trying other options first because asking a human beat-box to create the beats seemed "too obvious" (*The Inner or Deep Part of an Animal or Plant Structure*, dir. Gestsdóttir 2004).

However, in some instances, One Little Indian had less ability to overcome constraints of the industry. For example, with the exception of 'It's Oh So Quiet' (dir. Jonze 1995), Björk's music videos rarely featured on music television due to the lesser power of an independent record company to place their videos, compared to the majors (Birkett 2006). And while radio airplay had never been a major element in the promotion of her music, the absence of the three-minute format from Björk's later music mitigated against radio airplay. Nor did Björk engage in promotional activities around albums to the same extent as other international artists, finding the demands of switching between different types of promotional activities too stressful.[6]

Political Engagement

Björk's relationship with an independent record company, and her twenty-year involvement with Bad Taste, indicate Björk's commitment to counter-cultural values. Both Kukl (1983–1986) and the Sugarcubes (1986–1992) explicitly declared their aesthetic and political ambitions: Kukl aimed to use music as a means to cause change in society and exhibited a non-conformist attitude; and as part of the Bad Taste ('Smekkleysa') collective, the Sugarcubes aimed to revitalize the Icelandic pop music scene and redefine what constituted "good taste". These values were also evident in Björk's solo career through her refusal of sponsorship or use of her music in product advertisement. It is also evident in her clothing: Björk often wore one-off designs by relatively unknown designers because "wearing jeans and a T-shirt was a big part of the white, male imperialism — you know, like drinking Coca-Cola and eating hamburgers? It's a bit sort of giving in to the empire" (Björk cited in Davis 2004). Wearing the infamous swan dress to the Oscars and laying eggs on the red carpet was a humorous challenge to fashion industry norms (Kellner 1995).

Björk's compositional style can also be seen as political, because it challenges the norms of the popular music industry. Her increasingly "experimental" style made for less easy listening;[7] the changes in instrumental palette and collaborators from one album to another risked losing previous audiences; and the difficulty in classifying her output worked against industry norms of genre categorization. A record company's marketing plan for an international artist often plays down the national origins of the performer to create the idea of a pop star who transcends their national background. Simultaneous with this, the "world music" category was formulated to provide a market for diverse musics that affirmed a sense of place: effectively this was a re-territorialization of "domestic" music for consumption in other places (Negus 1999: 165). Björk's artistic output challenges such systematization of the music market by bringing together different musical worlds and foregrounding her own nationality in her music and performances.

Contribution 163

The international success of the Sugarcubes and Björk raised awareness of the Icelandic popular music scene, facilitating the success of other artists such as Sigur Rós, and contributing to Iceland's attractiveness as a tourist destination. Björk directly supported new Icelandic pop music through her involvement with the non-profit-making organization Bad Taste, which released both Múm's and Sigur Rós's first albums. The Sugarcubes' reunion gig in Reykjavík in 2006 raised money for Bad Taste so that it could continue to support Icelandic poetry and music. Within this larger context, the emphasis Björk placed on her artistic control and ability to take artistic risks constituted a display of national independence; she expressed her experimental approach through metaphors drawn from Icelandic tropes of ships and of Vikings "waving a pirate flag" (Gunnarsson 2004), and attributed her independent attitude to her Viking heritage (Rüth 1997), thereby explicitly aligning a mythologized Icelandic identity with her self-perceived artistic innovation.

Björk also increasingly communicated the idea that music could be made by anyone, thereby undermining a dominant ideology in which music is the domain of specialists and a commodity – an ideology which sustains the economic basis of the music industry. This attitude is enshrined in Bad Taste's manifesto, and its continued aspirations twenty years after its formation (Eldon 2006), although it only gained explicit expression in Björk's output from *Medúlla* onwards. The non-synchronous layering of voices on *Medúlla*, and the use of choir (associated with amateur music-making), promotes the idea that music can be made by everyone – a notion supported by the music video 'Triumph of a Heart' (dir. Jonze 2005), which includes a scene of Björk and friends singing *a cappella* inside the Reykjavík club Sirkus, and by Björk's anecdotes in interviews around *Medúlla*'s release, which referred to singing with her extended family and friends.

This participatory ideal was taken a step further in One Little Indian's use of open competitions to elicit material from her audience. The compilation of remixes of 'Army of Me', the first single from *Post* (1995), on *Army of Me-Xes*, was elicited by an invitation posted on bjork.com, and the selection from the 600 submissions was made by Björk and co-writer of the original track, Graham Massey. A similar process of open competition elicited videos for singles from *Volta*, because Björk "wanted to involve fans, but in a way where they are making things just like me, not in a Björk-worship kind of way" (Björk cited in Hilferty 2007). These open competitions can be seen as one way in which Björk propagated Bad Taste's DIY aesthetic, and its intended subversion of music's status as product. In addition, Björk's commitment to "re-versioning" her songs for remixes and live performance can be seen as a way to resist commercialism: by taking advantage of live performance as a distinct space for music-making (performance of music from her solo studio albums rarely recreates a studio sound) she renders her material open to continuous development in a way which undermines the notion of the fixed musical "product".

Nonetheless, participating as she does within the economic structures of the music industry, it would be naïve to suggest that Björk consistently articulated anti-capitalist and counter-cultural values. While the wearing of one-off designer items promotes individualism and counters fashion industry norms, designer fashion is situated within corporate fashion cultures in a way that her wearing of homemade and found-items as a teenage performer was not. Similarly, while One Little Indian is an independent record company it still operates on a profit-making basis. The incompatibility between counter-cultural values and a position as an international artist is unbridgeable for any artist.

A second domain in which Björk has political significance for many people is as an icon for gender equality: she has a public persona which avoids the clichéd sexualization of many other female pop stars; she exerted increasing control over the making of her music, yet successfully collaborated with others; and was also a mother and wife. Many writers focus on her position as a female musician: Reynolds and Press describe the way that during her career with the Sugarcubes, fans and critics focused on Björk's projected psychological imbalance (1995: 270); Whiteley (2005) remarks on Björk's reception as child-like figure; and Marsh and West (2003) argue that Björk's blurring of the distinction between technology and nature in her artistic output dissolves the polarization of masculinity and femininity. The British music press also focused on Björk's unconventional female image, particularly during the mid-1990s when the idea of "Girl Power" was an important part of the British pop music scene, and Björk's music appears on compilations promoting women's music, such as *Girl Monster*, released by Chicks on Speed Records (2006).[8]

Nonetheless, critical reception of Björk in the press has been marked by many of the diversionary treatments often allotted to female artists. Hence, the music press tended to focus on her motherhood and sexual relationships, particularly in her early career, with headlines such as 'Björk – Success and the solo mother' (Harding 1995), 'Freaky momma' (Tility 1996), and 'Love bites Bjork and Goldie' (Marcus 1996). Similarly, representations of her in the media as child-woman, elf, alien, eccentric and vocalist, rather than composer or producer, arguably diminish her status as an artist. On many occasions she forcefully rebutted assertions that her male collaborators were the originators of her music. For example, one journalist claimed that Björk "does weird, waily [sic] pop diva. Her producers do the rest. Often they do even more than that. Which leaves her free to turn on the kooky gamine charm" (Elliott 1997: 5). Such evaluations belie patriarchal values pertaining to the "significance" of various types of musical contribution: as a female artist who released music containing beats made by a male her authorship was questioned; but the authorship of music released by a male artist who included a female vocalist is rarely challenged. Collaborative work by females is viewed as "creatively suspect" and is heightened when, as sometimes in Björk's case, there was a personal relationship between collaborators.

Within production contexts, male and female participants tend to be aligned with an essentialized gendered subject: whereas male producers are valued for their technical objectivity, the female artist is valued for her emotional expression (Mayhew 2004). Björk is interestingly positioned with regard to this dichotomy, and in the *Volta* tour she confronted it. On the one hand, her author-image prioritizes her emotional authenticity, and her voice as signifier of the "natural" and "pre-technological", congruent with dominant constructions of the female subject in Euro-American culture. Furthermore, she attributed the conceptual character of *Medúlla* to her experience of pregnancy and birth,[9] describing the album as "blood, bones and meat" (*The Inner Part of an Animal or Plant Structure*, dir. Gestsdóttir 2004), and affirming constructions of the female subject as natural and pre-technological. On the other hand, Björk's artistic output and discourse projects a much more controlling image than is often the case for a female artist. She avoids clichéd sexual stereotyping in visual material, as others have noted (Hawkins 1999; Whiteley 2005): she does not wear conventionally revealing clothes, nor adopt conventionally sexualized poses or looks, even though her music videos have sometimes been erotically explicit (for example, 'Pagan Poetry' (directed by Knight, 2001) shows beads sewn into her naked flesh). From the start of her solo career, and even prior to that with the Sugarcubes, she was represented visually as an active agent. For instance, in 'Big Time Sensuality', directed by Stéphane Sednaoui (1993), she dances on the back of a flatbed truck driving around the streets of New York; the camera is static while she engages with it from various distances, looking directly into the camera – an image reinvigorated by director Dawn Shadforth's treatment of 'Who Is It?' in 2004; and in 'Army of Me' (dir. Gondry 1995) she is shown driving a tank, wrestling a dentist-gorilla for a diamond that belongs to her, and exploding a bomb in a museum to wake her sleeping boyfriend.

Given Björk's strong authorial image and avoidance of clichéd sexualization, one might expect her to be an ardent activist for women's rights. Prior to the birth of Ísadóra, Björk expressed ambivalence towards feminist agendas. For example, in 1993 she spoke admiringly of the work of film director Jane Campion praising her identity as a director portraying "feminine strength" rather than "moaning and complaining about everything" and "attacking blokes all the time", as she characterized other feminist films (Björk interviewed in Morton 1994). After the birth of her daughter, Björk articulated her awareness of the difficulties experienced by women in relation to work and family life, and of the cultural pressures on the development of young women.[10] This heightened awareness of gender inequalities influenced her artistic output from 2002; for instance, it drew her to commission film director Dawn Shadforth, known for capturing powerful and seductive performances by female vocalists, to create the music video for 'Who Is It?' (2004), as Shadforth recalled:

> She wanted to make a performance video, . . . not really too heavily conceptual – and I'd done a lot of work with performance video featuring female artists where they had become, had a presence, quite iconic. . . . Kylie and Goldfrapp, I think she particularly mentioned. Something to do with femininity as well, although I'm not sure if that's necessarily what we ended up expressing in the end. But that was the journey, that's mainly why she approached me in the first place. (Shadforth 2006)[11]

The final video realization of 'Who Is It?' is perhaps less focused around projecting a strong seductive female image than was the original intention, as Dawn Shadforth notes, but the very fact that Björk chose to work with this video director, renowned for her distinctive and powerful film work with female pop stars, is an indication of Björk's growing consciousness of her self-identity as a female artist.

Despite participating in a number of politically motivated musical events,[12] Björk's artistic output only became explicitly politicized after the terrorist attack on the World Trade Centre in New York in September 2001. Her first lyrical reference to real-world political events was in 'Mouth's Cradle' on *Medúlla* ("I need a shelter to build an altar/away from all Osamas and Bushes"). The interviews about *Medúlla* were also the first in which she discussed politics, motivated by the strength of her response to the events surrounding 9/11:[13]

> I would prefer that music was abstract rather than standing on a podium pointing a finger at what's wrong with the world. I'm an example of someone who always said they would never get involved in politics. But then situations can become too much so that even someone like me has to stand up and say 'wait a minute'. It reached a moment when I'd had enough.
> (Björk interviewed in Williamson 2005)

Björk's view was that music should offer an optimistic vision of the future: "Rather than point out what's wrong with the planet all the time, I'd rather make something new that becomes more of a positive statement about life rather than criticising" (Williamson 2005).

"Flags and Trumpets": A Vision of Music's Social Function

Björk's belief that music should communicate an optimistic vision of life is realized in her artistic output as an attempt to create "a possible moment of utopia" (liner notes to *Family Tree* 2002). One aspect of this is the overwhelmingly optimistic character of her music, discussed previously; another is her belief in music's therapeutic potential, both personally, to the extent that singing, composition and music listening offer a form of personal therapy, and in terms of music's function in contemporary society. Evidence for the therapeutic function of music-making for Björk herself resides in her statements about the place of music in her life, and in correspondences between biographical events and artistic output. The most stressful year of her life was 1996 during which she felt pressured to write another album, she hit a reporter who was trying to interview her son, and was sent a letter bomb by a fan who then videoed himself committing suicide to her music. These events were followed by a psychologically damaging period in which she filmed *Dancer in the Dark*. *Vespertine*, the album that followed, contained her most "introvert" music to date (symbolized in the album cover which was the only one at that time in which Björk did not meet the viewer's gaze), which she described as an attempt to make herself a sanctuary in which to heal after the rigours of these personal events.[14]

Just as music functions as a therapy of sorts for herself, so her declared motivation for making music is to make other people happy, as expressed in interviews and lyrics (for example in 'Alarm Call' from *Homogenic* she declares "I want to go on a mountain-top/with a radio and good batteries/play a joyous tune/and free the human race from suffering"). This affirming function for music is realized in different ways in each recording project and reveals her increased politicization.

As part of the Bad Taste collective, the Sugarcubes' pranksterish pop was not directed at real-world events, although it did embody a politicized consciousness which found expression in the collective's attempt to question what was accepted as "good taste", and (initially) to work outside corporate culture through DIY artistic projects. Elements of this pranksterism and freedom of imagination are evident in Björk's subsequent career, but she invests much more heavily in the idea that music is a means by which to create a better (utopian) world. The expression of unity, articulated throughout her solo career, is part of this utopian vision.

Björk described *Vespertine* as a "cocoon", a "paradise", and a moment of hibernation (Toop n.d.). Musically, these utopian ideals can be heard in the album's stylistic references to ideas of transcendence and plenitude. For example, the instrumentation of strings and harp suggests romantic art music, and its utopian appeal,[15] while the wordless male choir, and the album's title *Vespertine*, locate it in the realm of the sacred. Alongside lyrical intimacy, the virtual space of some tracks positions the listener close to Björk's whispered vocals and other small sounds, within a space "cocooned" from the outside world. *Vespertine*'s realization of utopia draws upon romantic ideals and symbols: it emphasizes the grandiose and the gigantic, at the same time as it celebrates smaller, more intimate forms, thereby suggesting the "vastness of the individual world" (Stewart 1984: 79–80), and retreating from the world outside the self.

Selmasongs, and the soundtrack to *Dancer in the Dark*, also display a utopian function for music, but the difference between these two projects is instructive. Within the diegesis of *Dancer in the Dark* (the narrative portrayed on screen), music and cinema are portrayed as a way to escape the harsh realities of life, thereby allowing the imagination sovereignty over everyday life for the character Selma (played by Björk), and by extension for the film audience as well.[16] For instance, a dull and exhausting shift on the factory floor is transformed in Selma's imagination into a song and dance sequence from a musical ('Cvalda'); conversely, a silently turning turntable foregrounds music's absence during Selma's struggle with Bill ('It's My Money', 'Show Some Mercy' and 'Scatterheart') illustrating that terrible things happen in the real-world (as opposed to the world of the imagination which is liberated by music). In *Dancer in the Dark* music's utopian function is brutally undercut when, in the final scene ('I'm Scared') Selma's singing abruptly ends with her execution: her voice is cut off mid-vocalization as the rope snaps taut. In this interpretation of the narrative, music is a tool of fantasy, which, while it offers escape from the harsh realities of life for Selma, and for audiences more generally, cannot overcome real-life injustices.

Hence, the treatment of music within *Dancer in the Dark* can be seen as a critical commentary on the utopian function assigned to music within the Hollywood film and film musical that it explicitly references.[17] As Carolyn Flinn has argued in her account of Hollywood Film, music, as it functions within film, has the ability to "ameliorate the social existence it allegedly overrides" and offers a sense of something better; it "extends an impression of perfection and integrity in an otherwise imperfect, unintegrated world" (Flinn 1992: 9). According to this view, music exceeds conventional language, allowing glimpses of a better world or a more profound experience than our own (Flinn 1992: 91). In *Dancer in the Dark*, music literally allows Selma to escape to a more perfect world, realized in musical numbers which constitute Selma's imagined, fantasy world where "nothing bad ever happens". Music's ultimate failure, enacted through Selma's death, is a critique of music's utopian function.

Two aspects of these projects reveal Björk's utopian vision for music: the absence of 'I'm Scared' from the soundtrack album *Selmasongs*, and Björk and Lars von Trier's disagreement over the final credit sequence to the film. Significantly, the song 'I'm Scared' which features in the execution scene is absent from the soundtrack album. One reason for this could be that it would reveal the film's denouement. However, another is that its absence allows *Selmasongs* to present a much more positive version of Selma's experience and of music's ability to offer her a sanctuary. Furthermore, whereas von Trier wanted the credits to roll in silence, Björk wanted music ('New World') to be present. The absence of music during the credits would have been congruent with the film's critique of music used as an escapist fantasy. However, Björk argued that music should be played during the credits to reconcile the audience, by suggesting that Selma's voice lives on. The presence of 'New World' during the credit sequence therefore communicates a life-affirming function for music, counter to the bleaker reading of the narrative and contradicts the critique of music's utopian function otherwise manifested in the film.[18]

The utopia represented by *Medúlla* has a very different character to that in *Vespertine* and *Selmasongs*, because it constitutes a "return" to a mythical moment prior to politics. Björk's response to 9/11 and the subsequent occupation of Afghanistan and Iraq, was to focus on things apparently outside or beyond that situation. Explaining the circumstances under which *Medúlla* was made she said:

> By playing with the whole raw thing, it was an attempt to come up with music that exists outside of all that, that isn't linked to any culture, religion and ideology. To me, being anti-war is just as war-minded as being pro-war. It's the same thing, it's still allowing yourself to be drawn into the fight. (McGeoch 2004: 96)

Her compositional response was to explore "primitive elements, in something that was before all this happened. Or like an individual before entering society. When you use no tools, nothing. Only what you have. The voice" (interviewed in *The Inner of Deep Part of an Animal or Plant Structure*, dir. Gestsdóttir 2004). Just as her lyrics on 'Mouth's Cradle' refer to a "shelter...away from all Osamas and Bushes", so the idea of music purveyed by these statements presents music as an escape to an alternative, utopian world. Avoiding the terms of an argument set by others has an emancipatory potential, but the danger is that it denies the extent to which one is implicated within and complicit in such actions.

Volta constitutes a much more confrontational response to social injustice, and references broader topical content: the lyrics reference suicide bombers, the death and destruction wrought by the tsunami that hit South East Asia in 2004, and colonialism:

> Maybe I felt that up to here things would be okay and the « good » would win in the end if only it persists. But things are not looking so good right now. It is time to go up on a mountain with a flag and a trumpet and insist on justice.
> (Scrudator 2007)

The metaphorical "flag" and "trumpet" were realized in the *Volta* tour through material characteristics of the performance: the presence of a female brass ensemble (literally playing trumpets and waving flags), Björk's playing of the Reactable, the confrontational lyrics, punk shouts, industrial beats, and head-banging and stage-encompassing movements in performance are all interruptive of patriarchal femininity; the eclectic ensemble of performers, and instrumental and stylistic palette works against ethnic, national and genre divisions; and lyrics and content directly engage with injustices.

This discussion of Björk's changing political engagement is a reminder of the extent to which her music is embroiled within ideologies of authenticity, nature, and nationalism, but also the extent to which it changed, becoming more explicitly confrontational and engaged with world events. Björk's voice and artistic identity are defined by ideas of the natural and instinctive, set up in partial opposition to the technological, yet she took increasing ownership of the technological within musical creation and performance; she posited an Icelandic identity based on an ideological image of the Icelandic nation, yet later rejected nationalism in favour of the idea of the global "tribe"; and her artistic output which once advocated music as therapy and escape became a clamour for justice. The development of the compositional style and conceptual content of her work reveals an artistic freedom that has led aspiring and established artists alike to claim her influence on them.[19]

Exploring the character and significance of Björk's artistic output also sheds light on more generic issues. It reveals how concepts and political beliefs can be embodied and communicated through multi-media works and performances. It shows how social circumstances, technologies and processes within which studio-based music is made influence the character of the resulting music. It also questions the relationship between an artist's biography and their music – a reminder that there is much more to be understood about how artistic identity (in Björk's case, her gender, national and personal identity) is mediated through music. It highlights the way that an artist's desire to communicate something "truthful" and sincerely felt is enmeshed within a music industry predicated on selling emotional authenticity, how this influences the sound of the music, and is complicit in the continuance of media intrusion into the private lives of pop icons.

Björk's artistic output and her performances are an incitement to anyone who will listen to take risks, to treat fear as a part of life (however unwelcome) rather than a constraint to it, to express individuality rather than be ruled by norms, to be strong but not afraid to show vulnerabilities, to be creative and determined, and (increasingly) to challenge injustice. This is an inspiring and life-affirming legacy.

Notes

Introduction

1. This recording, made in 1996 at the Verbier Festival in Switzerland, remained unreleased in 2008.

Chapter 1

1. Björk's naming follows the Icelandic convention of taking the father's first name (Guðmundur), plus the suffix "dóttir" (daughter).
2. The album has never been reissued and original vinyl copies are rare and expensive, although copies are available to download from online suppliers.
3. The cover tracks include 'Alta Mira' by the Edgar Winter Group, 1973; 'Álfur Út Úr Hól' (Elf on a Hill), a cover of the Beatles' 'Fool on a Hill'. The settings of children's tales include 'Búkolla', which consists of lyrics from an Icelandic folk story, set to the tune 'Your Kiss is Sweet' (co-written by Stevie Wonder in 1974), 'Fúsi Hreindýr' (Fusi the Reindeer), 'Himnaför' (Heavenbound), and 'Óliver'.
4. "Fame has never really been my thing. I have always been a bit bothered by it. In Iceland when I was 11, I did a record and people started recognising me in the street and kids in school started talking about me, in a nice way, but I just couldn't deal with the attention. It was a platinum seller in Iceland and they wanted me to do another one and I said 'no'" (Björk cited in Peachy 1993).
5. Historically, the single State radio station provided little access to popular music. The first weekly programme on Icelandic State radio dedicated to popular music (rock 'n' roll) was in 1956, prior to which exposure to pop came from the radio station at the American military base established at Keflavík in 1941, and from crews of Icelandic boats and aircraft who brought back records from journeys abroad. Thus, Icelandic popular music was largely influenced by American rock, and subsequently by the Beatles and the British Invasion in the mid-1960s.

6. Kukl also released *Kukl á Paris 14.9.84* (V.I.S.A., 1985) in France only.

7. The word "Úrnat" is described on Björk's official website as "A rather undefined and untranslatable word taken from Papu-ish, meaning something like 'trip' or 'holiday'" (Fritsch 2001).

8. Members of the Sugarcubes were friends, artists, and writers, rather than musicians first and foremost. Sjón's subsequent novels, *Augu þin sáu mig* (*Thine Eyes Did See Me*, 1994) and *Með titrandi tár: Glæpasaga* (*With a Trembling Tear: A Crime Story*, 2001), have been critically acclaimed for their use of imagery and imagination (Eysteinsson and Dagsdóttir 2006).

9. One track on *Debut* (1993) was produced solely by Björk, and one other was co-produced by Björk and Nellee Hooper. All other tracks were produced by Nellee Hooper, with the exception of 'Play Dead' which was added to later releases of *Debut* and was taken from the soundtrack album to the film *The Young Americans* and produced by David Arnold, Danny Cannon and Tim Simenon.

10. The child-like character of some of the material on *Debut* may also be attributable to its source in Björk's teenage years: "After the Sugarcubes, I guess I had a mixture of liberation and fear. It had been obvious for a while in the band that I had different tastes than the rest. That's fair enough – there's no such thing as correct taste. I wrote the melody for 'Human Behaviour' as a kid. A lot of the melodies on Debut I wrote as a teenager and put aside because I was in punk bands and they weren't punk. The lyric is almost like a child's point of view and the video that I did with Michel Gondry was based on childhood memories" (Björk cited in Hemingway 2002: 40).

Chapter 2

1. Other research based on demographic data suggests that population rates and deaths in Iceland were not dramatically worse than elsewhere in Europe, with the implication that late nineteenth- and early twentieth-century constructions of Icelanders' harsh existence and triumph against adversity may be largely mythical and in the service of a nationalist agenda (Vasey 1996).

2. Nationalist ideals about the beauty of the Icelandic landscape are expressed by early romantic poets (for example, Jonas Hallgrimsson (1807–1845)) and the "pioneers" of Icelandic painting: Þórarin B. Þorláksson (1867–1924), Ásgrimur Jónsson (1876–1958) and Jóhannes Kjarval (1885–1972).

3. According to Gísli Pálsson, some Icelandic scholars in the early and mid-twentieth century were influenced by the eugenics movement of Western

Europe and North America, and argued for the purification of the Icelandic race, essentialized Iceland's literary heritage on a genetic basis, and took up methods for preventing racial "degeneration" depicted in the sagas (Pálsson 2000: 11–13).

4. Paradoxically, Björk's appearance is unlike that of other Icelanders who tend to have the fair hair and blue eyes typical in neighbouring Scandinavian countries. Thus, her claim to an Icelandic identity based on racial categories is questionable on genetic as well as ideological grounds.

5. One hundred and fifty-two English language items of online and print journalism on Björk, published between 1984 and 2006, were analysed by noting recurrent topics in the texts. The seventeen topics identified from this analysis were then used as the target categories within a word count of the text using a customized internal dictionary within the Linguistic Inquiry and Word Count software (Pennebaker, Francis et al. 2003). The proportion of text consisting of the target words is less than one per cent for each topic, as shown below.

Topic	Words	Mean %	Std. Dev.
Landscape	ice snow thaw arctic polar freeze glacier landscape fire lava volcano erupt stone geyser cliff mountain earth island sky earthquake	.3	.26
Folklore	fairy saga tale curse goddess sprite imp elf goblin troll pixie siren god odin	.23	.33
Ice	ice snow cold thaw arctic freeze glacier polar	.22	.21
Eccentricity	odd sci-fi cyborg weird eccentric crazy bizarre mad outlandish bonkers	.21	.28
Northern people	eskimo innuit Viking Scandinavian icelandic	.18	.18
Nature	tree moss animal whale forest creature moth nature bird web cocoon blossom bear	.18	.18
Light	sun night sparkle shine shimmer twilight light bright dark daylight	.17	.2
Water	pirate geyser sea aqua ocean ship boat river stream water tide harbour anchor current wade	.13	.18
Magic	fairy curse siren magic mystery riddle puzzle charm code hidden secret enchant potion	.11	.19

Gender	fairy goddess schoolgirl diva princess queen child ingénue waif siren	.1	.16
Viking	pirate Viking ship boat explore hunt rebel	.07	.12
Exploration	viking explore map compass search	.05	.09
Fire	fire lava volcano spark cinder ash fuel electric erupt burn explode fireworks	.05	.1
Travel	ship boat locomotive aeroplane travel journey	.04	.08
Supernatural	alien heaven spirit sci-fi cyborg extra-terrestrial other-world supernatural	.03	.07
Violent movement	erupt explode geyser break burst earthquake	.03	.06
Sanctuary	cocoon sanctuary shelter altar	.01	.05

6. The frequency of topics varies across press reports in different languages which indicates that specific characterizations of Björk's Icelandic identity are projected on to her artistic output by whoever is interpreting it: reference to elves is equally common across all languages examined here, but English-language critical reception makes more reference to eccentricity.

7. Comparing the frequency of occurrence of topics across her career reveals that the period 2002–2006 was marked by significantly less reference by critics to ice, landscape, and movement, and significantly more reference to water, Vikings, and northern people.

Press reports were divided into periods corresponding to her pre-solo career (10 articles), a period including the albums *Debut* and *Post* and *Telegram* (40 articles), another including *Homogenic* and *Vespertine* (41 articles), and another including the *Greatest Hits, Family Tree, Medúlla* and *Drawing Restraint 9* (61 articles). Comparison across these four periods using a one-way ANOVA (Analysis of Variance) reveals a significant difference in the frequency of occurrence of words in critical reception of Björk's work relating to "ice" ($F(3, 151) = 5.72$, $p = .001$), "landscape" ($F(3, 151) = 7.49$, $p < .001$) and "movement" ($F(3, 151) = 4.25$, $p = .006$). Post-hoc tests reveal that the topic "ice" occurs significantly less in 2002–2006 than in her pre-solo career, 1993–1996, or 1997–2001 ($p<.05$); "landscape" occurs significantly less in 2002–2006 than in 1993–1996 or 1997–2001 ($p<.05$); "movement" occurs significantly less in 2002–2006 than in her pre-solo career or 1997–2001 ($p<.05$).

There are also significant differences in the frequency of occurrence of words relating to "water" ($F(3,151)=2.62$, $p = .05$), "Vikings" ($F(3,151)=2.6$, $p = .05$), and "northern people" ($F(3,151)=2.61$, $p = .05$). Post-hoc tests reveal that reference to water by critics and reviewers is significantly more frequent in 2002–2006 than 1997–2001; "Viking" is significantly more frequent in 2002–2006 than 1997–2001 or 1993–1996; and "northern people" is significantly less frequent in 1993–1996 than her pre-solo career or 2002–2006 ($p<.05$). These shifting thematic emphases reflect changes to the lyrical and visual content of her artistic output, but may also indicate increased emphasis on Björk's profile as an innovative artist as her work has accumulated.

8. "Musica Per Laptop E Ghiaccio Spezzato".

9. "Frau Gudmundsdottirs Inspirations-Quellen sprudeln offenbar wie die Geysire ihres Heimatlandes".

10. "Tatsächlich explodiert die Gefühlswelt der Isländerin mit jedem Lied aufs Neue, und immer in neuen, ungeahnten Formen, fast wie einer der unzähligen Vulkane ihrer Heimat".

11. "C'est là le défaut et la qualité de Björk: ne pas se fixer de limite, franchir les frontières du raisonnable, convoquer le feu et l'eau dans un même tourbillon d'impudeur instinctive".

12. "était aidée en par quelques elfes et lutins tout entiers dévoués à sa cause".

13. See Davidson (2005) and Spufford (1996) for accounts of how the North was conceived in terms of heroism by Europeans in the nineteenth and twentieth centuries.

14. "Als isländische Wikingerin ("Meine Familien-Stammbaum der vergangenen 1000 Jahre enthält ausschließlich Isländer") liebt Björk den radikalen, wenig auf Kompromisse bedachten Charakterzug ihres Heimatvolkes".

15. "Tøjet, hendes næsten overjordiske ansigt og accent efterlader det indtryk, at Björk er et fremmed væsen, der lige er landet på vores planet".

16. The documentary *Screaming Masterpiece* (dir. Magnússon 2005) tells a history of collaboration between pagan poets and pop bands, from the 1970s onwards. The poet Sjón likens the way that Björk performs his poetry all over the world to an ancient tradition whereby each European Court had its own Icelandic poet. Also shown are clips of a performance of *Odin's Raven Magic* (*Hrafnagaldur Óðins*) composed by Hilmar Örn Hilmarsson in collaboration with Sigur Rós. The performance on *Screaming Masterpiece* features a lithophone (a marimba made of stones which Sigur Rós refer to

as a "stone harp") made and played by the sculptor Páll Guðmundsson, which has no history of use in Iceland, but symbolizes a pagan past.

17. Björk also reportedly sang the 'Anchor Song' at Þingvellir in 1994 on the occasion of the celebration of fifty years of Icelandic independence. Notably the idea of being "anchored" in her homeland Iceland draws on the recurrent motif of ships.

18. The use of choirs in *Vespertine* and *Medúlla* can also be seen as having been influenced by the choirs that dominate Icelandic (classical) musical life. Male voice choirs, founded in the late nineteenth and early twentieth centuries, performed at all the significant national celebrations, such as the granting of home rule (1918), and full independence (1944), and were a symbol of the nationalist romantic movement and calls for Independence from Danish rule (I. R. Björnsdóttir, 'Hin karlmannlega raust og hinn hljodlati máttur kvenna: Upphaf kórsöngs á Íslandi', *Saga* 39 (2001): 7–50, cited in Faulkner and Davidson (2004)).

19. For a comprehensive scholarly account of Icelandic literature, see Neijmann (2006).

20. "In 'Human Behaviour', she's a little girl. In 'Isobel', she moves to the big city and big lights. She functions with her intuition which isn't very good in cities and crashes with a lot of ill-behaved people. So she goes back and trains a lot of moths and sends them back, as messengers of intuition, into the city to people who are not working with their intuition. In 'Bachelorette' she takes over and trees grow over the city. It's part autobiography part storytelling" (Björk cited in Hemingway 2002: 40). *Björk* describes this as an autobiographical trilogy which depicts her experience as the girl from the country who comes to the big city (Toop and Björk 2002), something which the music video realizations (all directed by Michel Gondry) affirm.

21. The synchrony between Björk's movements in the dress with bell sounds in the audio track (provided by the Bustaokirkja Bell Choir) mean that she embodies the bell, and becomes the source of the music, in a surrealist image reminiscent of the Sugarcubes.

22. The brief given to Dawn Shadforth by Björk was that it should be a performance video featuring bells. Björk said that she was inspired to use bells after witnessing a religious festival while visiting a Greek island after her performance at the Athens Olympic Games.

23. *Íslandsklukkan* was published in 1943, the year before a referendum in which the Icelandic people voted for independence from Denmark, and contributed to nationalist fervour (Magnússon 2000: 66). It may be no

coincidence that *Iceland's Bell* was only published in English in 2004, the same date that this video was made.

24. Like the music video 'Jóga', the documentaries *Inside Björk* (dir. Walker 2003), and *Screaming Masterpiece* (dir. Magnússon 2005) intercut mobile aerial shots of landscape with documentary footage of performances, continuing a tradition in which the Icelandic landscape is the central visual representation of, and way of understanding, Icelandic music.

25. This focus on the detail of the Icelandic landscape is evident in contemporary visual arts as well: for example, the projected video environment *Lava and Moss* by Steina Vasulka (2000).

26. Davið Oddsson, Prime Minister of Iceland, Introduction to Ingólfur Margeirsson, *Þjóð á Þingvöllum* (*Nation at Þingvellir*) (Reykjavík, 1994), p. 7 (Hálfdanarson 2000: 2).

27. Despite at times playfully humouring media characterizations of Iceland as a land of elves and puffin-eaters Björk has elsewhere criticized such portrayals: ". . . this marketing of what is Icelandic, this whole elfin thing, and we are this naïve race. And I'm just against it. ... And I never said that in the press that I saw elves, I never did see elves. Tolkien based his *Lord of the Rings* on Iceland and maybe that exists in the imagination of a lot of English-speaking people, so maybe it's English-speaking people projecting that on to Iceland" (Barton 2007: 9).

Chapter 3

1. In this respect the chapter is influenced by Julian Johnson's account of the idea of nature in the music of Webern (Johnson 1999).

2. Björk's accounts of singing outdoors ("I love to sing in the wind, in the rain, during a storm, at sea, on a lava flow... me against the elements" (Aston 1993)) may not be as idiosyncratic as they at first appear and may reflect broader patterns of understanding the relationship between singing and nature in contemporary Icelandic society. A study of the experience of men in Icelandic male voice choirs revealed that the physical environment was a common theme in their vocal self-identity, as the following examples from interviews with the men illustrates: "It's pretty good to sing there, with the rocks and the mountains to throw the sound between"; "I sing by myself and for myself when I'm alone in the barn. Experimenting with the voice, even make up text and melodies simultaneously and spontaneously, happened just the other day, out of the blue, and then went off with the wind" (Faulkner and Davidson 2004: 237).

3. Contemporary Icelandic art makes use of indigenous materials: for example, Ragna Róbertsdóttir's relief sculptures comprise chips of lava attached to a wall; an installation by Ólafur Elíasson incorporated a hanging curtain of moss; Georg Gudni created tonal paintings of valleys and mountains which dissolve in light in a revival of the Nordic sublime (Swain 2001). Ólafsdóttir argues that contemporary artists' focus on the miniature, closeness, emotion and the feminine reveals an interest in "nature" rather than the "landscape" of the pioneers of Icelandic painting, defined by its wide, omniscient views (Ólafsdóttir 2001: 34).

4. Björk's ambivalent relationship with urban environments is expressed in *Vessel* (dir. Sednaoui 1994): "First time I come to a city I was eighteen year old [sic] and I was terrified. I came to London and I couldn't believe that you can't just stand up and walk out of it. You can even go on a train or a car and you have to travel for hours and you're still inside the city and this completely freaked me out. I was so claustrophobic, and I got so obsessed with oxygen, I couldn't breathe, and I was trying to touch the buildings and scrape off the grease, and try to get in touch with things, and it was very scary. But then I learned to relax all about it, and I find it kind of kinky. You know, kind-a sticky. And I buy a bag of chips, which I usually hate, and I get all greasy alone with it. And ever since, I've been completely addicted to cities."

5. In October 2002 Björk's mother, Hildur Rúna Hauksdóttir, went on a hunger strike in protest at the building of the hydro-electric development, Kárahnjúkarvirkjun; in 2005 Björk's father, Guðmundur Gunnarsson, leader of the Union of Icelandic Electricians, publicly criticized the Icelandic government's failure to protect the rights of workers at Kárahnúkarvirkjun; in 2006 and 2008 Björk performed at concerts in aid of protecting the Icelandic wilderness and released a single 'Nattura' (2008) in support of an environmental protection campaign.

6. "I'd always wanted to work with music boxes but it was waiting for the right occasion. I'd been collecting them and stuff. The main thing was that I wanted to write my own songs in music boxes. In the beginning, the music box company weren't very excited. They'd made wooden boxes for eons and I wanted see-through plexiglass. They couldn't get their head round it – they were like 'Why?' They wanted to make the plonky sound softer with wood but I wanted it as hard as possible, like it was frozen" (Björk interviewed in Hemingway 2002: 43). For a history of the association between ice and glass see Davidson 2005.

7. The original treatment for the music video, as set out by directors Lynn Fox (Patrick Chen, Bastian Glassner and Christian McKenzie), imagines a retelling of the story of Adam and Eve set in the "primordial soup": Eve "drifts gently in the amniotic fluid..., primordial debris swirling about her like flies... The climax comes with the revelation of the first human growing inside Eve's womb" (Lynn Fox 2002). Given the subject matter of the music video it is tempting to read the track in terms of Björk's pregnancy during 2002. The song was originally released in December 1997 prior to Björk's pregnancy, under the title 'My Snare' as a B-side on the 'Bachelorette' single (December 1997). The directors were influenced by a book of scientific photography *A Child is Born* by Lennart Nilsson, as well as by the *Blue Planet: A Natural History of the Oceans* BBC television series narrated by David Attenborough.

8. The song was first recorded by pianist Nico Muhly in a version for "duelling lounge-lizard pianists" (Muhly 1994–2005) and only later did the choral version of the song realize Björk's subsequent vision of the sirens of Greek mythology whose singing lured mariners to their death: "It wasn't til the last day of mixing that I thought – oh! I need the sirens, if [sic] the Greek mythology! So we called up an English choir, and we got 16 women. I had done an arrangement for piano on the computer that was insane, impossible for a piano to play, and I got them to sing that, a bit like sirens" (Björk on XFM, 25 August 2004 ("Lyrics" 1995–2004)).

9. In Björk's idea of the track she is "a polar bear and I'm with five hundred polar bears, just tramping over a city. The lyric is about people who feel sorry for themselves all the time and don't get their shit together. You come to a point with people like that where you've done everything you can do for them, and the only thing that's going to sort them out is themselves. It's time to get things done. I identify with polar bears. They're very cuddly and cute and quite calm, but if they meet you they can be very strong. They come to Iceland very rarely, once every ten years, floating on icebergs" (Savage 1995).

10. The rhythmic pattern is similar to that of the bolero, but here it is in 2/4 rather than the 3/4 meter of the traditional bolero dance.

11. Other examples of Björk's embodiment of the natural world through visual material are the merging of Björk's face into a cybernetic landscape in the video for 'Hyperballad' (dir. Gondry 1996); the video of 'Alarm Call' (dir. McQueen 1998) in which Björk floats through a watery jungle and bites back at the fish; the video of 'It's in Our Hands' (dir. Jonze 2002) which shows Björk in night-vision, among oversized plants and insects, her eyes

reflective like an animal's; and the cover art to *Volta* in which flames emanate from Björk who is dressed in colourful knitted costume.

12. In his account of "revised naturalism" (influenced by philosopher Páll Skúlason's phenomenology of natural encounters), Árnason argues that "wild" nature represents the most alien form of nature and therefore provides a powerful encounter with the non-human, only through which can we truly know ourselves as human beings (2005: 27–28). The representation of "wild" nature in Björk's artistic output can therefore be seen as one way she addresses questions of what it is to be human, and dramatizes the distinction between human and non-human.

Chapter 4

1. The front cover art of the album *Homogenic* (1997) has flowers (nature) against silver (metallic) which suggests a state of metamorphosis between "nature goddess" and "technology's cyborg" (Marsh and West 2003: 195), and the insides of the CD art are red and organic suggesting nature, but as seen through science, i.e. a microscope. Marsh and West note that live performance of *Homogenic* emphasized the distinction between nature and technology: through placement of the Icelandic string orchestra on one side of the performance space, and Mark Bell (live mixer) on the other; through ordering of material (the performance opened with a traditional Icelandic ballad and ended with 'Pluto', the most "technological"); and by movement between these two kinds of material, which suggests neither has primacy.

2. In an essay about *Vespertine* (2001), Toop remarks that "Despite a passing Oval sample or rhythm tracks constructed by teams that define state of the art beats, this is a collection of overpoweringly emotional songs, gorgeous melodies and exquisitely inventive arrangements" (Toop n.d.). The same idea is implicit in the rhetoric used by Björk's collaborators, much of which emphasizes musical practices that will introduce "human feeling" into the results of digital technology. For instance, commenting on his string arrangements for 'Hunter', Eumir Deodato remarked that "she really wants a colour, the humanizing factor into tracks that are basically sequenced using electronic sounds" (*Bravo Profile*, dir. Walker 1997).

3. According to Alistair Beattle the video treatment also encapsulates the integration of technological and natural forms: "choice of a techno-bear ... has more to do with the idea of the beating heart of technology. Björk's music often has a dialogue between organic forms and techno forms, and we share this interest" ("Björk Family Tree and Greatest Hits: Hunter" 2002).

4. This same idea is reiterated by Valgeir Sigurðsson, studio engineer with Björk from 1998 to 2004 in relation to studio set-ups: "I like working with technology, but I want to have it set up so it never gets in the way. So it's a tool that, if you have an idea, it's not going to stop the creative process by slowing it down or by being too complicated or difficult" (Sigurðsson 2006).

5. The phonograph appears in cinematic contexts of female sexual transgression in which the woman is subsequently punished. For example, in *Pulp Fiction* (dir. Tarantino 1994) a record plays while Mia Wallace accidentally overdoses, and Vincent Vega talks himself out of potential adultery with her. In *Written on the Wind* (dir. Sirk 1956), Marylee, having been discovered to be picking up men, dances while crosscuts to another location show her father having a heart attack (Robertson Wojcik 2001: 441–4). In *Dancer in the Dark*, a record player is seen and heard shortly after Selma is (falsely) accused of propositioning Bill. The silence of the record can be read as an indication of the falsity of the accusation. Wojcik argues that the act of playing music on a phonograph is also a classic cinematic marker of female lack (often implicated to be a consequence of woman's transgressive sexuality) for which music acts as a consolation. For example, in *Breakfast at Tiffany's* (dir. Edwards 1961) Holly Golightly puts on a record as she describes how Tiffany's represents security ("nothing bad can happen there"), recalling Selma's statement that "nothing bad ever happens in musicals". And in *The Bride Wore Black* (dir. François Truffaut 1968) Julie plays a mandolin record before killing each of the men who murdered her husband. Although Selma kills Bill, the record player's silence in *Dancer in the Dark* suggests this is not revenge or intended murder. The fact it is Bill (not Selma) who theoretically has control over the record player can be read as a familiar trope of male authority and control through technology, which contrasts with Selma's music-making which relies on her voice. Against a context in which auditory power is gendered masculine, the silence of the record player symbolizes Bill's "lack": it is Selma who owns the money and shows self-discipline and self-sacrifice. It also signals that Bill has been trying to console himself, by being in a fantasy world in which the money is his.

6. See Sterne's account of three varieties of time implicit in recordings (Sterne 2003: 310).

7. "I think the only thing I said was that I wanted... I thought it was white, I was sure it was very, very white. And I'm trying to describe some sort of a heaven. But I also wanted to have the other level there, there would be like lust. It wouldn't be just clean. And I think I brought those like ivory

statues, that are, I think they're Chinese, of like people making love, like sort of erotic things. And I think I mentioned that I think it should be white, hard surface. There's something that's white and frozen and then it sort of melts because of love and making love" (Björk interviewed in *The Work of Director Chris Cunningham*, dir. Cunningham 2003).

8. "I knew them and liked them [a book of Chinese Kama Sutra prints that Cunningham recalls Björk bringing to him], but I couldn't figure out how to keep the explicit sexuality and still make it broadcastable. . . . It's a combination of several fetishes: industrial robotics, female anatomy, and fluorescent light in that order. It was perfect, I got to play around with the two things I was into as a teenager: robots and porn" (Cunningham cited on bjork.com ("Björk Family Tree & Greatest Hits: All is full of love" 2002)).

9. Only the eyes and mouth are Björk's own, the rest having been modelled in three dimensions using computer graphics.

10. "...her pronunciation is oddly toneless. She sings the way I imagine an alien would, or a mutant. Her voice is ethereal, almost disembodied. It seems to float in mid-air, as if it had come from a vast distance" (Shaviro n.d.).

11. Abbate notes the critical consensus that wordless music symbolizes absence of rationality, excess of passion, and the female in her analysis of the Queen of the Night aria *The Magic Flute* (Abbate 2001: 86).

12. The Golden Section is the proportion in which one section is to another as that is to the whole $(x/(1-x)=.618$ or $x/(1-x)=(1-x)/1)$. Here, the Golden Section can be taken as either bar 44/45 of the 72-bar track (counted from the first entry of the beat), or as 2:32 of the total 4:05 duration of the track. Both fall within the first bar of the third repeat of the chorus and coincide with the "money-shot".

13. The accordion has other, less benign historical associations. In the early twentieth century, the accordion became associated with the musette, which through various musical, physical and social transformations, has its roots also in musical automata (Abbate 2001: 219–28). The robotic machinery, then, is marked by its rationality, its lack of subjectivity in contrast to the cyborgs, but in the context of music and visuals the more benign associations win out.

14. "I usually work a lot with a QR20.... And you have 8 tracks and 100 noises and you can make as many songs as you want. A lot of my tunes the last 4 years I wrote on that. It's so incredibly convenient. You put the batteries in and you can take it, you can ride on the aeroplane, your

grandmother's house, top of a volcano, or in a club or in the tube" (Björk interviewed in *Bravo Profile*, dir. Walker 1997).

15. Dickinson argues that manipulation of the human voice in this way acts as a symbolic bridge between human and machine and goes against the cultural stereotype of women as instinctive and pre-technological (Dickinson 2004). Yet, arguably Cher's lack of authorial agency ultimately undermines the track's emancipatory potential.

Chapter 5

1. For a discussion of the fallibility of such definitions see Middleton (1990).

2. Björk's earliest instrumental compositions were written for instruments she learnt at school: 'Jóhannes Kjarval' was composed for recorder and piano, and is the only self-authored track on *Björk*; and 'Glóra' is a multi-tracked flute piece from 1980 performed by Björk but not released until 2002 on the *Family Tree* collection.

3. The "belt" style of singing originated as a means for female singers to produce a loud sound which would carry over an orchestra or band, prior to the use of microphones. It is best known through its use in Broadway musicals (exemplified by the singer Ethel Merman), and the vocal style of pop divas such as Celine Dion.

4. Sheila Whiteley notes the similarities between the "little girl" vocal tone used by Björk, and other female pop singers such as Tori Amos and Kate Bush. She also notes that critical reception has often focused on Björk's little-girl voice as evidence of her "girlish femininity" and tended to ignore the full range of vocal timbres Björk employed. This is one way in which critical reception downplayed Björk's status as a skilled musician in favour of representing her as child or elf (Whiteley 2005: 117).

5. Compression is a commonly used treatment which keeps the overall dynamic range of a performance fairly constant, but which therefore increases the volume of quieter sounds such as breaths and lip smacks that would otherwise pass unnoticed.

6. An example of expressive use of breath control can be heard at climactic sections of the track 'Play Dead' (*Debut*): each phrase of the wordless vocalize ends with a noisy expiration of excessive air, immediately followed by an inspiration for the next vocal phrase in a single gesture such that the vocal becomes a continuation of Björk's breathing.

7. Fellow Icelandic musicians, Sigur Rós, also make use of an imaginary language, which they call "hopelandic". But whereas Sigur Rós' use of

wordless singing is a refusal of language and the naming that is part of the global language of rock, as demonstrated in their album title *()*[empty parentheses], Björk's wordless singing often occurs at climactic moments in tracks, where it has a heightened expressive effect.

8. A recording of this performance can be viewed on YouTube (Sugarcubes 'Birthday' (Live in Reykjavik 2006)), although the analysis was based on the authors' own attendance at the gig. Added 19 November 2006 by eddiecurry (www.youtube.com/watch?v=PzUUzd0sbh8). Accessed 3 August 2007.

9. I use the Icelandic version as the basis for the comparison here, since the 2006 performance was given in Icelandic. Although one is a recording and the other a performance, Björk's performance in 2006 is representative of Björk's vocal style at this time.

10. "On the first album tour she sung every gig within an inch of her life and I think probably at a certain level physically you can't keep that up and you have to develop a different voice. And I think that was always exciting but you sense that and on the second album tour she had a lot of times when she just, we had to cancel gigs because she lost her voice. And I think she then had a lot of lessons . . . . And it wasn't that she wanted to change in the sense of, you know, sing in the conventional way that people did, but she knew that she had to start really taking care of it" (Sigsworth 2006).

11. The exception to this general descent is the music for *Drawing Restraint 9*, which includes only three vocal tracks featuring Björk, some of which are heavily processed.

12. Many of the vocals on *Volta* were recorded using the industry standard Shure SM58, a unidirectional dynamic microphone which minimized pick up of background sound. This was vital given that recordings often happened in non-studio settings (boats, cabins, hotel rooms) and with Björk singing without headphones. An exception to this was the recording of Björk's quieter and whispered vocals, such as those on *Vespertine*, which were recorded using a NU-47 condenser microphone. The NU-47, which has a distinctive wooden outer casing, was a prototype designed and built by the Finnish sound engineer Martin Kantona: the NU-47 made for Björk was one of very few such microphones in the world.

13. Describing the improvisational character of his part in a performance of 'Hope' with Toumani Diabaté on the *Volta* tour, keyboardist Jónas Sen remarked: "my role in 'Hope' is to be 'the Lydian front' which will give Toumani the freedom to do what he wants. Björk's music is usually in the Lydian mode (which is a normal major scale but with a sharp fourth note –

for instance, a C major scale would have an F sharp, not F natural) and my improvisation is supposed to emphasise that characteristic" (Sen 2007).

14. "*Medúlla* was my way of pulling out of that, refusing to be categorized as 'Oh what rhythm is she going to do next?' Just feeling the pressure of all these young drum programmers or producers or whatever you call them contacting me, like, who was going to be the flavor of the month. It had become this kind of fashion statement, it just wasn't right" (Björk quoted in Stosuy 2007). The move away from duple structures is even more explicit in the music to *Drawing Restraint 9*: 'Cetacea' uses a repeated seven-bar figure, while 'Storm' uses a five-beat bass line.

15. "...Björk wanted the morse code for 'Wanderlust, relentlessly craving Wanderlust'. She was more into the effect of the dots and dashes layering over each other than specifically trying to communicate words in morse code, . . . I'm not sure if many or any of the full phrase found their way onto the record" (Damian Taylor quoted in "Wanderlust" 2007).

16. As discussed previously, the importance of "the foreign" within Björk's compositional aesthetic appears to be born out of two related responses to her Iceland identity: her desire to acknowledge the global context of her own and others' national and musical identity, and to challenge the isolationism she perceived in Icelandic culture: "I come from an island that's quite proud to be isolated and separated from the rest of the world. And when I grew up a little bit I just thought it was silly and isolating us unnecessarily. If you have a strong sense of identity you are much more able to communicate without losing any of your identity" (Björk interviewed on *Live at Canal+* 2004).

17. "It was tricky because when I sat down and it was of course, 'Okay, now I'm doing a Japanese film score, okay...' And then part of me doesn't like that sort of stuff because coming from Iceland I've always been treated as this exotic elf, which I never really got, but there you go... And I sort of felt that maybe you've got countries in the world like the States and Great Britain and France and Germany who are sort of not exotic, and the rest of the world, which is probably 85%, is exotic. And South America's exotic, and Africa's exotic, and Asia's exotic, and Iceland's exotic, and probably Canada... no, probably not. [laughs]

So I didn't want to sort of treat Japan like it's been treated a lot, which is sort of this clichéd, kind of exotic-ness, and tons of shakuhatsi and, you know, that sort of stuff. So I wanted to treat it as an equal, as I would like if somebody from, I don't know where, Bulgaria was making an Icelandic film soundtrack and they would ask me to collaborate. You know, how I would like to be treated, as an equal human being" (Björk 2005).

18. According to Taylor, "collaboration" is a rhetorical trope which was established by Paul Simon's *Graceland* whose inclusion of non-Western musicians continues to cause debate about the exploitation of non-western by western musicians (Taylor 2007: 127–9). Mientjes (1990) points out in her analysis of *Graceland* that the social relationships involved in music-making have their sonic manifestation in musical "hybridity", and are projected to audiences through the meta-commentary which accompanies record releases. According to Erlmann, Paul Simon is cultivating his authority as a "cosmopolitan artist and world cultural intermediary by evoking the authentic and primordial" (Erlmann 1999: 215).

19. Exceptions to this treatment are 'Who Is It?' from *Medúlla*, which treats throat singing as one sound sample within a larger collection, and 'Pearl' from *Drawing Restraint 9*, in which it is associated with a film narrative of sorts.

20. Kukl's tracks generally avoided clear sectional repetition, with the exception of 'Dismembered' from *The Eye*, in 4/4 which uses a traditional phrase structure grouping of 16-bar sections, subdivided into two eight-bar sub-sections, each consisting of four two-bar phrases.

21. Her early music references dance music through its musical materials, and its lyrics: 'There's More to Life Than This' was recorded in toilets at the Milk Bar, in Covent Garden, London (Gittins 2002: 45), and features Björk singing along to (rather than singing) a track in the background, the lyrics recounting a reportedly semi-autobiographical experience of leaving a dull nightclub to experience the harbour at night and a visit to an early morning bakery.

22. Unusual for a track at this time, 'Human Behaviour' combines a lyrical vocal melody with an electronic dance sound, and plays with the timing of the vocal line in a way completely at odds with the regularity of the underlying bass and percussion pattern. The harmonic structure of the track is also unusual: the bass riff heard throughout is in A minor, with the exception of the first four bars of the B section (bars 19–22 and subsequent repetitions) where the bass riff suddenly shifts up a semitone to B flat minor. The synthesized guitar sound (heard first in the two-bar introduction) introduces the major 3rd, giving the track an unusual major/minor ambiguity. Furthermore the vocal line rarely resolves on to the tonic, lingering instead on the fourth and fifth degree of the scale, avoiding harmonic closure. Added to this, the

unusual timpani bass riff is slightly off-key, pitched between A and A flat, creating further dislocation between voice and instrumental material.

23. Tracks on *Vespertine* combine cyclic material with material that avoids repetition; the first tracks that are completely through-composed appear on *Medúlla*. The avoidance of repetition on *Vespertine* and *Medúlla* is anticipated by earlier songs that consist of a single (repeated) section (for example, 'The Anchor Song' and 'Cover Me').

24. "When we started to do stuff that turned into the *Vespertine* sessions, we were really into things that grew from improvisation; you could call it kind of aphoristic improvisation – trying to get things so that literally the first riff I would play she would respond to – and that's why we got into lyric things which were basically just reading something out of a book. . . . I came across Cummings and I could see that in a way it's very naïve but it sort of breaks the grammar and undoes the language and breaks the language open in a really interesting way. And I knew it had this kind of erotic subtext which I knew Björk would love as well. So I bought her that collection of the poems and she would just sort of read out and sing the poems – find one at random and it would be whatever we'd play. So, I think that the loosening of the sort of song moulds was a lot to do with bringing in a kind of improvisation into things" (Sigsworth 2006).

25. "We wanted to do this song that we used to talk about on the tour bus which was called 'The Boho Dance', basically because actually we really liked this trumpet line on it. . . . What we wound up doing was I hired a clavichord and then what I did was, just because it was just her, me and tape, I got the guy to, after we'd, we just kept playing until we'd got a basic take that we liked, and then I asked him to run the tape at half speed and at double speed and I just played extra parts. . . . Then that was the first thing I took back to my Pro-Tools and started editing it. . . . You'll hear a lot of what happened later is kind of based on that track I think in a way. . . . I think it was like the kind of celesta thing. That was the first use of it ever. And it also, and a lot of that digital editing thing that you hear in *Dancer in the Dark* sort of was a development of what I'd being doing with the Joni Mitchell thing and it was partly just an on the spot feeling of 'OK, how can I take this even further?'" (Sigsworth 2006).

26. The language used by Björk and her collaborators in the recording and mix stages emphasizes the need to "preserve" the live character of the music. One strategy Björk used to counteract this with *Medúlla* was that she did not let Mark "Spike" Stent hear any of *Medúlla* prior to the mix stage. Stent's description of attempting to mix tracks from *Medúlla* highlights the

primacy of "liveness" to the process: he recalled that the "timing" within one track he worked on was "all over the place" because all of the materials were human performances, including the beats. His first reaction was to try to edit the sounds to provide a regular metric grid for the track, but in doing so realized that he had robbed the materials of their distinctiveness and that "what made it extraordinary was the performance and the fact that every beat *wasn't* the same." So what he did was take longer loops "so it felt like definitely a performance" (Stent 2006).

Chapter 6

1. Other examples of Björk's artistic integrity cited by Derek Birkett include her rejection of offers to use her music for product advertisement, her refusal to cut tracks to enable a better fit to the three-minute airplay slot required by radio; her decision to perform *Vespertine* on tour with a 75-piece orchestra and a choir, and perform in opera houses, despite the financial loss this incurred.

2. Moore (2002) identifies three types of authenticity in performance: "first-person authenticity" in which the listener perceives an originator as conveying the impression that her utterance has integrity and attempts to communicate in an unmediated form (or, "what it's like to be me"); "third-person authenticity" in which a performer conveys the impression of accurately representing the ideas of another within a tradition of performance; and "second-person authenticity" in which the performer gives the idea that the music validates the listener's experience ("what it's like to be you, the listener").

3. For a discussion of the idea of the "star-text" see Evans and Hesmondhalgh (2005).

4. "With *Debut* I was really a beginner so a lot of it was just learning about the studio even though obviously I had been in studios since I was eleven so I was very comfortable there. But usually I had just taken care of my vocals and lyrics. I was usually there during the mix with the Sugarcubes, and I had ideas but I never been [sic] responsible for the whole thing. So *Debut* was the first time I talked about arrangements and towards the end of *Debut* I talked about rhythms and towards *Post* I got braver in that way and produced more. *Homogenic* was the first album where I knew how the whole production, not the whole detail, but the big picture I knew what it was going to be before it started. So it was more of a case of playing little roles inside that picture. Where with *Debut* and *Post* sometimes I would have half the song and I would ask someone to complete it, so it was like

a duet or a collaboration. I guess in *Homogenic* I started to get a little more bossy" (Toop and Björk 2002). From this perspective she can be situated as one in a long line of producer-artists (Moorefield 2006: 111).

5. For example, sessions involving Björk and the harpist Zeena Parkins in 2000 varied from laying down pre-written parts to co-composition of the track 'Generous Palmstroke'. Zeena Parkins first encountered 'Palmstroke' as a CD recording of a bassline, chords and melody and was asked by Björk to "do what she wanted" with it. She described "working on this idea of doing the bending of the strings" and using this as an introduction section to the song, then going to the studio where they played through it numerous times: "We just kept coming up with more ideas of how to make it better based on the thing that we'd just done. We did a lot of takes and that was the only time we ever really worked on it, was actually recording it" (*Vespertine Live at the Royal Opera House*, dir. Barnard 2001).

6. "I felt funny about having an album out that said 'Björk' on it and it wasn't my work. I'd been collaborating and wrote just one song, but I sort of promised to myself that I would never do that again unless I felt it was my album, not just something I fronted" (*Inside Björk*, dir. Walker 2003).

7. Given the evident tensions surrounding the topic of collaboration, the manner in which promotional material presents Björk's collaborative work is interesting for the ways in which it maintains her authorial image. Björk's descriptions of her collaborative processes position her as the author, identifying, directing and crafting what amounts to a virtual ensemble in recording, and stressing continuities between her ideas and those of her collaborators. For instance, Björk's description of Matmos's involvement in *Vespertine* emphasizes their skills while acknowledging her own use of the same techniques: "I had taken recorded things around the house before. I guess it's what people have been calling non-instrument instruments, where you take any object around the house, as long as it's not a musical instrument, and make music with it. I guess Matmos had been doing these kind of beats and using these kind of noises for eight years, and I sent them songs and they would send them back to me where the beats, where they had added things that made it a lot more alive. Sort of like a virtuoso spark" (*Miniscule*, dir. Gestsdóttir 2001). Elsewhere in the same interview, Björk's authorship is further emphasized through the distinction between Matmos's "virtuoso" additions to the album, and their role in the *Vespertine* tour for which they reportedly spent eight months programming and replacing Björk's beats with their own noises, resulting in "more of a Björk-Matmos collaboration" (*Miniscule*, dir. Gestsdóttir 2001). The potential danger which this kind of

meta-narrative tries to dispel is the perception that Björk is not the author of the work in her name.

8. "The only brief she really gave me was 'I want to remake this track with bells, and I like the idea of using bells in the video as well.' The reason for making the track with bells was because of a sort of visual, I mean obviously from her point of view it was the idea of the voices of the bells replacing the voices in the music, and that was something she'd been playing with on that album" (Shadforth 2006).

9. "With Björk you can do whatever you want really, I mean you're not confined by the pop world or the hip-hop world or anything. That doesn't really come into it. You can do anything to get the emotion of what she's trying to convey across, you know. You're trying to basically support the vocal in the most interesting and unusual way I guess. You know, realising what's in her head really" (Stent 2006).

10. "It's like she has strong ideas, and because she has strong ideas and firm vision, then there's a lot of freedom within that. She's not like nervous about her work being maybe destroyed or things going wrong as a result of people trying out different things" (Sigurðsson 2006).

11. "...it wasn't quite like she gave me a brief and let me run with it. I mean I did give her a couple of ideas initially which weren't quite right and so the idea was refined. It wasn't like 'Oh yeah fine, go and do it'. We went on a journey from shooting here versus there. And it was a journey of discovery for me because her brief was so open but still, once I'd thought it through it wasn't quite right, . . . so maybe it's a case of her discovering too and needing to be presented with something to know that" (Shadforth 2006).

12. Seven percent of Björk's lyrics consist of affect words compared to five percent in test norms for emotion-writing. Test norms are taken from the manual by Pennebaker, Francis et al. (2003). This analysis software is based on the idea that the way individuals talk and write provides insight into their emotions and thoughts. A long history of psychological research has shown that talking or writing about emotional experiences is associated with improvements in mental and physical health, therefore this text-based method was developed to aid study of individuals' language use. The software analyses written text word by word, and calculates the percentage of words from the text which fit eighty-two specified categories, some of which are super-ordinate or subordinate to other categories. Results are reported only for the English-language lyrics from the solo studio albums because studio

albums tend to be thought of by listeners as autobiographical in comparison to film soundtracks.

13. An analysis of variance conducted on the lyrics of Björk's studio albums (1993–2004) on each of the dimensions of LIWC2001 reveals a significant difference in the percentage of words concerned with affect in the different albums ($F(4,46) = 2.8$, $p = .04$). Post-hoc comparisons of the percentage of affect words in the five studio albums reveals a significantly higher proportion of affect words in *Debut* than in all other albums except *Medúlla*, and a significantly greater proportion of words concerned with optimism in *Medúlla* than in any other album (at an alpha level of $p<.05$).

14. "I've always liked Ella [Fitzgerald] because she's really happy. I've never been into all these suffering artists, I think it's a bit pathetic. You have your problems, but you have to go one step further, and see the funny side of it. Everybody has problems, not only Morrissey. That's why I've always preferred Ella to Billie [Holiday], even though Billie is the singer of the century and all that shit, but I think it's much braver to be happy than to be suffering, taking heroin and all that. Ella was strong enough not to bore the audience with her own difficult life" (Aston 1993: 42).

15. The lyrics of 'So Broken' dwell on imminent heart-break ('Here I go/ trying to run ahead of that heart-break-train') and the failure of a relationship ('I'm trying to land this aeroplane of ours/gracefully/but it seems just destined to crash'), leading critics to interpret the track as 'a sorry lament to the end of her relationship with Goldie' (Gittins 2002: 138). However, according to an interview with Björk in 1997, 'So Broken' was written subsequent to her learning of fan, Ricardo Lopez', letter bomb and suicide: "I recorded 'So Broken' that infamous week for me, the week of the bomb. The only way for me to write a song about it was just to take the piss. I wrote it in my house hitting the table singing, 'I'm so broken (in corny, overwrought voice), olé!' I was going to have the sound of washing dishes and three kids screaming; it would be a soap opera" (Björk cited in Micallef 1997). "I wrote it as a cliché then I went to Spain to record it because it was a Spanish cliché. And then it became real, that's what Ramundo [the guitarist] did to it" (Björk interviewed on *Later with Jools Holland*, 1997 ("Homogenic" 1995–2003)).

16. According to the psychoanalytic theories of Sigmund Freud, the term "oceanic" refers to the feeling of oneness with the world that arises from a childhood need for protection. He argued that the distinction between inside and outside was a crucial stage in psychological development, which allowed the developing child to recognize a reality separate from itself.

17. For instance, the title of the documentary *Inside Björk* (dir. Walker 2003) illustrates the way that audiences are offered an illusion of access to the interior of the "real" person behind the star-text. The title also refers to being within interior rather than exterior environments. This coincides with the concept behind the *Vespertine* and *Selmasongs* recording projects which were concerned with the idea of interiority, and which preceded the documentary release by two and three years respectively.

Chapter 7

1. "She'll go back and say 'Some of those things that I did, or agreed to do, or was persuaded to do, were right for me at that time, but where I am now they don't really fit in. And I'm really interested in presenting this vision, and as far as I'm concerned some of those things cloud that, obscure it, make it less clear and focused. So I'd like to delete them and not have them available.' . . . She would be really happy erasing some bits of the past" (Birkett 2006).

2. From *Homogenic*, album titles are invented or obscure words with connotations relevant to the main theme of that project. The word "Homogenic" expresses the idea that the album is on a single theme, but also resonates with the idea of cultural homogeneity, so central to nationalist conceptions of identity. "Vespertine" is an invented word which references the idea of heavenly paradise and evening, as appropriate to the utopian, Icelandic-domestic theme. "Medúlla" refers to the biological "marrow" in all living things, appropriate to the idea of primordial commonality among all humans. "Volta" has multiple meanings relevant to the energetic, multicultural agenda of the album: electricity, a river in Africa, and a dance.

3. *Vespertine* and *Medúlla* were certified Gold in France in 2001 and 2004 respectively and are her only albums to have been certified as such in France ("Charts in France" 2002–2007).

4. Recording engineer Valgeir Sigurðsson, a record label owner himself, explained the rarity of this relationship among international artists and labels: "She's stayed really loyal to him and he gives her all the freedom to do whatever she wants to do and I think that's a really rare relationship between an artist and a label. Because for me she was the first international actor I'd worked with and so seeing it from that angle as well how the label just doesn't get involved at all and then I work with other people and the label is breathing down your neck the whole time and trying to make something" (Sigurðsson 2006).

5. "…one of the problems that you have when you get into relationships with people like that is there's several other people that creatively want to control what's happening and, because they're putting up money, some of these things cost a lot for us to do, they want the right of veto and whatever else. And the relationship I have with her, with Björk, because we were both in punk bands, and had a punk label, was we never asked anybody anything" (Birkett 2006).

6. Evidence suggests this is not a primadonna-ish affectation but a consequence of a personality trait, which means that Björk devotes all of her energy to one type of activity at a time. One way this was resolved was by holding press conferences and releasing documentaries, which include footage and documentary material in partial replacement of the huge number of press interviews that would otherwise be demanded. *Inside Björk* was specifically commissioned by Derek Birkett for this purpose (Birkett 2006).

7. The prime example of this is the album *Medúlla* (2004) in which apparently simple materials (primarily voices only) belie their conceptual difficulty within the pop genre: *a cappella* material does not fit within a pop music industry geared towards guitar-based rock or electronic sources, and the tracks themselves lack some elements of the gloss of mainstream studio production practices, sounding closer to the idiosyncrasies more commonly found in live performance (for example, the wavering tuning and splashy entrances and exits in 'Submarine'), or which are confrontational in their nakedness (for example, the *a cappella* solo 'Show Me Forgiveness').

8. This compilation includes the track 'Storm' from *Drawing Restraint 9* written by Björk and Leila Arab, which counters the more frequent situation in which electro-vocal compositions are composed by men using female voices. See Bosma for a critique of the gender stereotyping in electro-vocal composition (Bosma 2003).

9. Björk said that the song 'Mouth's Cradle' was about breast feeding, and 'Submarine' was an expression of her re-awakening of her artistic identity after her absorption in motherhood (Kennedy 2004).

10. "It's interesting for me to bring up a girl. You go to the toy store and the female characters there – Cinderella, the lady in Beauty and the Beast – their major task is to find Prince Charming. And I'm like, wait a minute – it's 2005! We've fought so hard to have a say, and not just live through our partners, and yet you're still seeing two-year-old girls with this message pushed at them that the only important thing is to find this amazing dress so that the guy will want you. It's something my mum pointed out to me

when I was little – so much that I almost threw up – but she's right" (Björk interviewed in Hoggard 2005).

11. Whereas Kylie often presented a soft and passively alluring image in performance, Dawn Shadforth encouraged her to give a stronger and more sexually aggressive performance in the video of 'Can't Get You Out of My Head' (2001), resulting in an image of Kylie not previously seen. Although the open fronted dress worn by Kylie was extremely riské, choice of edits made sure that it was never revealing:

"I enjoy the working with women and I think it's quite liberating for them working with me that they are able to sort of express their power and sexuality at the same time. And at the same time I think it's to do with the way that I edit, in the choices that I make in the edit – on my own as well as with the artist – in terms of how far to go, so someone can feel quite free in front of the camera. . . . That's where *my* femininity comes into play and I make different choices to those a man would. You know, just because I'm projecting myself into the woman and sort of being how I wanted, if I was her, I'd want to be seen, rather than looking at her" (Shadforth 2006).

12. Björk was involved in a number of politically motivated musical activities during her career. She performed at a number of *Free Tibet* benefit concerts. She described *Medúlla* (2004) as her most political album to date, influenced by her experience of living in New York during and after 9/11. In 2005 an album of remixes of the track 'Army of Me' was released as a benefit record for UNICEF to raise money for victims of the Asian Tsunami in 2004, and as an attempt to make a difference after the powerlessness felt at Bush's re-election (Williamson 2005). In April 2005 Björk made available two remix tracks from *Medúlla* through the not-for-profit organization WarChildMusic to raise money for programmes working with children who had been affected by conflict. In July 2005 she performed live for the first time in two years at the Japan *Live8* concert (one of a series of simultaneous free concerts given world-wide to coincide with the meeting of the G8 Summit held in Edinburgh, Scotland, and intended to "make poverty history"). In January 2006 she performed at a concert at Reykjavík's Laugardalshöll to support the Icelandic Nature Preserve (a cause for which Björk's mother, Hildur Rúna Hauksdóttir, went on hunger strike in 2002). And in 2008 she participated in, and sponsored, concerts and seminars in aid of the *Náttúra* campaign for sustainable environmental and economic development in Iceland (Dibben, in press).

13. Describing the extremity of her feelings regarding the war on Iraq she remarked: "J'ai été furieuse, très choquée par la guerre en Irak. Mais on en parle tellement dans le monde occidental. On en parle, on en parle, on

pense à Bush, qui dégage une telle énergie négative ! Vous pouvez répéter: ce n'est pas bien, ce n'est pas bien, mais il vaut mieux arriver avec d'autres propositions, positives. Peut-être est-ce le rôle de l'artiste" (Mortaigne 2004). [I was furious, very shocked by the war in Iraq. But everyone is always talking about it in the western world. One talks about it, talks about it, one thinks about Bush, which releases such negative energy! You can repeat: this is not good, this is not good, but it is better to come up with other positive suggestions. Maybe this is the role of the artist. (Translation by the author)]

14. "I think looking back on *Vespertine* now, and having started my next project it becomes more obvious what I was aiming for... I think I was aiming for how you can express yourself when you are absolutely, you exploded five thousand times and there's nothing left, and you're just lying there like the ruins of you, but you still want to make something but you have no muscle and you have no blood and you still want to create beauty. So you end up using instruments like harp, celesta, microbeats and whisper [sic], so you are creating music with no physicalness and no body. And that's supposed to calm you and soothe you, like hibernation to wait, to help you to wait until you become strong again" (*Miniscule*, dir. Gestsdóttir 2001).

15. The prominant use of harp on the album was the result of technological convenience (the harp sounded "pretty" when downloaded to her laptop), a reaction against the sounds of the guitar she "overdosed on" as a child, and her long-term interest in the harp and its romantic associations: "I think I've always been obsessed with the harp since I was a little girl – I think probably the utopian element it brings – sort of a sugary sweet thing" (*Miniscule*, dir. Gestsdóttir 2001).

16. Emma Bell (2006: 214) argues that Selma's ability to bring together reality and fantasy allows her to survive hardship and to overcome disability thereby enabling cinema to represent and be a substitute for the imagination. However, I argue that it is music, and the cinematic musical, which represents the imagination, and that Selma's execution reveals the danger and ultimate futility of music's escapism as a strategy.

17. Björk's embrace of the utopian character of the film musical was anticipated in the award-winning music video for the single 'It's Oh So Quiet' (dir. Jonze 1995).

18. "As far as the story goes, Bjork believes there was a way to redeem Selma's suffering, by raising her sacrifice to a beatific level. It should have seemed, by the end, that the world could no longer hurt her. And this, at least, would have made the film truer to the dreamy genre of musical. 'Instead everyone walked out of that movie feeling miserable and they felt

miserable for one or two days. I don't think that is necessary. I think if Selma reached that saint-like elevation you would have walked out of that cinema feeling miraculous. She still died but you would have felt "up". It is that tiny little detail where we disagreed. When this plant we planted became too big he began to chop it down. I think it was fear, if you ask me. I think it is some sort of minority complex. You are an artist and you should believe in your work and let it stand for what it is. You don't need to put extra pain and suffering in there just so that the critics will say, "This is art."'" (*Evening Standard*, 15 August 2001 ("About & About: Dancer in the Dark" 1995–2006)).

19. Established recording artists claim to be inspired by Björk's refusal to conform to norms of the rock/pop genre and fashions, rather than by her music, although many aspiring and emerging acts do claim a musical influence (see promotional quotations ("About & About: Other people about Björk" 1995–2007)). In addition, visual artists she worked with claim to have been influenced by her thinking: Alexander McQueen stated in an interview with *Vogue* in 2000 that one of his collections for Givenchy was influenced by his work with Björk on the cover art for *Homogenic*.

References

"4orum" (n.d.). *bjork.com*. http://4um.bjork.com/. Accessed 6 January 2006.
Abbate, C. (1999). "Outside Ravel's tomb." *Journal of the American Musicological Society* 52(3): 465–530.
——— (2001). *In Search of Opera*. Princeton and Oxford: Princeton University Press.
"About & About: Björk" (1995–2007). *bjork.com*. http://www.bjork.com/facts/about/. Accessed 21 August 2007.
"About & About: Dancer in the Dark" (1995–2006). *bjork.com*. http://www.bjork.com/facts/about/. Accessed 27 August 2007.
"About & About: Debut" (1995–2007). *bjork.com*. http://www.bjork.com/facts/about/. Accessed 23 August 2007.
"About & About: Other people about Björk" (1995–2007). *bjork.com*. http://www.bjork.com/facts/about/. Accessed 28 August 2007.
"About & About: Selmasongs" (1995–2007). *bjork.com*. http://www.bjork.com/facts/about/. Accessed 20 August 2007.
"About & About: The Sugarcubes" (1995–2007). *bjork.com*. http://bjork.com/facts/about/right.php?id=1338. Accessed 27 August 2007.
"About & About: Vespertine" (1995–2007). *bjork.com*. http://www.bjork.com/facts/about/. Accessed 27 August 2007.
Ahonen, L. (2006). "Authorial voices, faces and media images in popular music." PhD thesis, University of Helsinki.
"Always Been Special: An interview with Björk's grandma and grandpa" (17 July 1993). *Björk's Page*. http://home-1.concepts.nl/~sinned/bjork2.htm. Accessed 25 January 2006.
"An interview with Björk" (7 April 2007). *Brooklyn Vegan*. http://www.brooklynvegan.com/archives/2007/04/an_interview_wi_18.html. Accessed 26 July 2007.
Anderson, B. (1983). *Imagined Communities: Reflections on the Origin and Spread of Nationalism*. London: Verso.
Árnason, T. (2005). "Views of nature and environmental concern in Iceland." Doctoral thesis. *Linkopings Studies in Arts and Science No. 339*. Linkoping: Linkopings Universitet, Institutionen för Tema.

Aston, M. (1993). "Björk Gudmundsdottir's record collection." *Q Magazine*. October: 40–42.
——(1996a). *Björkgraphy*. London: Simon & Schuster.
——(1996b). "Ssshhh! Quiet everybody. Björk's talking." *Raw*. 17 January: 22–29.
Bailie, S. (1993). "Lock up your Gudmundsdottirs." *NME*. 25 December. http://www.ebweb.at/ortner/tia/93/nme931225/nme931225.html. Accessed 27 August 2007.
Barton, L. (2007). "The Björk interview: 'I had a little bit of cabin fever'." *The Guardian*. 27 April. Film and Music: A Special Issue Edited by Björk: 8–9.
Bell, E. (2006). "The passions of Lars Von Trier: Madness, femininity, film." In C. C. Thomson, *Northern Constellations: New Readings in Nordic Cinema*, 205–216. Norwich: Norvik Press.
Benston, M. L. (1988). "Women's voices/men's voices: Technology as language." In *Technology and Women's Voices: Keeping in Touch*, ed. C. Kramarae, 15–28. London and New York: Routledge & Kegan Paul.
Berry, C. (1998). "Sno-koan." *Wired*. June. http://www.wired.com/news/culture/0,1284,12921,00.html. Accessed 8 November 2001.
Biddle, I. (2004). "Vox Electronica: Nostalgia, irony and cyborgian vocalities in Kraftwerk's Radioaktivität and Autobahn." *Twentieth Century Music* 1(1): 81–100.
Birkett, D. (2006). Personal interview. 4 October.
Bjork (1996). "Bjork meets Karlheinz Stockhausen. Compose yourself." *Dazed & Confused*. http://www.stockhausen.org/bjork.html. Accessed 8 November, 2001.
——(2001). The Call of the Wild, a conversation with Sir David Attenborough. *Björk. A project by Björk*. New York and London: Bloomsbury.
——(2002). Interview with Robert Sandall and Mark Russell. *Mixing It*. BBC Radio 3, London. 17 March.
——(2005). Interview with Robert Sandall and Mark Russell. *Mixing It*. BBC Radio 3, London. 5 August.
——(2007). Interview. *Later with Jools Holland*. BBC2. 8 June 2007.
"Björk & Medúlla & Oceania & Olympics" (2004). *bjork.com*/news 2004. 13 August. http://bjork.com/news/?id=480;year=2004. Accessed 25 January 2007.

"Björk Family Tree & Greatest Hits: All is full of love" (2002). *bjork.com.* http://unit.bjork.com/specials/gh/SUB-01/index.htm. Accessed 11 August 2006.

"Björk Family Tree & Greatest Hits: It's in our hands" (2002). *bjork.com.* http://unit.bjork.com/specials/gh/SUB-15/index.htm. Accessed 2 December 2006.

"Björk Family Tree & Greatest Hits: Hunter" (2002). *bjork.com.* http://unit.bjork.com/specials/gh/SUB-10/index.htm. Accessed 16 December 2006.

"Björk Family Tree and Greatest Hits: Jóga" (2002). *bjork.com.* http://unit.bjork.com/specials/gh/SUB-04/index.htm. Accessed 25 January 2006.

Bohlman, P. V. (2004). *The Music of European Nationalism: Cultural Identity and Modern History.* Santa Barbara, CA: ABC-Clio.

Bosma, H. (2003). "Bodies of evidence, singing cyborgs and other gender issues in electrovocal music." *Organised Sound* 8(1): 5–17.

Broughton, F. (1994). "Björk's big night out." *i-D* 132. 2 September: 28–30, 33.

Brydon, A. (2006). "The predicament of nature: Keiko the whale and the cultural politics of whaling in Iceland." *Anthropological Quarterly* 79(2): 225–60.

Calcutt, A. (1999). *White Noise: An A-Z of the Contradictions in Cyberculture.* Basingstoke: Macmillan.

"Celebetty:Bjork" (2000). *BeatBoxBetty.com.* October. http://www.beatboxbetty.com/celebetty/bjork/bjork/bjork.htm. Accessed 23 August 2007.

"Charts in France" (2002–2007). *chartsinfrance.net.* http://www.chartsinfrance.net/certifications/. Accessed 11 January 2006.

Cockburn, C. and S. Ormrod (1993). *Gender and Technology in the Making.* London: Sage.

"Cocoon Special" (2001). *bjork.com.* http://unit.bjork.com/specials/cocoon/. Accessed 6 January 2006.

Collins, K. E. (2006). "Flat twos & the musical aesthetic of the Atari VCS." *Popular Musicology Online,* www.popular-musicology-online.com

Connolly, P. (2001) "Off the wall? Interview." *The Times.* 18 August. Section: Play, 4.

Cronshaw, A. (1999). "Iceland: Waiting for the thaw." *In World Music: The Rough Guide. Africa, Europe and the Middle East,* S. Broughton, M. Ellingham and R. Trillo, vol. 1: 168–69. London: Rough Guides.

Cumming, N. (2000). *The Sonic Self: Musical Subjectivity and Signification.* Bloomington and Indianapolis: Indiana Press.
Davidson, P. (2005). *The Idea of North.* London: Reaktion Books.
Davis, J. (2004). "Björk again." *Sunday Times.* 22 August: 12–15.
deCordova, R. (1991). "The emergence of the star system in America." In *Stardom: Industry of Desire,* C. Gledhill, 17–29. London and New York: Routledge.
Deevoy, A. (1994). "Hips. Tits. Lips. Power." *Q magazine.* May: 90–94, 97.
Demby, E. (2001). "Bjork says new record allowed her to clear her head." *MTV News.* http://www.mtv.com/news/articles/1441258/20010302/bjork.jhtml. Accessed 14 March 2006.
DeMuth, S. (2006). "Saving Iceland interview with Björk." *Saving Iceland.* January. http://www.savingiceland.org. Accessed 1 April 2008.
Dessange, L. (2004). "Le chant des possibles." *Voir ca.* http://www.sofftchevaliers.net/presse2004/voir.htm. Accessed 12 September 2006.
Dessau, B. (1992) "Still crazy after all these beers." *Vox.* February. http://www.abc.se/~m8996/cubes/interviw/vox9202.html. Accessed 27 August 2007.
Dibben, N. (2006). "Subjectivity and the construction of emotion in the music of Björk." *Music Analysis* 25(1-2): 171–97.
Dibben, N. (in press) "Nature and nation: National identity and environmentalism in Icelandic popular music video and documentary film" *Ethnomusicology Forum.*
Dickinson, K. (2004). "'Believe': Vocoders, digital female identity and camp." In *Music, Space and Place: Popular Music and Cultural Identity,* S. Whiteley, A. Bennett and S. Hawkins, 163–79. Aldershot: Ashgate.
Diva, M. (2007) "'I'm just doing my best to escape boredom": DIS questions Björk about Volta and beyond." *Drowned in Sound.* http://www.drownedinsound.com/articles/1900868. Accessed 25 July 2007.
Doerschuk, R. L. (1997) "Björk – Saga you can dance to." *Musician.* http://www.ebweb.at/ortner/tia/97/musician9712/musician9712.html. Accessed 27 August 2007.
Durrenberger, E. P. (1996). "Every Icelander a special case." *In Images of Contemporary Iceland: Everyday Lives and Global Contexts,* G. Pálsson and E. P. Durrenberger, 171–90. Iowa: Iowa University Press.
Edensor, T. (2002). *National Identity, Popular Culture and Everyday Life.* Oxford and New York: Berg.

Eldon, S. (2006). "The war against frugality: An interview with Einar Örn." *The Reykjavík Grapevine.* http://www.grapevine.is/Features/ReadArticle/The-War-Against-Frugality. Accessed 8 October 2008.

Elliott, P. (1997). "Who the hell does Bjork think she is?" *Q Magazine.* November: 5–7.

Erlmann, V. (1999). *Music, Modernity and the Global Imagination. South Africa and the West.* Oxford: Oxford University Press.

Evans, J. and D. Hesmondhalgh, eds. (2005). *Understanding Media: Inside Celebrity.* Maidenhead: Open University Press.

Eysteinsson, Á. and Ú. Dagsdóttir (2006). "Icelandic prose literature 1940–2000." In *A History of Icelandic Literature. Vol. 5. Histories of Scandinavian Literature,* D. Neijmann, 404–470. Lincoln: University of Nebraska.

Faulkner, R. and J. Davidson (2004). "Men's vocal behaviour and the construction of self." *Musicae Scientiae* 8(2): 231–55.

Faulkner, R. S. C. (2005). "The vocal construction of self: Icelandic men and singing in everyday life." PhD thesis, University of Sheffield.

Fay, L. (1994) "Björk on the wild side." *Hotpress.* Interview, 10 August. http://www.abc.se/~m8996/bjork/interviw/hotpress.html. Accessed 14 March 2006.

Fern, R. (1997) "Björk, don't run." *Mixmag.* September: 122–25. http://www.ebweb.at/ortner/tia/97/mixmag9709/mixmag9709.html. Accessed 27 August 2007.

Flinn, C. (1992). *Strains of Utopia: Gender, Nostalgia, and Hollywood Film Music.* Princeton, NJ: Princeton University Press.

Flint, T. (2001). "Musical differences." *Sound on Sound.* November: 70–72, 74, 76, 78–79.

Frith, S. (1986). "Art versus technology: the strange case of popular music." *Media, Culture and Society* 8(3): 263–79.

———(1996). *Performing Rites: Evaluating Popular Music.* Oxford: Oxford University Press.

Fritsch, O. (2001). "77island – complete discography." *bjork.com.* http://unit.bjork.com/77island/kukl/index.htm. Accessed 30 March 2007.

Frost, M. (2001, 2004). "Eruptive Schaffenskraft." *CD-Kritik.de.* http://www.cd-kritik.de/frameset/frset.htm?/kritiken/kuenstler/bjork.htm. Accessed 13 September 2006.

Gibson, R. (1987). "Sweet sensation." *Sounds.* September: 41–42.

Gittins, I. (2002). *Björk Human Behaviour: The Stories Behind Every Song.* London: Carlton.

Gledhill, C., ed. (1991). *Stardom: Industry of Desire.* London and New York: Routledge.

"Gold & Platinum" (2006). *Recording Industry Association of America.* http://www.riaa.com/goldandplatinum.php. Accessed 11 January 2006.

Grimley, D. M. (2005). "Hidden Places: Hyper-realism in Björk's *Vespertine* and *Dancer in the Dark.*" *Twentieth Century Music* 2(1): 37–52.

Guðmundsson, G. (1990). *Rokksaga Íslands: Frá Sigga Johnnie Til Sykurmolanna 1955–1990 (The Story of Icelandic Rock: From Sigga Johnnie to The Sugarcubes 1955–1990).* Reykjavik: Forlagid.

Gunnarsson, V. (2004). "Waving a pirate flag. Björk: seditious superstar." *Rekyavik Grapevine.* http://unit.bjork.com/specials/albums/medulla/pirate/. Accessed 13 March 2006.

Hálfdanarson, G. (1995). "Social distinctions and national unity: On politics of nationalism in nineteenth-century Iceland." *History of European Ideas* 21(6): 763–9.

———(2000). "Thingvellir: An Icelandic 'Lieu de Mémoire'." *History and Memory* 21(1): 4–29.

Haraway, D. (1991). *Simians, Cyborgs and Women: The Reinvention of Nature.* London: Free Association Books.

———(2000). "A manifesto for cyborgs: Science, technology, and socialist feminism in the 1980s." In *The Gendered Cyborg: A Reader,* G. Kirkup, L. Janes, K. Woodward and F. Hovenden, 50–57. London and New York: Routledge/The Open University.

Harding, L. (1995). "Björk – Success and the solo mother." *You.* 12 November. http://www.ebweb.at/ortner/tia/95/you951112/you951112.html. Accessed 27 August 2007.

Hawkins, S. (1999). "Musical excess and postmodern identity." *Musiikin Suunta* 2: 43–54.

Hedetoft, U. and M. Hjort, eds. (2002). *The Postnational Self: Belonging and Identity.* Minneapolis and London: University of Minnesota Press.

Helgadóttir, G. (n.d.). "The image of a Northern destination: the Eyjafjördur region." Hólar University College.

Helligar, J. and J. Griffiths. (1995). "Out of the shadows." *People,* 25 September. http://allbjork.com/gb/spe/itw/index.php?itw=13. Accessed 27 August 2007.

Hemingway, D. (2002). "Björk: The Icelandic singer guides David Hemingway through her forthcoming Greatest Hits." *Record Collector.* August: 38–43.

Henten, A. and T. M. Kristensen (2000). "Information society visions in the Nordic countries." *Telematics and Informatics* 17(1-2): 77–103.
Herbert, M. (2005). "Personal contract for the composition of music (incorporating the manifesto of mistakes)." *matthewherbert.com*. http://www.matthewherbert.com/pccom.php. Accessed 20 August 2007.
Herman, J. P. (1997). "Icelandic divine." *Elle*. December. http://www.ebweb.at/ortner/tia/97/elle9712/elle9712.html. Accessed 27 August 2007.
Hilferty, R. (2007). "Quirky Bjork relocates her innocence, explains video contest." *Bloomberg.com*. http://www.bloomberg.com/apps/news?pid=20601088&sid=akoDn9u_w6w4&refer=muse. Accessed 3 October 2007.
Hoggard, L. (2005) "'Maybe I'll be a feminist in my old age'." *The Observer*. http://observer.guardian.co.uk/review/story/0,6903,1436296,00.html. Accessed 27 August.
"Homogenic" (1995–2003). *bjork.com*. http://unit.bjork.com/specials/albums/homogenic/. Accessed 23 August 2007.
"Icelandic National Flag." http://eng.forsaetisraduneyti.is/state-symbols/icelandic-national-flag/design. Accessed 1 April 2008.
Inglis, S. (2001). "Music after Midi." *Sound on Sound*. March: 190–92, 194–5.
Ingólfsson, Á. H. (2003). "'These are the things you never forget': The written and oral traditions of Icelandic Tvísöngur." PhD thesis, Harvard University.
———(2005). "Drawing new boundaries." *Nordic Sounds* 4.
"Interview on Japanese TV" (2002). *bjork.com*/news. 21 January. http://bjork.com/news/?id=208;year=2002. Accessed 23 August 2007.
Jackson, R. (2004). "Hallgrímur Helgason." *The Reykjavík Grapevine*. http://www.grapevine.is. Accessed 1 April 2008.
Jenkins, P. (2004). "Creativity = Bad taste?" *I Love Icelandic Music*. http://icelandicmusic.blogspot.com/2007/05/history-of-smekkleysa.html. Accessed 6 August 2007.
Jóhannesson, I. Á. (2005). "Icelandic nationalism and the Kyoto Protocol: An analysis of the discourse on global environmental change in Iceland." *Environmental Politics* 14(4): 495–509.
Johnson, J. (1999). *Webern and the Transformation of Nature*. Cambridge: Cambridge University Press.
Kaarst-Brown, M. L. and D. Robey (1999). "More on myth, magic and metaphor: Cultural insights into the management of information technology in organizations." *Information Technology & People* 12(2): 192–218.

Karlsson, G. (2000). *Iceland's 1100 Years: History of a Marginal Society*. London: Hurst & Co.
Kavenna, J. (2005). *The Ice Museum: to Shetland, Germany, Iceland, Norway, Estonia, Greenland and Svalbard in Search of the Lost Land of Thule*. London: Penguin.
Kellner, D. (1995). *Media Culture*. London: Routledge.
Kennedy, J. (2004). "Bjork on 'Medulla'." *Xfm Online*. http://www.xfm.co.uk/Article.asp?id=37313. Accessed 29 June 2006.
Koestler, D. (1995). "Gender ideology and nationalism in the culture and politics of Iceland." *American Ethnologist* 22(3): 572–88.
Kot, G. (2007). "Björk and the beats behind 'Volta'." *Metromix.com*. 9 May. http://www.metromix.com. Accessed 29 July 2007.
Kramer, L. (2001). "The mysteries of animation: history, analysis and musical subjectivity." *Music Analysis* 20(2): 153–78.
Kvaran, Ó. and K. Kristjánsdóttir, eds. (2001). *Confronting Nature: Icelandic Art of the 20th Century*. Reykjavík: National Gallery of Iceland.
Lacasse, S. (2005). *Persona, Emotions and Technology: The Phonographic Staging of the Popular Music Voice*. CHARM Symposium 2: The art of record production. University of Westminster.
Lagambina, G. (2002). "Björk: Look back in wonder." *Filter Mag*. September. http://allbjork.com/gb/spe/itw/index.php?itw=18. Accessed 27 August 2007.
Lee, L. (2004). "Björk 'Medulla'." *Flakmagazine*. http://www.flakmag.com/music/bjorkmedulla.html. Accessed 14 August 2006.
Lester, P. (2007). "'I have a lot of respect for people like Debussy'." *Living.Scotsman.com*. 25 August. http://living.scotsman.com/music.cfm?id=1350132007. Accessed 27 August 2007.
LynnFox. (2002). "Björk: Nature is Ancient: Abstract." *bjork.com*. http://unit.bjork.com/specials/natureancient/nia_treatment.html. Accessed 22 March 2006.
"Lyrics" (1995–2004). *bjork.com*. http://www.bjork.com/facts/lyrics/. Accessed 4 December 2006.
Magnússon, M. Á. (2000). "Nordic and British reluctance towards European integration." MPhil thesis, University of Cambridge.
Marcus, T. (1996). "Love bites Bjork and Goldie. Get your teeth into this." Interview by Tony Marcus. *i-D*. July: Front cover.
Marsh, C. and M. West (2003). "The nature/technology binary opposition dismantled in the music of Madonna and Björk." In *Music and Technoculture*,

R. T. A. Lysloff and L. C. Gay, 182–203. Middletown, CT: Weslyan University Press.

Mayhew, E. (2004). "Positioning the producer: gender divisions in creative labour and value." In *Music, Space and Place: Popular Music and Cultural Identity*, S. Whiteley, A. Bennett and S. Hawkins. Aldershot: Ashgate.

McDonnell, E. (1997). "Björk: The saga of Iceland's fierce faerie." *Request*. http://www.ebweb.at/ortner/tia/97/request9712/request9712.html. Accessed 20 August 2007.

———(2001). *Army of She: Icelandic, Iconclastic, Irrepressible Björk*. New York: Artrandom.com.

McGeoch, C. (2004). "Voices from within – Bjork." *Dazed & Confused* 2: 90–96.

Micallef, K. (1997). "Home is where the heart is." *Raygun*. http://ebweb.at/ortner/tia/97/raygun9709/raygun9709.html. Accessed 23 August 2007.

Middleton, R. (1990). *Studying Popular Music*. Philadelphia: Open University Press.

Mientjes, L. (1990). "Paul Simon's Graceland, South Africa, and the mediation of musical meaning." *Ethnomusicology* 34(1): 37–73.

Moore, A. (2002). "Authenticity as authentication." *Popular Music* 21(2): 209–223.

———(2005). "The sound of popular music: Where are we?" *CHARM Symposium 1: Comparative perspectives in the study of recordings*. Royal Holloway: University of London.

Moorefield, V. (2006). *The Producer as Composer: Shaping the Sounds of Popular Music*. Cambridge, MA: MIT Press.

Mortaigne, V. (2004). "Björk á la recherche de l'énergie tellurique." *Le Monde*, 31 August, L'Été du Monde Musique: 27.

Morton, R. (1994). "Björk – Love & Hate." *The New Musical Express*. 26 February: 24–25.

Muhly, N. (1994–2005). "Nico Muhly. Pianist on 'Oceania'." *bjork.com*. http://unit.bjork.com/specials/albums/medulla/nicomuhly/. Accessed 22 March 2006.

Negus, K. (1999). *Music Genres and Corporate Cultures*. London: Routledge.

Neijmann, D. (2006). *A History of Icelandic Literature. Vol. 5. Histories of Scandinavian Literature*. Lincoln: University of Nebraska

Ólafsdóttir, A. (2001). "Visions of Nature in Icelandic Art." In *Confronting Nature: Icelandic Art of the Twentieth Century*, Ó. Kvaran and K. Kristjánsdóttir, 23–38. Reykjavík: National Gallery of Iceland.

Oslund, K. (2002). "Imagining Iceland: narratives of nature and history in the North Atlantic." *British Journal for the History of Science* 35: 313–34.
Óttarsson, G. K. (2005). "Dense Time – Press Release." http://www.islandia.is/gko/DENSE-ISL.pdf. Accessed 30 March 2007.
Pálsson, G. (1995). *The Textual Life of Savants: Ethnography, Iceland, and the Linguistic Turn.* Chur, Switzerland: Harwood.
———(2000). "Genomes and genealogies: Decoding debates about deCode." *Paper presented to a conference of the International Association for the Study of Common Property, Constituting the Commons: Crafting Sustainable Commons in the New Millennium, Bloomington, Indiana, May 31 – June 4, 2000.* Reykjavík: Institute of Anthropology, University of Iceland.
Pareles, J. (2007) "At home again in the unknown." *New York Times*, 29 April, late ed. – final, section 2: 1.
Pattison, L. (2007). "Music/artists and albums: Bjork, Volta." *bbc.co.uk.* 5 July. http://www.bbc.co.uk/music/release/mwvr/. Accessed 23 August 2007.
Peachy, M. (1993). "New Björk, New Björk." *Vox.* http://www.abc.se/~m8996/bjork/interviw/vox9312.html. Accessed 27 August 2007.
Pennebaker, J. W., M. E. Francis, et al. (2003). *Linguistic Inquiry and Word Count 2001.* Mahwah, NJ: Erlbaum.
Pfaffenberger, B. (1988). "Fetishized objects and humanised nature: Towards an anthropology of technology." *Man* 23: 236–52.
"Post" (1995–2003). *björk.com.* http://unit.bjork.com/specials/albums/post/. Accessed 23 August 2007.
Powell, M. (2007). "Interview." *Stylus.* 26 April. http://www.stylusmagazine.com/articles/interview/bjork.htm. Accessed 30 July 2007.
Prevignano, A. (2001). "Björk, musica per laptop e ghiaccio spezzato." *KataWeb.* 20 June. http://www.kwmusica.kataweb.it/kwmusica/pp_scheda.jsp?idContent=71470&idCategory=2028. Accessed 15 August 2006.
Procenko, S. (2000) "Iceland balks at island freebie for Björk." *The Independent.* Section: Foreign News. 10 February: 15.
Pytlik, M. (2003). *Björk: Wow and Flutter.* London: Aurum Press.
Reynolds, S. (1993). "Jazzy love songs tinged with an oceanic feeling." *The New York Times.* 22 August. Section 2: 25.
Reynolds, S. and J. Press (1995). *The Sex Revolts: Gender, Rebellion and Rock 'n' Roll.* London: Serpent's Tail.
Riley, M. (2002). "Rustling Reeds and Lofty Pines: Elgar and the Music of Nature." *19th-Century Music* 26(2): 155–77.

Roberts, C. (1987). "Single of the week and it's not the primitives." *Melody-Maker* 62: 30.
Robertson Wojcik, P. (2001). "The Girl and the Phonograph; or the Vamp and the Machine Revisited." In *Soundtrack Available: Essays on Film and Popular Music*, P. Robertson Wojcik and A. Knight, 433–54. Durham and London: Duke University Press.
Rodgers, T. (2003). "On the process and aesthetics of sampling in electronic music production." *Organised Sound* 8: 313–20.
Ross, A. (2004). "Bjork's saga." *The New Yorker*. 23 August: 48.
Rüth, S. (1997). "Björk – 'Wir Wikinger sind die größten Rebellen aller Zeiten'." *Zillo*. October. http://www.ebweb.at/ortner/tia/97/zillo9710/zillo9710.html. Accessed 27 August 2007.
Ryming, P. E. (1993). "The siren from the volcano-island." *Agenda*. September. http://home.concepts.nl/~sinned/d4.htm. Accessed 27 August 2007.
Ryzik, M. (2008). "Bjork in 3-D: The 'Wanderlust' Video." *The New York Times*. 3 April. http://video.on.nytimes.com/?fr_story=cae6cd1d56ad61cd2686baeba62701d9f7a8d2ae. Accessed 5 April 2008.
Sabatier, B. (1997). "Une femme sort d'influences." *Technikart* 15. http://www.technikart.com/article.php3?art_uid=925&id_rubrique=24. Accessed 27 August 2007.
Sandall, R. (2004). "This time it's intuition only – no brain please." *Daily Telegraph*. 14 August: 4.
Savage, J. (1995). "The always uncjorked Bjork – interview with pop singer Björk." *InterWOMAN*. http://www.zinkle.com/p/articles/mi_m1285/is_n6_v25/ai_17231482. Accessed 20 February 2006.
Scrudator, K. (2007). "Army of She: Planting flags with Björk." *Filter Magazine*. 24 April. http://www.bjork.fr/filter-mag-com.html. Accessed 25 July 2007.
Sen, J. (2007). "The Lydian front." *The Journey Itself is Home: a Volta Tour Blog*. http://blog.bjork.com. Accessed 24 July 2007.
Shadforth, D. (2006). Personal interview. 11 December.
Shaviro, S. (n.d.). "Robotic: Björk and Chris Cunningham." *Stranded in the Jungle*. http://www.shaviro.com/Stranded/31.html. Accessed 3 March 2006.
Sherburne, P. (2004). "Digital discipline: Minimalism in house and techno." In *Audio Culture: Readings in Modern Music*, C. Cox and D. Warner, 319–26. New York and London: Continuum.
Sigsworth, G. (2006). Personal interview. 13 November.

Sigurðsson, G. (1996). "Icelandic national identity: From romanticism to tourism." In *Making Europe in Nordic Contexts*, P. J. Anttonen, 41–76. Turku: Nordic Institute of Folklore, University of Turku.
Sigurðsson, H. (1997). *Infotactics as Art: Extrinsic Implantations within the Rhizomatic Field of Media*. Lofoten, Iceland. http://www.art.is/. Accessed 1 November 2006.
Sigurðsson, V. (2006). Personal interview. 23 October.
Simonart, S. (1995). "Trolden, excentrikeren, barnet Björk." *Politiken*. Section: Magasinet. 8 October: 6–7.
Simpson, B. (2000). "Imagined genetic communities: Ethnicity and essentialism in the twenty-first century." *Anthropology Today* 16(3): 3–6.
Spufford, F. (1996). *I May Be Some Time*. London: Faber & Faber.
Steingrímsson, H. (2000). "Kvædaskapur: Icelandic Epic Song." Ed. D. Stone and S. L. Mosko. http://music.calarts.edu/KVAEDASKAPUR/main.html. Accessed 25 January 2007.
Stent, M. S. (2006). Personal interview. 5 October.
Sterne, J. (2003). *The Audible Past: Cultural Origins of Sound Reproduction*. Durham and London: Duke University Press.
Stewart, S. (1984). *On Longing: Narratives of the Miniature, the Gigantic, the Souvenir, the Collection*. Baltimore: John Hopkins University Press.
Stosuy, B. (2007). "Interview." *Pitchfork*. 23 April. http://www.pitchforkmedia.com/article/feature/42181-interview-bjrk. Accessed 24 July 2007.
Stuart, C. (2003). "Damaged sound: Glitching and skipping compact discs in the audio of Yasunao Tone, Nicolas Collins and Oval." *Leonardo Music Journal* 13: 47–52.
Swain, M. (2001). "Updating the Nordic sublime." In *Confronting Nature: Icelandic Art of the Twentieth Century*, Ó. Kvaran and K. Kristjánsdóttir. Reykjavík: National Gallery of Iceland.
Swenson, K. (2004). "Breath control." *Remix*. 1 October. http://remixmag.com/artists/remix_breath_control/. Accessed 15 March 2006.
Tagg, P. (1994). "From refrain to rave: The decline of figure and the rise of ground." *Popular Music* 13(2): 209–222.
Taylor, D. (2006). "Forum: So much gear, so little time! Thread: Anyone familiar with vocal tracking for The Knife and or Bjork?" *gearslutz.com*. 26 September. http://www.gearslutz.com/board/. Accessed 15 January 2007.
Taylor, T. D. (1997). *Global Pop: World Music, World Markets*. New York and London: Routledge.
——— (2001). *Strange Sounds: Music, Technology and Culture*. New York: Routledge.

―――(2007). *Beyond Exoticism: Western Music and the World.* Durham and London: Duke University Press.
"The somewhat complete Bad Taste saga" (n.d.). *Bad Taste.* https://www.smekkleysa.net/. Accessed 24 May 2006.
Thompson, B. (1997). "Quiet fireworks." *Mojo.* November: 66–67, 69–70.
Thomson, P. (2003). "Atoms and errors: Towards a history and aesthetics of microsound." *Organised Sound* 9(2): 207–218.
Tility, J. (1996). "Freaky momma." *Bust.* August: Front cover.
Toop, D. (n.d.). "Björk: Vespertine biography." *bjork.com.* http://www.bjork.com/specials/vespertine/pictures/vespbio/index.htm. Accessed 9 November 2001.
Toop, D. and Björk (2002). "Björk in conversation with David Toop." *bjork.com.* http://unit.bjork.com/specials/gh/extra/toop.htm. Accessed 13 March 2006.
van den Berg, E. (1997). "Homogenic is Ijsland, mijn vaderland, mijn thuis. (Homogenic is Iceland, my native country, my home)." *Oor.* September. http://www.ebweb.at/ortner/tia/97/oor9709/oor9709t.html. Accessed 16 November 2004.
Van Meter, J. (1997). "The outer limits." *Spin.* December. http://www.ebweb.at/ortner/tia/97/spin9712/spin9712.html. Accessed 9 February 2006.
Vasey, D. E. (1996). "Premodern and modern constructions of population regimes." In *Images of Contemporary Iceland: Everyday Lives and Global Contexts,* G. Pálsson and E. P. Durrenberger, 149–70. Iowa: Iowa University Press.
Visiticeland.com. (n.d.). "Iceland discoveries: Natural wonders." *Your official travel guide to Iceland.* http://www.visiticeland.com/default.asp?cat_id=270. Accessed 1 November 2006.
Wade, I. (2001). "Bjork – Vespertine." *dotmusic.* http://uk.launch.yahoo.com/l_reviews_a/21556.html. Accessed 2 June 2006.
"Wanderlust" (2007). *Bjork.fr.* http://www.bjork.fr/Wanderlust.html. Accessed 6 August 2007.
Westwood, M. (2008). "Made to mingle with electricity." *The Australian.* http://www.theaustralian.news.com.au/story/0,25197,23029169-16947,00.html. Accessed 25 January 2008.
Whitelaw, M. (2001). "Inframedia audio." *Artlink* 21(3): 49–52.
―――(2003). "Sound particles and microsonic materialism." *Contemporary Music Review* 22(4): 93–100.
Whiteley, S. (2005). *Too Much, Too Young: Popular Music, Age and Gender.* New York: Routledge.

Whiteley, S., A. Bennett, et al., eds. (2004). *Music, Space and Place: Popular Music and Cultural Identity*. Aldershot: Ashgate.

Williamson, N. (2005). "Born again Bjork." *Scotland on Sunday.* 16 July. http://living.scotsman.com/music.cfm?id=1639722005. Accessed 11 August 2006.

———(2007). "Björk: the sonic explorer unleashes her new creation." *Songlines* 44: 21, 23.

Zak III, A. J. (2001). *The Poetics of Rock: Cutting Tracks, Making Records.* London and Berkeley: University of California Press.

Þorvaldsson, E. (2006). "Icelandic poetry since 1940." In *A History of Icelandic Literature. Vol. 5. Histories of Scandinavian Literature*, 471–502. Lincoln: University of Nebraska.

Discography and Filmography

Björk (all CD unless stated otherwise)

Bjork. Falkinn Records, 1977. [LP]
Gling Gló. Björk Guðmundsdóttir and Tríó Guðmundar Ingólfssonar. Smekkleysa, 1990.
Debut. One Little Indian, 1993.
Vessel (dir. S. Sednaoui), 1994. *Björk: The Live Archive.* Wellhardt/One Little Indian, 2005. [DVD]
Post. One Little Indian, 1995.
Telegram. One Little Indian, 1996.
Homogenic. One Little Indian, 1997.
Volumen. Björk Overseas/One Little Indian, 1999. [DVD]
Selmasongs. One Little Indian, 2000.
Miniscule (dir. R. Gestsdóttir). Wellhardt/One Little Indian, 2001. [DVD]
Vespertine. One Little Indian, 2001.
Vespertine Live at the Royal Opera House (dir. D. Barnard). Wellhart/One Little Indian/BBC, 2001. [DVD]
Family Tree. Wellhart/One Little Indian, 2002.
Greatest Hits. One Little Indian, 2002.
Volumen Plus. One Little Indian, 2002. [DVD]
Inside Björk (dir. C. Walker). Wellhart/One Little Indian, 2003. [DVD]
LiveBox. One Little Indian, 2003.
Medúlla. Wellhart/One Little Indian, 2004.
The Inner or Deep Part of an Animal or Plant Structure (dir. R. Gestsdóttir). Wellhart/One Little Indian, 2004. [DVD]
Army of Me-Xes. One Little Indian, 2005.
Triumph of a Heart: The Stories Behind the Video (dir. R. Gestsdóttir). Björk: The Medúlla Videos 2004–2005. The Archive DVD Series, Elektra, 2005.
The music from Drawing Restraint 9. Wellhart/One Little Indian, 2005.

Björk: The Live Archive. Wellhart/One Little Indian, 2005. [DVD]
Björk: The Television Archive. Wellhart/One Little Indian, 2005. [DVD]
Surrounded. One Little Indian, 2006.
Volta. Wellhart/One Little Indian, 2007.

Music videos

'Birthday' (dir. Kristin Jóhannesdóttir, 1987). *Sugarcubes: The DVD.* One Little Indian, 2004. [DVD]

Björk: Volumen. Björk Overseas Ltd/One Little Indian, 1999 [DVD]:
'Big Time Sensuality' (dir. Stéphane Sednaoui, 1993).
'Human Behaviour' (dir. Michel Gondry, 1993).
'Venus as a Boy' (dir. Sophie Muller, 1993).
'Violently Happy' (dir. Jean-Baptiste Mondino, 1994).
'Army of Me' (dir. Michel Gondry, 1995).
'Isobel' (dir. Michel Gondry, 1995).
'It's Oh So Quiet' (dir. Spike Jonze, 1995).
'Hyperballad' (dir. Michel Gondry, 1996).
'Possibly Maybe' (dir. Stéphane Sednaoui, 1996).
'Bachelorette' (dir. Michel Gondry, 1997).
'Hunter' (dir. Paul White, 1997).
'Jóga' (dir. Michel Gondry, 1997).

Björk: Volumen Plus. Wellhart/One Little Indian, 2002 [DVD]:
'Alarm Call' (dir. Alexander McQueen, 1998).
'All is Full of Love' (dir. Chris Cunningham, 1999).
'Hidden Place' (dir. Inez van Lamsweerde and Vinoodh Matadin and M/M (Paris), 2001).
'Pagan Poetry' (dir. Nick Knight, 2001).
'Cocoon' (dir. Eiko Ishioka, 2002).
'It's In Our Hands' (dir. Spike Jonze, 2002).
'Nature is Ancient' (dir. Lynn Fox, 2002).

Björk: the Medulla Videos. Elektra, 2005 [DVD]:
'Oceania' (dir. Lynn Fox, 2005).
'Triumph of a Heart' (dir. Spike Jonze, 2005).
'Who Is It? (Carry my joy on the left, carry my pain on the right)' (dir. Dawn Shadforth, 2005).

Others:
'Declare Independence' (dir. Michel Gondry, 2007).
'Wanderlust' (dir. Enyclopedia Pictura, 2008).

TV programmes

Bravo Profile (dir. C. Walker, 1997). South Bank Show. ITV, London. 9 November.
Live at Canal+. 25 October 2004.

Kukl

The Eye. Crass Records, 1984.
Holidays in Europe (The Naughty Naught). Crass Records, 1986.

Tappi Tíkarrass

Bítið Fast í Vítið. Spor, 1982. [12 inch EP]
Miranda. Gramm, 1983. [12 inch EP]

The Sugarcubes

Life's Too Good. One Little Indian/Elektra, 1988.
Here Today, Tomorrow, Next Week! One Little Indian/Elektra, 1989.
It's It. One Little Indian/Elektra, 1992.
Stick Around for Joy. One Little Indian/Elektra, 1992.
Sugarcubes: The DVD. One Little Indian, 2004. [DVD]

Other Artists

2001: A Space Odyssey (dir. Stanley Kubrick, 1968).
Alien (dir. Ridley Scott, 1979).
Rokk í Reykjavík (dir. Friðrik Þór Friðriksson, 1982).
Ex:El. 808 State (ZTT Records, 1991).
The Young Americans (dir. Danny Cannon, 1993)
Bedtime Stories. Madonna (Maverick, 1994).
Diskont. Oval (Thrill Jockey, 1994).
Mass Observation. Scanner (New Electronica, 1995).
Songs from the Cold Seas (Hector Zazou, 1995).
Nearly God. Tricky (Island, 1996).
Systemisch. Oval (Thrill Jockey, 1996).
Being John Malkovich (dir. Spike Jonze, 1999).

Dancer in the Dark (dir. Lars von Trier). Fine Line Features, 2000. [DVD]
The Juniper Tree (dir. Nietzchka Keene, 1990). Rhino, 2002. [DVD]
The Work of Director Chris Cunningham (dir. Chris Cunningham, 2003). Palm Pictures. [DVD]
Eternal Sunshine of the Spotless Mind (dir. Michel Gondry, 2004).
'Prayer of the Heart', *A Portrait: John Tavener*. Naxos, 2004.
Drawing Restraint 9 (dir. Matthew Barney, 2005). [Film: not on general release]
Screaming Masterpiece (dir. Ari Alexander Ergis Magnússon, 2005). Soda Pictures. [DVD]
Back to Basics. Christina Aguilera (RCA, 2006).
A Tribute to Joni Mitchell (Nonesuch, 2007).

Index

'5 Years' (Björk) 112
808 State 15, 122 *see also* Massey, Graham
2001: A Space Odyssey (film) 90

'Aerodeck' (Oval) 82–3
'Aeroplane' (Björk) 112, 121
AI (film) 91
'Alarm Call' (Björk) 22, 168
Alien (film) 91
'All is Full of Love' (Björk) 39, 72, 86, **90–95**, 108–9, 183–4 nn.7–9
'Ammæli' (Sugarcubes) *see* 'Birthday'
'Amphibian' (Björk) 103
'Ancestors' (Björk) 115
'Anchor Song' (Björk) 15, 37, 63, 68, 178 n.17
'An Echo, A Stain' (Björk) 115, 124, 147
Arab, Leila 16, 42
'Army of Me' (Björk) 17, 67, 139, 143, 166
Army of Me–Xes (Björk) 21, 143, 163
Árnason, Sævar 5–7
'Aurora' (Björk) 61–2, 78
authenticity 30, 51, 69, 131–9, 144, 151–4, 158, 171–2

'Bachelorette' (Björk) 38, 57, 69, 103
Bad Taste 12–14, 16, 23, 101, 162–4
Baldursson, Sigtryggur 10, 12–13
Barney, Matthew 20–1, 67, 140
'Bath' (Björk) 113
beats 33, 114–17, 119
    and the idea of the technological 73–4, 94, 98
    microbeats **78–85**, 128
    on *Debut* 18–19, 74–7

on *Homogenic* 46–7, 59–61, 77–8
on *Medulla* 78, 161
on *Vespertine* 20, 78, 147
on *Volta* 21
Bedtime Stories (Madonna) 17
'Believe' (Cher) 98
Bell, Mark 18–19, 22, 46, 49, 77, 115, 119
bells 39–40, 64, 77
Benediktsson, Einar Örn 9–10, 12, 14–15, 35, 101, 104
Bernstein, Howard *see* 'Howie B'
'Big Time Sensuality' (Björk) 75–6, 103, 114, 139, 161, 166
Birkett, Derek 9–11, 14, 16, 132, 134, 137–8, 160–1, 195 n.5
'Birthday' (Sugarcubes) 13–14, 68, 104–5
Björk (Björk) 6–8, 16, 44, 135
Björk (M/M Paris) 20
Björk
    and cover versions 7, 9–10, 126, 135, 155–6, 173 n.3
    and politics 57–8, 70, 162–7, 180 n. 5
    as a mother 12, 20, 141–2, 116, 166
    as an actress 13, 19, 21, 68
    as childlike 14, 16, 88, 102, 104–5, 110, 112, 164–5
    assaults on journalists 18, 154
    awards 1, 17, 19–20, 50, 155
    childhood 5–8, 54, 63
    clothes 19–20, 32, 162
    on animals 66–8
    on art music 8, 33–4, 100–1, 128, 159
    on her Icelandic identity 41–2, 65–6, 187 n.16

218 Björk

on popular music 100–1
pregnancy 11, 116, 141, 165,
  181 n.7
schooling 5–6, 8
voice 18, 31, 54, 73–8, 91, 98,
  101–9, 109–14, 119, 144,
  147–8, 170
bomb 18, 140, 143
Brodsky Quartet 19–20
Brown, Rahzel M. (see 'Rahzel') 20, 116

celesta 61, 126
Chippendale, Brian 22
'Cocoon' (Björk) 22, 82, 147–50
collaboration 22, 37, 42, 48, 115,
  119–21, 133–8, 140–1, 157–8, 165,
  188 n.18, 190 n.4, 191 n.5
compositional process 8, 15, 30, 53–4,
  83–5, 98, 101–3, **109–10**,
  115–17, 122–8, 131–2, 134–8,
  189 nn.24, 25, 26, 191 nn.5, 7
compression 102, 147, 185 n.5
Corsano, Chris 22
cover art 14, 16, 21, 72, 140–1, 146,
  182 n.1
'Cover Me' (Björk) 38, 66
Crass 11–12
'Crying' (Björk) 57, 114
Cunningham, Chris 90–2
'Cvalda' (Björk) 85, 87
cyborg 90–1, **94–6**, 98, 108

DAF 122
Dancer in the Dark (film) 19–20, 72,
  78–9, 85, **87–90**, 139, 160,
  168–70
Debut (Björk) 15–17, 121–4, 139,
  142–4, 152, 158, 160
'Declare Independence' (Björk) 115, 142
Denmark 24, 29, 39, 142
Deodato, Eumir 17
'Desired Constellation' (Björk) 115
'Deus' (Sugarcubes) 35
Diabaté, Toumani 21
Dokaka 20
'Do While' (Oval) 126
Drawing Restraint 9 (film) 21, 38, 120,
  128

'Earth Intruders' (Björk) 106, 108, 115–16,
  142
Einar Örn *see* Benediktsson, Einar Örn
'Einn Mol' á Mann' (Sugarcubes) 14
electronic dance music 114, 123–5
Elgar Sisters, The 11–12, 35, 110
'Enjoy' (Björk) 17, 113
Erlings, Friðrik 12–14
Ex:El (808 State) 15
Exodus 9
Eye, The (Kukl) 11, 31, 121

Fálkinn 6–7
Fall, The 9
Family Tree (Björk) 20, 33–34, 40, 155,
  158
Flux of Pink Indians 9, 11
'Frosti' (Björk) 62, 126

Gaultier, Jean-Paul 17
gender 97–9, 142, 164–7, 171, 195
  n.10, 196 n.11
'Generous Palmstroke' 191 n.5
Gillis, Tanya *see* 'Tagaq'
Glennie, Evelyn 17
Gling-Gló (Trió Guðmundur Ingólfssonar)
  15, 39, 155
glitch *see* 'micro-beats'
'Glóra' (Björk) 6
golden section 92–4, 184 n.12
Goldie 18, 42
Gondry, Michel 16, 22–3, 42, 49, 57
Gramm 9
Greatest Hits (Björk) 20, 135, 155–6,
  160
Gunnarsson, Guðmundur 5, 137, 180
  n.5

Hale, Corky 16–17
'Handa Tjolla' (Kukl) 121
harmonic style 110–14
harp 16–17, 61, 80, 168, 197 n.15
Harvey, PJ 17
Hauksdóttir, Hildur Rúna 5–7, 63, 180
  n.5, 196 n.12
'Headphones' (Björk) 17
Hegarty, Antony 21
Herbert, Matthew 83

Here Today, Tomorrow, Next Week! (The Sugarcubes) 35
'Hidden Place' (Björk) 22, 62, 81–2, 145–6
Hilmarsson, Hilmar Örn 35
Hipkin, Murray 18
Holidays in Europe (The Naughty Naught) (Kukl) 11, 119, 121
Homogenic (Björk) 18–19, 35, 41–42, 46, 48, 58–61, 115–16, 140–1, 152–3
Hooper, Nellee 16–17, 75, 113, 123, 174 n.9
'Hope' (Björk) 112, 116, 142
Horn, Rebecca 96
Howie B 17, 108
'Human Behaviour' (Björk) 16, 38, 57, 66–7, 115, 124–5, 174 n.10, 188 n.22
humour 129–30
'Hunter' (Björk) 36, 66–67, 79, 139
'Hyper-ballad' (Björk) 69

Iceland
  history 24–9
  independence 24–5, 49, 59, 163
  landscape 26–8, 31–3, 43–4, 58–62, 174 n.2, 179 nn.24, 25, 180 n.3
  literature 28, 35, 38–39
  mythology 32, 34–35, 97
  traditional music 35–37, 46–47, 112–14
Iceland's Bell (Laxness) 39
'I Go Humble' (Björk) 115
'I Know Who You Are' (Björk) 151
'I Love to Love' (Björk) 6
'I'm Scared' (Björk) 170
Independent People (Laxness) 28
'Innocence' (Björk) 116
Inside Björk 37, 179 n.24, 194 n.17, 195 n.6
intimacy 62, 82, 144–9, 154
Ishioka, Eiko 22
Íslandsklukkan (Kjarval) 39
'Isobel' (Björk) 38, 57, 178 n.20
'It's Not Up to You' (Björk) 81, 85

'It's Oh So Quiet' (Björk) 17, 19, 156, 161
'I've Seen It All' (Björk) 87

Jam 80 9
'Jóga' (Björk) 36, 41–50, 59–60, 114
Jónsson, Ásmundur 8–10, 35
Jónsson, Þór Eldon 12, 15
Jonze, Spike 17
Juniper Tree, The (film) 13

Kárahnjúkar 57–8, 180 n.5
'Kjarval' (Björk) 7, 44–5
Kjarval, Jóhannes 7, 26, 39, 44
Knak, Thomas 20
Kokosolaki, Sophia 65
Konono No.1 21
'Köttur' (Sugarcubes) 13
Kraftwerk 73
Kukl 10–12, 31, 35, 104, 110, 121, 162, 188 n.20

Lake, Oliver 16
Laxness, Halldór 28, 39, 142
Leifs, Jón 27, 36–37, 60–61, 114
LFO 18
Life's Too Good (Sugarcubes) 35
'Like Someone in Love' (Björk) 121
'Lucky Night' (Sugarcubes) 76
lyrics 41, 56, 63, 103, 142–3, 171, 185 n.7

Madonna 17, 153
magic 84–5
'Mama' (Sugarcubes) 110
Massey, Graham 15–17, 119, 122–3, 163
Mass Observation (Scanner) 17
Matmos 20, 136–7
McQueen, Alexander 22, 39–40, 198 n.19
Medúlla (Björk) 20–21, 40, 48, 54, 78, 114–16, 167, 170–1
Medúsa 12
Megas (Magnús Þór Jónsson) 11
Melax, Einar 10
melodic style 110–13

'Miðvikudags' (Björk) 112–13, 127
Miniscule (Björk) 80, 154
M/M Paris 22
modes 36–7, 111–13
'Modern Things, The' (Björk) 17, 72
Mogensen, Birgir 10
Mondino, Jean-Baptiste 16
Monk, Meredith 22, 127
Mosley, Tim *see* Timbaland
'Motorcrash' (Sugarcubes) 14
'Mouth's Cradle' (Björk) 127, 167, 171
music box 61–2, 83–5, 88–9, 126, 128, 180 n.6
music videos 57, 63, 66–8, 72, 129, 145–6, 161, 165–7
   'All is Full of Love' 90–5
   'Big Time Sensuality' 166
   commissioning of 136, 138, 163, 166
   'Human Behaviour' 16
   'Hunter' 67, 79
   'It's Oh So Quiet' 17, 19
   'Jóga' 41–9, 159
   'Nature is Ancient' 63–4, 77–8
   'Oceania' 64
   'Triumph of a Heart' 163
   'Who is it' 39–40, 136, 138, 166–7

Nagano, Kent 18
'Nature is Ancient' (Björk) 63–4, 77–8, 115
Nearly God (Tricky) 17
'New World' (Björk) 170
northernness 37–8, 51, 67

'Oceania' (Björk) 21, 64, 69, 113
Ólafsson, Braggi 12
'Öll Birtan' (Björk) 103
Olympic Games 21, 64–5
One Little Indian 14, 16, 160–2, 194 n.4
Organ 37, 83–4
Örnolfsdóttir, Margaret 15
Óttarson, Guðlaugar Kristinn 10–11
Oval 80, 82–3, 126

pagan mythology 28–9, 35, 40, 50–1, 55, 69, 178 n.16

'Pagan Poetry' (Björk) 61, 85, 103, 145, 147, 165–6
Parkins, Zeena 136–7, 191 n.5
Patton, Mike 20
peace summit 13
Pejowski, Marjan 20
personification
   of nature 45–6, 64, 66–69, 101 n.11
   of song character 139–40, 152
   star persona 144–5, 153–4
Pierrot Lunaire (Schoenberg) 18, 127, 153
'Play Dead' (Björk) 57, 143, 185 n.6
'Pluto' (Björk) 39
'Prayer of the Heart' (Tavener) 18–19, 127, 155
Popp, Markus *see* Oval
'Possibly Maybe' (Björk) 17, 63, 72, 111–12, 113–14, 143
Post (Björk) 17–18, 41, 56, 68–9, 77, 106, 123, 139, 142–3, 152, 160
punk 8–10, 22–3, 34
Purrkur Pillnikk 9–10, 12

Rahzel 20
Reactable 128
record player 87–8, 183 n.5
record sales 160
recording process 106–9, 145, 186 n.12
reversioning 17–18
Rimbaud, Robin *see* 'Scanner'
Rock 6, 8, 11, 35, 80
Rokk í Reykjavík (film) 9

Scanner (Robin Rimbaud) 17
'Scatterheart' (Björk) 87–9
Schlomo 20
Schoenberg, Arnold 18
sea 63–5
Sednaoui, Stéphane 40
Selmasongs (Björk) 19, 78–9, 85, 115–16, 121, 139, 169–70
Sen, Jónas 22
Shadforth, Dawn 39, 136, 138, 166–7, 196 n.11
'Show Me Forgiveness' (Björk) 115, 126
'Siðasta Ég' 12, 110

Index

Sigur Rós 163, 185 n.7
Singh, Talvin 16–17, 42
Sigsworth, Guy 16, 19, 76, 80, 82–4, 111, 126, 189 nn.24, 25
Sigurðsson, Valgeir 19, 138, 194 n.4
Sjón (Sigurjón Birgir Sigtryggur) 13, 19, 64, 103, 174 n.8
Smekkleysa *see* Bad Taste
'So Broken' (Björk) 143, 193 n.15
song structure 123–7, 149
Songs of the Cold Sea (Zazou) 35
'Sonnets/Unrealities XI' (Björk) 115, 126
soundbox 80–1
Spit and Snot 8
Stent, Mark "Spike" 90, 126–7, 131–2, 134, 138, 189 n.26
Stick Around for Joy (Sugarcubes) 35
Stockhausen, Karlheinz 8, 18
'Storm' (Björk) 111
Story of the Eye (Bataille) 11
string arrangements 17, 34, 46–7
'Submarine' (Björk) 115, 141
Sugarcubes, The 11–12, 14–16, 31, 35, 68, 76, 101, 104, 110, 162–3, 168
'Sun in My Mouth' (Björk) 85, 111, 124
Surrealism 11–12, 14, 35, 101
swan dress 19–20, 67–8, 162
Sykurmolarnir *see* Sugarcubes

Tagaq 20, 38, 120
Tappi Tíkarass 9–10, 104, 122
Tavener, John 18–19, 128, 155
Taylor, Damian 22, 108
Telegram (Björk) 18
Thaws, Adrian *see* Tricky
'The Boho Dance' (Mitchell) 126, 189 n.25
'The Pleasure is All Mine' (Björk) 120, 127, 141
'There's More to Life Than This' (Björk) 63, 114, 121, 188 n.21
throat singing 38, 120
'Tidalwave' (Sugarcubes) 35

Timbaland 21, 116, 129–30, 137–8
timbre 104–5, 115–17
titles 194 n.2
tours 11, 15–16, 18, 19–20, 128
Tricky 17, 42
Trier, Lars von 19, 68, 132, 137, 160
Trió Guðmundur Ingólfssonar 15
'Triumph of a Heart' (Björk) 78, 127, 129, 141, 163
Triumph, Johnny 13

Um Úrnat frá Björk (Björk) 11, 174 n.7
'Unison' (Björk) 68, 82, 115, 117, 129
unity 51–2, 70–1, 117–22, 130, 150–1, 156–9

'Venus as a Boy' (Björk) 16, 63, 113, 139
Vespertine (Björk) 20–21, 61–2, 67–8, 78, 80–1, 84, 98, 115–16, 124–6, 145–6, 153, 168–9, 197 n.14
Vessel (Björk) 40
'Violently Happy' 56, 63, 114, 131, 139
virtual space 147–9
'Vísur Vatnsenda-Rósu' (Björk) 35
'Vökuró' (Björk) 61
Volta (Björk) 21–2, 48, 65–6, 100, 115–17, 120–1, 127, 142, 171

'Walkabout' (Sugarcubes) 35
'Wanderlust' (Björk) 65, 115, 117–18, 136
'Water' (Sugarcubes) 35
'Where is the Line?' (Björk) 113, 116
'Who Is It?' (Björk) 39–40, 126, 136, 138, 166, 192 n.8
Wyatt, Robert 20

Zazou, Hector 35

Þeyr 10, 35, 101
Þingvellir 24, 27, 29, 39, 44, 47

www.ingramcontent.com/pod-product-compliance
Lightning Source LLC
Chambersburg PA
CBHW050551160426
43199CB00015B/2615